Erv and Andrea,

What a joy to have shared the journey with you! We celebrate our "common denominators," the privilege of working with you, and now being close, in and with our extended family. I, with you celebrate those grandchildren of ours to whom His book is dedicated.

Jack

6/25/10

John Calvin as Biblical Commentator

John Calvin as Biblical Commentator

An Investigation into Calvin's Use of John Chrysostom
as an Exegetical Tutor

John R. Walchenbach

WIPF & STOCK · Eugene, Oregon

JOHN CALVIN AS BIBLICAL COMMENTATOR
An Investigation into Calvin's Use of John Chrysostom as an Exegetical Tutor

Wipf & Stock
An Imprint of Wipf and Stock Publishers
199 W. 8th Ave., Suite 3
Eugene, OR 97401
www.wipfandstock.com

ISBN 13: 978-1-60899-328-4

Manufactured in the U.S.A.

For

Ben and Olivia

Cole and Nate

for "tomorrow"

Contents

Foreword

IT IS A PLEASURE to commend this significant study of "John Chrysostom as an Exegetical Tutor to John Calvin." Jack Walchenbach and I have been friends since the 1970s at Pittsburgh Theological Seminary when we were both in the joint PhD program with the seminary and the University of Pittsburgh. I respected Jack then as both a scholar and a pastor whose commitment to the Reformed tradition was deep and whose studies of John Calvin set a high standard for others of us in the doctoral program.

This work was written under the direction of one of the premier Calvin scholars of the twentieth-century, Dr. Ford Lewis Battles. Jack and I both studied under Dr. Battles. But Jack entered into the intracies of doctoral studies under Dr. Battles' tutelage. It was quite a work-out! As a classicist and Rhodes scholar, as well as the renowned translator of the best contemporary translation of Calvin's 1559 *Institutes of the Christian Religion*, Dr. Battles was a Calvin scholar without peer. He expected high standards for academic work. But as a teacher and guide was imbued with great gentleness and care for students. I know Jack would not trade his experience with Dr. Battles for any other in the academic and even "spiritual" realms. So it is a personal pleasure to commend Jack's work here and to express the debt we both owe to Ford Lewis Battles as well as the affectionate regard with which we held our great teacher.

What Jack Walchenbach produced is this fine study that examines John Calvin's use of the exegetical insights of the great Greek early church theologian, John Chrysostom. This work documents Calvin's grateful dependence on Chrysostom at many places, building on the interpretations of the great eastern church father on a range of Scripture passages in the Old and New Testaments. Walchenbach examines these in detail, showing points where Calvin agreed with the ancient exegete; as well as where he did not present the fullness of Chrysostom's views, or plainly rejected them. Calvin's engagement with this important figure from the early church was substantial and Walchenbach's work clearly lays out the lineaments of this interplay, forthrightly and accurately.

Calvin leaned most heavily on Augustine for theological interpretations. As is well-known, Calvin's theological views drew on Augustine's, especially on contentious points such as sin, election, and predestination. But as an exegete of Scripture, Calvin found Augustine to be "over-subtle." Calvin was also not a fan of Augustine's penchant for allegorical interpretive moves.

But of all the ancients, Calvin found in John Chrysostom a biblical interpreter from the early church who looked primarily to the historical sense of Scripture and who made the teachings of Scripture available to the common people. This outlook accorded with Calvin's own desire to provide commentaries on Scripture and his commitment to Scripture's plain and natural sense. As Walchenbach translates Calvin's words: "The outstanding merit of our author, Chrysostom, is that it was his supreme concern always not to turn aside even to the slightest degree from the genuine, simple sense of Scripture and to allow himself no liberties by twisting the plain meaning of the words."

A measure of Calvin's esteem for Chrysostom, a matter dealt with thoroughly by Walchenbach, was Calvin's desire to publish a French translation of Chrysostom's Homilies. This never materialized. But we do have a Latin preface to the intended French translation. This is where Calvin made the case for Chrysostom's worthiness as an exegete and justified this intended edition of Chrysostom's sermons. Calvin wanted these to be available in French so ordinary Christian people (Lat. *plebem christianam*) should not be robbed of the Word of God and could avail themselves of the aids God has provided through the preaching of John Chrysostom.

In this Preface also, Calvin indicated places where he disagreed with Chrysostom and found his theological viewpoints unsatisfactory. Among these were the early theologian's views on free will, rewards for works, grace, and election. Calvin sought to explain Chrysostom's shortcomings on these points and, as Walchenbach says, he "stretches every nerve to exonerate Chrysostom's theological deficiencies." But Calvin was willing to overlook Chrysostom's problematic viewpoints in light of his overall greatness as a biblical interpreter and his proclamation and exposition of the Word of God in Scripture to the people of God. As Walchenbach writes:

In Chrysostom Calvin found an interpreter who kept closely to the meaning of the words, refusing to turn neither to the right or left of their clear intent. Calvin had found in Chrysostom a servant of the church with whose intentions Calvin himself could identify. Among the Fathers of the church East and West, Calvin assigned first place as an exegete to the Preacher of Antioch.

While some Calvin scholars have known Walchenbach's work as a dissertation, this splendid study has not, till now, been so accessible to a wider audience of those interested in Calvin. This is fortuitous—or providential!

Interest in Calvin as an interpreter of Scripture has increased in the years since Walchenbach's work was written. Now, the nature and scope of Calvin's use of Chrysostom as an "exegetical tutor" can be recognized by a wider audience of those interested in Calvin and also by those who focus on the history of biblical interpretation. The strength and clarity of Walchenbach's work will be a boon both to Calvin scholars and biblical scholars. Now the breadth of Calvin's use of the ancient theologian will be clear—even as the points of theological disagreement will become crystallized. As Calvin himself adopted the Humanist motto: *Ad fontes!*—"To the Sources," now Calvin scholars will be able to study the sources of Calvin's own exegesis at a number of points where the Genevan reformer turned for guidance and support to the ancient Antiochene preacher. This work is a significant contribution to Calvin studies and to our understandings of biblical interpretation in both the early church and Reformation periods.

Walchenbach's work is first-rate scholarship. This study sheds light on Calvin's use of John Chrysostom as an exegetical tutor. With Chrysostom, Calvin joined in common cause to make the message of Scripture accessible for the world to which the Word of God is given, ever old, ever new.

Donald K. McKim

Preface to the Second Edition

IT IS A PLEASURE to welcome to a wider audience this work that in 1974 constituted a PhD dissertation submitted to the Graduate Faculty of Arts and Sciences of the University of Pittsburgh, a degree offered in conjunction with Pittsburgh Theological Seminary.

Since the completion of that initial work, an enormous amount of Calvin scholarship has appeared affirming the importance of Calvin as a biblical exegete, and that exegesis then, in a back-and-forth manner, formed the basis for his theological "system." Born into an age in which the Latin Bible was the only known translation of Scripture, and then known primarily by priests only, Calvin was convinced that the understanding of Scripture by the common layperson was of first importance. This was not just because the spirit of the age in good humanist fashion was *ad fontes*—back to the sources—but because knowledge of the Bible was a matter of appreciating the meaning of the term "good news," a matter of claiming for one's self the promises of God, a matter of eternal salvation and indeed life and death itself. Therefore the church is to be the "school of Christ," where laypersons as well as clergy, and particularly young people, would come under the influence of the primary curriculum in this school, sacred Scripture.

But one can study Scripture and become confused! In response to this easily confirmed observation by all who have embarked on such an adventure, Calvin decided to do three things. First, as he observes in his *John Calvin to the Reader*, he would write a "guide" to help students of the divine Word, "in order that they may be able both to have easy access to it and advance in it without stumbling. For I believe I have so embraced the sum of religion in all its parts, and have arranged it in such an order, that if anyone rightly grasps it, it will not be difficult for him to determine what he ought especially to seek in Scripture, and to what end he ought to relate its contents." This "guide" of course turned out to be his massive *Institutes of the Christian Religion*.

Second, he determined to write and publish interpretations of Scripture, commentaries on almost every book of the Bible. Moreover he would do this with one goal in mind, "lucid brevity," meaning he would confine himself to the clear and straightforward meaning of the text, and include theological observations based on the text in his *Institutes*. Such determination is demonstrated again from his *John Calvin to the Reader*, where he says, "I shall always condense them [the commentaries], because I shall have no need to undertake long doctrinal discussions, and to digress into 'commonplaces' (theological topics). That he carried out this goal is confirmed in his preface to his Romans commentary, addressed to his friend Simon Gyrnaeus, where he says, "Three years ago, when we conferred together about the best sort of Scripture exposition, I remember that the approach that pleased you most was also acceptable to me beyond all others. We both thought that the chief virtue of an interpreter consists in lucid brevity."

Third, Calvin intended to translate and publish in French the homilies of John Chrysostom. Why Calvin chose the great Greek patristic bishop of Constantinople, and why Calvin saw Chrysostom to be the supreme exegetical tutor is of course the subject of this present work, but suffice it to say here that Calvin's choice of Chrysostom is consistent with his game plan of "lucid brevity," for in Chrysostom Calvin discovered an author who devoted himself to the "literal" and "historic" meaning of the Scriptures, who shied away from all allegorical interpretations and was content with the plain meaning of the text. Once again, Calvin saw in Chrysostom one who would contribute in a major way toward the edification of the "average layperson" in the school of Christ.

It is my hope that the publication of this work will make a humble contribution toward a wider appreciation of Calvin as an outstanding commentator and guide of sacred Scripture.

In such a work as this, there are always institutions and individuals to whom one owes a profound sense of gratitude.

Of the institutions, I would like to express profound appreciation to Hope College, New Brunswick Theological Seminary, and Pittsburgh Theological Seminary. All three, each in their own way, at specific junctures along the way, were formative for me in their Christian commitment, which was and continues to be a gift passed on to generations of students. Added to their high qualities are the attention to the personal needs of individual students and their commitment to excellence in scholarship.

I express my appreciation to the several churches it has been my honor to serve as Minister of Word and Sacrament, and who have invited me to teach a "Calvin class," which was always my joy and delight.

Of all the individuals I might name to whom I am singularly in their debt, one stands out, and that is Dr. Ford Lewis Battles, who was and always shall be, even after his death, "my father in Calvin." It was my honor to complete—the real word should be "survive"—both the ThM and PhD under his constant tutelage. He opened up for me, as he has for countless students, the worlds of classics, languages, patristics, research, humanism, a love of the Reformation, and honesty in scholarship.

I certainly want to express my appreciation to my wife, Pat, for her support through the two degree programs. During the master's studies we served a small church in Markle, Pennsylvania, and she was a delightful pastor's wife as well as the mother of our two very young sons, Tim and Jim. During the doctoral program, we moved onto the campus of Pittsburgh Theological Seminary, where she continued to oversee the growth and development of our two sons while I disappeared into the library of the seminary. When Waverly Presbyterian Church kindly offered me the pastorate with the understanding that I would be given time to write the dissertation, Pat put her RN to work in Pittsburgh hospitals to help financially sustain the family, and of course continued also to be Tim and Jim's mom.

I want also to thank Dr. Donald McKim for his friendship and encouragement. Don and I became friends while we were both PhD candidates at Pittsburgh Theological Seminary and the University of Pittsburgh, and have remained friends over the years. It was at a chance, no providential, meeting at Montreat during the Calvin Jubilee that Don encouraged me to write a curriculum on Calvin for the Presbyterian Church (U.S.A.), and explore the publication of the present work. This book would never have seen the light of day without Don's publishing expertise and wisdom. I thank Don for recommending two gentlemen at Wipf and Stock Publishers, Jim Tedrick, managing editor, and Christian Amondson, assistant managing editor, for their continued support through this project.

There are three individuals to whom I owe a profound debt of gratitude for their research abilities and their rigorous attention to detail. The first is Susan Carlson Wood, freelance copyeditor and Fuller Theological Seminary faculty publications specialist and ECD coordinator, who performed the enormous task of copyediting the manuscript, a monumental undertaking. I have so very much appreciated her patience in ensuring that all the footnotes, bibliography, and references to the original sources are correct. The second is Joel Albritton, who has taught at Fuller Theological Seminary as an adjunct instructor in Theological Latin, teaches at Sylmar High School Magnet in Los Angeles, and spent no small amount of time proofing all the Latin and Greek references in the manuscript against the original texts for accuracy. The third is Sharon Ralston, research librarian at the David Allan Hubbard Library, Fuller Theological Seminary, who helped Joel unearth the original texts in fragile books and massive databases. Without the devoted work of Susan, Joel, and Sharon, this book would never have become available to the general public.

Finally, I am dedicating this work to our four grandchildren, Cole and Nate Walchenbach, sons of Tim and Lisa Walchenbach, who live in Everett, Washington, and Ben and Olivia Walchenbach, son and daughter of Jim and Macy Walchenbach, who live in Poissy, France. In the spirit of Calvin's interest that young people become familiar with the sacred Scriptures, it is my hope that they may also, as the years progress, hear through the Scriptures God's Word to them, and know that their grandfather came from and stood for a great tradition.

Jack Walchenbach
February 2010

Preface to the First Edition

SUMMA IGITUR ERIT UT quos nobis praefecit Dominus, eos suspicia-
mus, eosque et honore et obedientia et gratitudine prosequamur." The
sentence from Calvin—"This, then, is the sum: that we should look up to
those whom God has placed over us, and should treat them with honor,
obedience, and gratefulness"—crystallizes for me not so much a duty as a
debt of profound gratitude I owe to many individuals and institutions. If
there is any one individual toward whom I feel as Calvin enjoins us, it is
Professor Ford Lewis Battles, who has been and always shall be my "father
in Calvin." He opened the door to the study of languages, intimacy with
the Fathers, and made *ad fontes* an exciting adventure.

Other men paved the way: Dr. Henry Voogd at Hope College, Dr.
Justin Vander Kolk at New Brunswick Theological Seminary, Dr. M.
Eugene Osterhaven at Western Theological Seminary.

Three men who serve on the faculty of the University of Pittsburgh
and the Pittsburgh Theological Seminary have provided stimulation and
critical evaluation of the work that follows. Dr. George Kehm has, in class
and seminars, been a most stimulating tutor in theological disciplines.
Dr. Arthur Cochrane provided constant encouragement and hours of
welcome friendly discussion as the work was in process. To the recently
appointed Chairman of the Graduate Program in the Study of Religion at
the University, Dr. Richard H. Wilmer Jr., I, as well as all students in the
program, owe a debt of gratitude for his willing spirit and leadership.

During several years of graduate study at the masters and doctoral
levels, the one person closest to me who gave of herself, sacrificed, and
supported me daily has been my wife, Patricia. Maintaining love at the
center of our home, assuming responsibilities for our two boys, she has

always done more than her share in order to allow me that most precious factor in graduate work, time.

I wish to express my deep appreciation to the Session and Congregation of Waverly United Presbyterian Church, Pittsburgh, who, in such a united and magnanimous spirit, granted me freedom from pastoral responsibilities and encouraged me to complete my studies.

I wish also to thank Mrs. Gail Clare, who typed the manuscript. Her expertise with English grammar and willingness to tackle the mechanics of Latin-English parallel column typing was of invaluable service, but her willingness to learn the typing of Greek was certainly a work of supererogation!

Finally, I wish to dedicate the work that follows to my parents. It was their encouragement, support, prayers, and love that sustained me every step of the way. Both my parents represent the spirit of Calvinism at its very best, and combine with that spirit a true humility, which history has accorded John Chrysostom.

[1974]

Introduction

IN THE YEAR 1500 only a relatively few individuals possessed a copy of the Bible. By the year 1600 it was at least possible for practically everyone in Europe who could read to have his or her own Bible. A number of achievements combined to make the sixteenth century the age of the Bible: the intensive study in the grammar and syntax of Hebrew, Greek, and Latin; the translation of Scripture into every major language group in Europe; the prodigious output of many humanist scholar-printers; the energy provided by the economic development and regional patriotism of the cities; the enthusiasm for learning that the Renaissance bequeathed to the common person. To an extent unequalled since the early years of Christianity, Scripture and commentaries on Scripture came into the hands of an educated laity.

In his 1971 publication, *Calvin's New Testament Commentaries*, T. H. L. Parker makes the observation that although the sixteenth century was, above all things, the age of the Bible, it is strange that this area of the century's history has, apart from some well-trodden paths, been neglected. To be sure, as Parker further remarks, the printed editions of the Bible are well known and have been fairly thoroughly investigated. Also, considerable work has been done on the translations of the Bible. It is when we come to commentaries on the Bible that the deepest poverty appears. While today there is a resurgence of interest in Erasmus, most studies center on Erasmus the "humanist." There exist only two or three works on Luther as an expositor, and the literature of Calvin as an interpreter of Scripture is also meager and disappointing. We are told repeatedly that Calvin is one of the greatest commentators in the history of the Christian church, that he kept to the *literalis sensus* of the biblical text, and that his commentaries are marked by sobriety and faithfulness. This manner of generalizing characterizes virtually every essay on the subject of Calvin as a biblical interpreter.

Expressing the hope that his own book will stimulate further study of the Bible in the sixteenth century, Parker sounds the following warning:

> Let it be said that we do most definitely not want to be told that X, Y, and Z wrote commentaries. We want to know why they wrote commentaries, how they wrote commentaries, where these were published and in what editions, what Greek text they used, how far they were influenced by the Vulgate or vernacular versions, what their principles of interpretation were, how they interpreted this or that word, this or that passage. Anything but such scientific and critical studies are henceforth not worth serious consideration.[1]

Taking seriously Parker's observation that there is a disturbing lack of interest in that branch of church history that deals with the continual reinterpretation of Scripture, and taking equally seriously the necessity of asking critical questions concerning the biblical commentaries produced in the sixteenth century, the following study seeks to examine Calvin as a biblical commentator from the standpoint of the sources he employed as he produced his commentaries. Part of the task of evaluating any commentator on Scripture necessitates an examination of the methodological principles that he employs upon his sources. Calvin's commentaries are a dialogue with the immediate and distant past, drawing on the authority of his contemporaries and predecessors, disassociating himself from false paths and exegetical quirks. At every point Calvin is conscious of his fathers and forefathers in the goodly fellowship of biblical interpreters.

Given Calvin's penetration into the Fathers, the question becomes, which of the sources should be studied in order to evaluate Calvin as a biblical commentator? While one instinctively is drawn to Augustine, we are drawn away from Augustine as an exegetical source by Calvin himself, and led to the Greek Father John Chrysostom. In the Corpus Reformatorum (9:831–38) appears a *Preface* by Calvin to the Homilies of Chrysostom. Apparently Calvin projected a translation of Chrysostom's homilies into French, of which only the Latin *Preface* remains. But in the *Preface*, Calvin speaks in glowing terms of the exegetical excellence of Chrysostom, and forthrightly states that Chrysostom is to be preferred as an interpreter of

---

1. Parker, *Calvin's New Testament Commentaries*, vii.

Scripture over such Greek Fathers as Origen, Athanasius, Basil, Gregory, Cyril, and Theophylact, and over such Latin Fathers as Tertullian, Cyprian, Jerome, Ambrose, and even the highly praised Augustine. Of Augustine, Calvin writes, "Beyond question Augustine is the greatest of all in the dogmas of faith; he is also outstanding as a devotional interpreter of Scripture; but he is over-subtle, with the result that he is less solid and dependable." But of Chrysostom, Calvin writes, "The outstanding merit of our author Chrysostom is that it was his supreme concern always not to turn aside even to the slightest degree from the genuine, simple sense of Scripture, and to allow himself no liberties by twisting the plain meaning of the words." Of all the Fathers we are led to the Greek preacher-patriarch as an exegetical source for the commentaries of Calvin.

Paraphrasing Parker's challenge and applying it to our study, we may say that we most definitely do not want to be told simply that Calvin used Chrysostom as an exegetical source. We want to know why Calvin turned to Chrysostom; on what grounds he was drawn to Chrysostom over against other patristic exegetes; what Calvin found in Chrysostom that was favorable or unfavorable; what methods of interpretation Calvin employed as he entered Chrysostomic material in the commentaries; how Chrysostom understood this or that word, and how Calvin made use of Chrysostom's interpretations; what text of Chrysostom Calvin used.

Part 1 of our study examines Calvin as a commentator on the Bible, the reasons Calvin was drawn to Chrysostom, and an evaluation of Calvin's assessment of Chrysostom based on the writings of Chrysostom himself. Part 2 examines Calvin's use of Chrysostom based on a critical reading of Chrysostom's Greek and Calvin's Latin exegetical work on 1 Corinthians. Proposed solutions to textual and methodological problems raised are offered in the remaining chapters of part 2.

The nature of this study necessitated a substantial amount of translating from either Greek or Latin into English. Wherever Calvin is quoted, the English translation is given in parallel columns. It was felt that the nature of chapter 3 did not demand the inclusion of Chrysostom's Greek, but the analysis of Chrysostom's Greek as it compared with Calvin's Latin in chapter 4, where a side-by-side reading of the commentaries of each exegete is offered, required the inclusion of the Greek, which is translated again in parallel columns. English translations of the material incorporated into this study, where they exist, have always been consulted, but unless specified otherwise, the translations offered here are my own.

T. H. L. Parker's research into the history of Calvin's commentaries proved to be an invaluable guide through the *Calvini Epistolae*, especially those letters that bear on the production of Calvin's commentaries. The first chapter includes much of the fruit of that research.

PART I

Calvin and Chrysostom

The Biblical Commentaries of Calvin

JOHN CALVIN WROTE COMMENTARIES on almost every book of the Bible. We begin our study of Calvin as a commentator on Scripture by examining the publication of Calvin's commentaries. Tracing chronologically the production of the commentaries, we wish to discover, as closely as possible, the intentions, the motivating factors, the historical circumstances that called forth Calvin's volumes. In the course of our historical review, we wish further to establish that the writing of commentaries was not a secondary issue with the Reformer. It will be seen that Calvin early in his literary career determined to write commentaries, and that this literary function was at least of equal importance as the production of the frequently revised *Institutio*.

Early in his career, from February 1535 until early in 1536, Calvin lived in Basel and established lasting friendships with many of the learned Reformers: Munster the Hebraist; Capito; and Simon Grynaeus, professor of Greek and Latin and intimate friend of Erasmus. The dedicatory preface of Calvin's first commentary, Romans, reveals the fact that as early as 1535 Calvin had discussed with Grynaeus methodological principles on which commentaries ought to be written:[1]

---

1. *Calvinus Grynaeo*, Ep. 191, CO 10:402.

Memini, quum ante triennium de optimo enarrandae scripturae genere inter nos familiariter commentaremur, eam quae plurimum tibi placebat rationem mihi quoque prae aliis probatam tunc fuisse. Sentiebat enim uterque nostrum praecipuam interpretis virtutem in perspicua brevitate esse positam.	I remember that three years ago we had a friendly discussion about the best way of interpreting Scripture. The plan which you particularly favored was also the one which at that time I preferred to any others. Both of us felt that lucid brevity constituted the particular virtue of an interpreter.

If Calvin had his mind made up as early as 1535 how commentaries should be written, it was not until 1539 that the first edition of Romans was published. The intervening years would find him concentrating on other matters. There was the *Psychopannychia*, which was strongly criticized by Capito, necessitating revision. The first edition of the *Institutio* was nearing completion and being prepared for publication. The first visit to Italy, the weeks in France to clear up family affairs, and the summons to Geneva all bode ill for work on the Romans commentary. It was undoubtedly the 1538 exile from Geneva and the sojourn in Strassburg that allowed Calvin time to complete and publish the Romans commentary. The dedication was written on October 18, 1539, and in the following March the commentary was published.

While no biblical commentaries were produced during the 1535–1539 interval, Calvin was asked to revise Olivétan's French Bible. Robert Olivétan, Calvin's cousin, was commissioned by the Waldensian church to translate the Bible into French. The work appeared in 1535 with a Latin and a French preface by Calvin, which at least strongly suggests that at that time Calvin was engaged in responsible work on the New Testament.

That Calvin had set his course as a commentator on the Bible is further established by the *Epistle to the Reader*, prefixed to the 1539 edition of the *Institutio* and altered in later editions to keep it up to date. The *Institutio*, Calvin informs the reader, was written to prepare and instruct candidates in sacred theology for the reading of the divine Word. Thereupon Calvin adds:[2]

---

2. *Epistola ad Lectorem*, OS 3:6.

Itaque, hac veluti strata via, siquas posthac Scripturae enarrationes edidero, quia non necesse habebo de dogmatibus longas disputationes instituere, et in locos communes evagari: eas compendio semper astringam.	If, after this road has, as it were, been paved, I shall publish any interpretations of Scripture, I shall always condense them, because I shall have no need to undertake long doctrinal discussions, and to digress into *loci communes*.

That Calvin was not simply pondering whether or not he might publish commentaries, but actually intended to do so is substantiated by this French translation:

> siquas posthac Scripturae enarrationes edidero . . . French trans.: Parquoy si doresenavant nostre Seigneur me donne le moyen et opportunité de faire quelques commentaires . . .[3]

Calvin fully intends to work further on the publication of biblical commentaries, "if only the Lord shall give me the means and opportunity."

Calvin was thirty years old at the publication date of the Romans commentary, March 1540. In addition to this first biblical commentary, he already had to his credit the *Commentary on Seneca's De Clementia* of 1532, the 1536 edition of the *Institutio*, the expanded and revised 1539 *Institutio*, as well as a few shorter treatises. With Romans completed, Calvin planned a set of commentaries on the Pauline corpus. He undoubtedly expected to produce a commentary on 1 Corinthians immediately, but other duties intervened. He attended the conference on Christian reunion at Frankfurt called by Charles V, and later represented the city of Strassburg at the colloquies of Hagenau, Worms, and Ratisbon. These conferences, aimed at reconciliation between Roman Catholics and Protestants, occupied much of his time between 1539 and 1541. In August of 1540 he married Idelette de Bure, and their child, Jacque, was born in July of 1542, only to live a few days. On his return to Geneva September 13, 1541, he began the work of continuing reform in the city. Here he recodified the Genevan laws and constitution; was instrumental in the negotiations with Berne that resulted in the treaty of 1554; entered into protracted controversy with such figures as Pighius, Bolsec, Castellio, and Servatus; and engaged in pastoral work that involved frequent preaching.

---

3. *Argument du Present Livre*, OS 3:8.

Such labors allowed little time for a man of poor health to continue his intended publication of commentaries on the Pauline Epistles.

In spite of all the duties to which Calvin was summoned, his friends never allowed him to give up on the production of the commentaries. Learned people would gather for study and ask when the commentaries would be published. Calvin's friends informed him that it was the work of Satan that prohibited the production of further biblical commentaries. As a commentator Calvin was allowed no respite. Indeed, it was Farel himself, the redheaded Reformer who threatened Calvin with the wrath of God if he did not take up the work in Geneva. In 1546 Farel coolly wrote to Calvin:[4]

Paulum perge familiarem omni-	Go on to make Paul familiar to
bus reddere pro gratia tibi data.	everyone, according to the grace
	given to you.

Almost in exasperation, Calvin replied:[5]

Quod me ad scribendum hortaris,	As to your exhorting me to write,
utinam plus esset otii aliquando et	I only wish I had more time and
valetudo robustior!	better health.

Calvin's commentaries were not so much offered as demanded. The human situation that produced the commentaries is to be described not as the outpouring of an author who wished to have his writings printed, but as the response of an already overworked pastor and ecumenical theologian to the demand and requests of a waiting public. Learned and humble folk alike considered Calvin's studied opinion on a text to be final and definitive. At one time an argument arose among some of the learned in Strassburg as to the meaning of 2 Corinthians 6:1: "We are fellow workmen with God." One of those involved in the discussion was Francis Bauduin, a civil lawyer, who placed before the group his own opinion on the meaning of the text, but was thereupon instructed to refer the sentence to Calvin for his opinion, which would end the matter:[6]

4. *Farellus Calvino*, Ep. 825, CO 12:379.

5. *Calvinus Farello*, Ep. 832, CO 12:391.

6. *Balduinus Calvino*, Ep. 4144, CR 20:379–80.

Incidit nuper disputatio in coetu doctorum virorum de illo ad Corinthios dicto Pauli: Dei sumus cooperarii sive συνεργοί. Hic omnes vehementer tuos commentarios qui totam contraversiam facile composuissent, desiderant. . . . Hanc sententiam iussus sum ad te referre ut pronuncies verane sit an minus. Quod ubi definieris nulla erit provocatio.

Recently an argument took place during a gathering of some learned men concerning the following words of Paul: "We are fellow workers with God." . . . I was instructed to refer this sentence to you, so that you may pronounce whether it is true or not. For when you give your interpretation, there will be no challenge to it.

The insistent demand for the commentaries, and the benefit they would have for the church, is well expressed by one Valerandus Pollanus. Pollanus, who described himself as *filius et discipulus* to Calvin, wrote to the Reformer in December of 1545:[7]

Wendelinus negat posse quod petis de commentariis ad Corinth. praestare. Si per nostrum Balduino misisses, nihil erat facilius. Sed in sequentes nundinas poterit res perfici. Et simul in utramque, quod multi optant. Numquam puto quidquam ardentioribus votis expetitum. Omnes docti, quoties me conveniunt, rogant, quando tandem illa commentaria sint habituri. Dicam aliquid: vos parum sapitis, dum ita permittitis vos a Satana rapi ad alia, non contemnenda illa quidem, sed tamen non tam utilia quam esset eiusmodi scripturae tractatio.

Wendelinus says that he cannot perform what you ask about the commentaries on Corinthians. If you had sent them by our friend Bauduin, nothing would have been easier. But in about three weeks he will be able to do what you ask, at the same time on both epistles, which many desire. I think there was never anything more ardently awaited. All the learned, when they meet, ask when those commentaries will finally be ready. Allow me to say something to you: you are not very wise in permitting Satan to tear you away into other matters. Although they certainly are not to be despised, they are not as useful as the discussion of Scripture.

7. *Pollanus Calvino*, Ep. 729, CO 12:216.

Idem dolent et queruntur de Bucero omnes pii et docti. Sed quid ego? Vide, mi pater: sic loquor quum mihi de Christi gloria et ecclesiae aedificio aliquid persuadeo. Vellem enim Calvinus semel hoc in animo destinasse nunquam interquiescere, donec perpetuos in epistolas Pauli, deinde in Prophetas, deinde in reliquos libros sacros scripsisset commentarios. Deus bone, quantum illa iuvarent ecclesiam! quantum ad gloriam Christi facerent! quam non abolendam immortalitatem compararent!	All the pious and learned complain and lament about Bucer in the same manner. But why am I saying this? Look, my father, I am speaking like this because I am persuaded that it is for the glory of Christ and the edification of His Church. I want Calvin to determine just one thing—that he will never rest until he has written commentaries on all of the Epistles of Paul, then on the prophets, then on the rest of the sacred books. Good God! How they would benefit the church! How much they would do for the glory of Christ! What inexhaustible immortality they would provide.

Just as Calvin was summoned to Geneva by a "dreadful imprecation," the commentaries on Paul, the prophets, and all of Scripture were demanded by a public that, seemingly, could not do without them. The learned would not allow Calvin a moment's rest until the next commentary was produced. With such requests based on the edification of the church, the greater glory to Christ, and indeed, immortality itself, how could Calvin avoid further work on his commentaries? If the letter from Pollanus is at all representative of the success that met the earlier commentaries, Calvin must have determined to work on the remainder of the Pauline corpus with more determination than ever. This supposition is supported by the speed with which the remaining New Testament commentaries were produced. Pollanus had written to Calvin in December of 1545. On January 24, 1546, Calvin wrote the dedication to the 1 Corinthians commentary, addressed to his friend de Fallais:[8]

8. *Calvinus Fallesio*, Ep. 753, CO 12:258.

Utinam hic noster Commentarius, quo Pauli epistolam non minus obscuram quam utilem conatus sum explicare, sicuti a multis pridem expetitus atque etiam subinde flagitatus, nunc in lucem prodit, ita spei votisque omnium similiter respondeat. Hoc ideo dico, non ut fructum inde aliquem laudis percipiam, quae ambitio a Christi servis longe abesse debet, sed quia prodesse omnibus ipsum cupio: quod fieri nequit nisi probetur. Ego quidem, ut citra ostentationem plurimum ecclesiae Dei prodesset, summa fide nec minore diligentia elaboravi. Quantum profecerim, iudicium ab ipsa experientia facient lectores. . . .

In this commentary of mine, I have attempted to expound an epistle of Paul's, that is no less difficult than valuable. Many people have been asking for it, and have indeed been making furious demands for it for a long time. Now that its publication has seen the light, I hope that it may measure up to the expectations of all. I say this, not in order to receive praise from the fruit of my labors, for such ambitions ought to be far from the servants of Christ; but because I desire that it might be useful to all, and the commentary cannot do that if it is not acceptable. For my own part, I have labored with the utmost faithfulness, and no less diligence, so that without any ostentation, the work might be of the greatest service to the Church of God. The degree to which I have succeeded, my readers will judge from their own experience with the work. . . .

The commentary on 2 Corinthians was completed by August 11, 1546. The fate of the manuscript was in question for some time, being lost on its way from Geneva to Strassburg. Stricken by the author's nightmare of a lost manuscript, Calvin wrote in near hysteria to Viret:[9]

9. *Calvinus Vireto*, Ep. 817, CO 12:368.

Scripsi ad te ante triduum quum adhuc de superioribus literis dubium esset, periissentne an tibi redditae fuissent. Iam alia quoque maioris momenti perdita fuisse video. Utinam mihi Ioannes Girardus indicasset se biblia missurum. Vetuissem. Ita salvae fuissent reliquae chartae.... De meo commentario nihildum audivi.... Ego, si intellexero lucubrationem meam fuisse perditam, Paulum non amplius attingere decrevi. Et tamen magnum est periculum. Mensis enim ab eius discessu elapsus erat, quum mihi scriptum est nondum illuc appulisse.

I wrote to you three days ago when there was still doubt about the earlier letter, whether it had been lost or delivered to you. Now I see that other and more important things have been lost. I wish that John Girard had told me that he was going to send his Bible. I certainly would have told him not to. Then the remaining papers would have been safe.... I have heard nothing yet about my commentary.... If I learn that all my labor is lost, I have determined to give up commentaries on Paul. And yet there is great danger. For it was a month after it left here before they wrote to tell me my commentary had not arrived.

The commentary on 2 Corinthians was apparently found, however, for it was published by Jean Girard in French in 1547. Calvin thereupon produced the remaining commentaries on the Pauline corpus with amazing speed. The "Galatians Group," consisting of Galatians, Ephesians, Philippians, and Colossians, was completed before February 1, 1548, the date of the dedication. The commentaries on 1 and 2 Timothy followed swiftly in the same year. In 1549 came Hebrews and Titus, and when the corpus was completed with 1 and 2 Thessalonians and the Catholic Epistles in 1551, the collected edition was finally published.

The collected and revised Pauline corpus called forth a letter of appreciation from a former pupil of Reuchlin, Ambrose Moiban of Bratislava:[10]

---

10. *Moibanus Calvino*, Ep. 1615, CO 14:307.

Gratulor tibi illud insigne Dei donum, quo tam feliciter ἐν ἐνεργίᾳ spiritus interpretaris scripturas sanctas. Non* est cuiusvis hoc Dei donum rarissimum. Sit laus omnipotenti patri coelesti. Tua scripta, virum nunquam visum, semper amavi, tametsi doctorum hominum consuetudinem semper quaesiverim. Tua lego et relego, nec capior ullo taedio. Et inprimis probo quod hoc anno totum Paulum tuis sanctissimis cogitationibus ornaris . . .	I congratulate you on the remarkable gift of God by which, in the power of the Spirit, you interpret the Holy Scriptures so felicitously. This gift of God to anyone is very rare. Praise be to the omnipotent Father in heaven. Although I have never met you, I always love to read your writings, notwithstanding the fact that I always seek the fellowship of learned men. I have read and re-read your works, and am never tired of them. And I am especially happy that this year you have adorned the whole of Paul with your most holy thoughts. . . .

* Certainly the context here demands that *non* must be a misprint, or the statement is a rhetorical question.

Having completed, revised, and collected his commentaries on the Pauline corpus, including Hebrews, Calvin determined to work on the remaining New Testament books while, at the same time, making inroads into the Old Testament. Acts was published in two parts, 1552 and 1554. In the intervening year came the commentary on John's Gospel; the New Testament commentaries were concluded with the *Harmony of the Synoptic Gospels* in 1555. With the *Harmonia* Calvin concluded his work on the New Testament. He had expounded on every book except 2 and 3 John and Revelation.

Calvin produced his first Old Testament commentary, Isaiah, in 1551. The commentary on Genesis was to take some time to write, being published in 1554. In 1557 came both Psalms and Hosea. A second and revised edition of Isaiah appeared in 1559, along with the first publication of all the Minor Prophets. In 1561 came Daniel; and 1563 saw the publication of Jeremiah, Lamentations, and the *Harmonia* on the rest of the Pentateuch. Joshua and Ezekiel (1–20) were published posthumously.

Thus we can affirm that Calvin devoted himself through his career to the writing, revising, and collecting of his biblical commentaries. It was Calvin's life-long penetration into Scripture that provided the foundation for his work in that other major production of his life, the *Institutio*.[11]

11. The question of the relationship between the commentaries and the *Institutio* is considered in chapter 4.

What motivated Calvin in such a prodigious undertaking? Perhaps the essential motivating spirit behind Calvin the biblical commentator is to be found in his 1551 dedicatory epistle of the Catholic Epistles[12] to Edward VI of England. It is in this dedicatory letter that we discover the driving force that impelled the already overworked Calvin toward the completion of the commentaries. Calvin was anxious to encourage the English rulers to give their full support to the Reformation. To this end he dedicated first the commentary on Isaiah, and then the commentary on the Catholic Epistles:[13]

En iterum ad te redeo, praestantissime Rex. Neque enim, si quos nuper in Iesaiam commetarios obtuli gratum Maiestati tuae speravi fore munus, ideo tamen animi mei voto satisfactum est. Ergo Epistolas canonicas (ut eas vocari usu receptum est) quasi auctarii vice quod iustam mensuram impleret addendas putavi: ut simul utrumque opus in manus tuas veniret. Et certe quum vel gentibus procul dissitis vel Iudaeis varias ac longinquas regiones sparsim incolentibus scriptae sint, nihil illis novum accidit, si et traiiciendum hodie sit mare, et superandi multiplices viarum anfractus ut ad tuam Maiestatem perveniant. Quanquam sic tibi, Rex inclyte, privatim offero meos labores ut sub tuo nomine publicati omnibus prosint.

Again I return to you, most excellent King. For though I did not expect that the commentaries on Isaiah, which I lately dedicated to your Majesty, would be a worthy gift, yet they were offered with the good wishes of my heart. I have, therefore, thought to add the Catholic Epistles (as they are commonly called according to standard practice) as a supplement to complete the full measure, so that both might come to your hands at the same time. Just as they were written either to Gentiles a great distance away, or to Jews who were residents of far scattered countries, it is nothing new for these letters to cross the sea today on their circuitous route to your Majesty. Thus, as a private individual I offer my labors to you, most illustrious King, in order that they may be published under your name, and profit all people.

---

12. The "Catholic" or "Canonical" Epistles consist of 1 and 2 Peter, 1 John, and the Epistles of James and Jude.

13. *Calvinus Regi Eduardo*, Ep. 1443, CO 14:30.

Following this introduction to the dedicatory epistle, Calvin launches into an extended discussion concerning the reason and necessity for writing biblical commentaries. Larger issues are at stake than meeting the wishes of those who enjoy learned opinions on the interpretation of Scripture. Against those who profess the new faith atrocious cruelty is everywhere displayed. In those places where the pure doctrine of religion does prevail, force and the use of arms seek to corrupt what has been established. But more than that, the pope himself is contemplating the continuation of the Council of Trent, temporarily in abeyance, which five years earlier had passed decrees elevating tradition to a position of authority in the church alongside Scripture. It is the church, and not the private citizen, said the council, that must judge the meaning and interpretation of Scripture:[14]

Praeterea, ad coercenda petulantia ingenia, decernit, ut nemo, suae prudentiae in- nixus, in rebus fidei, et morum ad aedificationem doctrinae christianae pertinentium, sac- ram scripturam ad suos sensus contorquens, contra eum sensu, quem tenuit et tenet sancta mater ecclesia, cuius est judicare de vero sensu, et interpretatione scripturarum sanctarum, aut etiam contra unanimem consensum patrum ipsam scripturam sacram interpretari audeat, etiamsi huiusmodi interpretationes nullo unquam tempore in lucem edendae forent. Qui contravenerint, per ordinarios declarentur, et poenis a jure statutis puniantur.

Furthermore, in order to restrain petulant spirits, the council decrees that no one, relying on his own skill, shall—in matters of faith and morals pertaining to the edification of Christian doctrine—wresting the sacred Scripture to his own senses, presume to interpret the said sacred Scripture contrary to that sense which holy mother Church,—whose it is to judge the true sense and interpretation of holy Scripture—holds and does hold; or even contrary to the unanimous consent of the Fathers; even though such interpretations were never (intended) to be at any time pub- lished. Those who contravene shall be made known by their Ordinaries, and be punished with the penalties established by law.

Calvin was not unwilling to bow before the judgments of a legiti- mate council, if, as he observes, such a council were possible. But when

14. Schaff, "Canons and Decrees of the Council of Trent," 83. Schaff translation; ibid.

the council allows those whom it deems to be heretics no appeal, and demands all to define religion at the whim and will of the council and not by the Word of God, submission to a council is impossible. If a council were called at which those advocating the reformed opinion might be allowed to speak and present in safety a suitable defense, then the authority of the council would not be questioned. But only the "anointed and mitred" are permitted at the council. Such prelates cannot bear to hear the "clear thunderings of truth." If the Word of God were heard, the "sacred ears of bishops would be so irreverently offended" that the indignity would be intolerable. If only Scripture were allowed its own authority, adversaries of the reform would be compelled to silence. Bishops at the council as much as admit this fact when they contend that owing to the ambiguous meaning of Scripture all people ought to stand solely on the judgment of the church. By laying aside the Word of God, the whole right of defining doctrine is thereby transferred to the ecclesiastical hierarchy. They kiss the closed copies of the Scripture as a kind of worship; yet when they charge it with being obscure and ambiguous, they allow it no more authority than if no part of it existed in writing. The Romanists thus do not allow to Scripture the authority that properly belongs to it. Their will alone is αὐτόπιστος, rather than the sure teaching of Scripture. Since Scripture is shamefully deformed by the false comments of the Sophists, and the hired rabble of the pope is bent on this stratagem, in order to obscure the light by their own smoke, it is right for the reformers to restore the brightness of Scripture. One scholar at least will devote his life and studies to this work:[15]

Ego sane quod mihi reliquum est vitae, si otium simul et libertas suppetet, huic praecipue studio destinavi. Primum huius laboris fructum ecclesia cui sum addictus ita percipiet ut longius deinde manet. Etsi enim a muneris mei functione perquam exiguum mihi tempus restat, id tamen, quantulumcunque est, institui ad hoc scriptionis genus conferre.	I soundly resolve to devote myself to this work as long as I live, if time and opportunity are afforded me. The church to which I belong shall receive the first fruit of my labor that it may endure the longer. For although the discharging of my duties leaves me very little time, yet, however short it may be, I have determined to devote my life to this kind of writing.

15. *Cal. Reg. Ed.*, Ep. 1443, CO 14:37.

Calvin wishes the king to understand his commentaries on the Catholic Epistles as a pledge of what is to come:[16]

Atque, ut ad te revertar, clarissime Rex, hoc mediocre pignus habes meos commentarios, quibus canonicas Epistolas, ubi multa obscura alioqui et recondita habebantur, ita explicare conatus sum ut lectori non prorsus ignavo familiaris ad verum sensum accessus pateat.	And, to return to you, most illustrious King, you have here a modest pledge in my commentaries on the Canonical Epistles, where many things, previously regarded as obscure and mysterious, I have so tried to explain that a ready entrance to the meaning may be opened up for the not utterly lazy reader.

Finally, Calvin eloquently charges the king:[17]

Sicuti autem pro sua facultate ad debellandum Antichristum arma suppeditant scripturae interpretes, has quoque Maiestatis tuae proprias esse partes memineris, quo integra vigeat religio, sinceram ac germanam scripturae interpretationem ab indignis calumniis vindicare. Non temere per Moisem Deus mandat, simul atque rex populi sui inauguratus fuerit, ut sibi describendum curet Legis volumen. Quid si privatus in eius se lectione iam diligenter exercuerit?	As interpreters of Scripture according to their ability supply weapons to fight against Antichrist, so you also must bear in mind that it is a duty which belongs to your Majesty, to vindicate from unworthy calumnies the true and genuine interpretation of Scripture, so that true religion may flourish. It was not without reason that God commanded through Moses that, as soon as a king was appointed over his people, he was to take care to have a copy of the Law written out for himself. Why so, if as a private individual he had already exercised himself diligently in reading it?

16. Ibid.
17. Ibid.

Verum ne ignorent reges, tum singulari doctrina se habere opus, tum peculiare eius tuendae et asserendae munus sibi iniungi, legi suae Dominus in eorum palatio sacrum domicilium assignat. Porro, quum aetatis tuae modum longe superet in hac parte heroica animi tui magnitudo, non est quod plus verborum in te acuendo consumam. Vale, Rex nobilissime. Dominus Maiestatem tuam protegere fide sua, ut coepit, pergat: prudentiae ac fortitudinis spiritu te et consiliarios gubernet, totumque regni statum incolumem pacatumque servet.

In order that kings might know that they themselves need this remarkable doctrine, and that it is their special duty to defend and maintain it, the Lord assigns to His Law a sacred habitation in their places. Moreover, since the heroic greatness of your mind far surpasses the measure of your age, there is no reason why I should add more words to stimulate you. Farewell, most noble King. May the Lord continue to preserve your Majesty in His faith as He has already begun. May He govern you and your counselors with the Spirit of wisdom and fortitude, and keep your whole kingdom in safety and peace.

These are not the words of a man who produced commentaries as an afterthought, or for whom they were a secondary issue. Calvin's own words belie the frequently found estimate of Calvin summed up in the words of Imbart de La Tour:

> The whole of Calvinism is in the *Institutes*, his principal work, the work most valued by Calvin . . . who spent his entire life revising and reshaping as well as enriching it. All his other works, commentaries, controversies, smaller dogmatic or moral treatises, are related to it like advanced redoubts meant to defend the heart of the place against the enemy.[18]

Or again, the very first sentence in the scholarly production of Luchesius Smits, "Calvin is a man of one book,"[19] can hardly stand against both the expressed intention and monumental output of Calvin. Calvin labored at the commentaries because they were called forth from a public that longed for the studied opinion of a man equipped to handle the languages

18. Imbart de La Tour, *Les Origines de la Réforme*, 4:55.

19. Smits, *Saint Augustin dans L'Oeuvre de Jean Calvin*, 1:1.

and able to lay open the mind and thoughts of the biblical authors. He labored at the commentaries because his readers affirmed they edified the church, were an instrument to the greater glory of Christ, and indeed, the immortality of the readers. He labored at the commentaries so that kings might maintain and uphold religion in their lands, and that common people might have a guide through difficult territory. Moreover, since to him the pronouncements of councils and the whims of prelates sought to confine within the hierarchical structure of the church the interpretation of Scripture, Calvin resolved to provide an access to the Word of God.

2

Calvin's *Praefatio in Chrysostomi Homilias*

H AVING WRITTEN OR INTENDING to write commentaries on almost all the books in the Bible, one might consider that Calvin would have rested in the conviction that he had accomplished or would indeed accomplish a life's goal, the publication of the Word of God to as many people as possible. On Scripture he had lectured; preached; written commentaries, treatises, catechisms; and he had organized "the sum of religion" in the *Institutio*. Was such a literary output not sufficient to establish the church once again on its proper foundation, the Word of God? Did not all people now have the words of Scripture and aids as an understanding of Scripture in sufficient supply? Apparently not.

At some time in his life[1] Calvin projected the publication of a monumental work that, according to his own words, was new and unusual. Calvin, in order to provide even further help to Christian understanding, piety, and training, proposed to publish in a French translation the homilies of the fourth-century Antiochene preacher and patriarch of Constantinople, John Chrysostom. Apparently the project was never carried through, but we do possess the Latin *Preface* to the intended French translation. We turn now to an examination of Calvin's *Praefatio in Chrysostomi Homilias*.[2]

Why should a Reformer of the sixteenth century make available to French-speaking Protestants homilies preached nine hundred years

1. See appendix A for a proposed dating of the *Preface*.
2. *Praef. in Chry. Hom.*, CO 9:831–38.

previously to a Greek culture of the distant East? Calvin knew that the publication of homilies from an ancient preacher would be seen as a strange project in the eyes of many of his contemporaries. Conscious of his ever-present detractors, Calvin begins the *Preface*:[3]

Quia inusitatum adhuc est hoc lucubrationis genus quod nunc in publicum edo, videor mihi operae pretium facturus, si consilii mei rationem breviter exponam. Video enim, quod in rebus novis evenire fere solet, quosdam non defuturos qui laborem hunc meum non modo supervacuum contemnant, sed etiam ut parum utilem ecclesiae repudiandum prorsus censeant, Quos tamen ipsos non diffido propitios mihi fore, si meis rationibus intendere paulisper animum sustineant.	Because this kind of study that I am now publishing is still out of the ordinary I think it will be worth my while to explain briefly my purpose and object; for I see that, as nearly always happens in the case of something new and unusual, there will not be lacking some men who will not only belittle this work of mine as pointless, but will also roundly consider that it should be rejected as of little use to the Church. But I do not doubt that these men will come to favor my point of view if they give their attention for a few moments to examining my purposes.

The reason Calvin proposes this new and unusual publication is synonymous with the intentions and goals to which he dedicated himself as a biblical commentator, namely, providing an access to Scripture for all people, and in particular the common people (*plebiis hominibus*). "We are well aware," notes Calvin, "of the chorus of objections raised by the untrained when the proposal was first made that the Gospel should be read to the common people." It was thought a dastardly crime to make available for all, that which had been so closely guarded by priests and monks. But now that the Scriptures have been published, those who were so displeased at the action give their resounding approval. Indeed, anyone with a "grain of piety" can see that people who were formerly being robbed of Scriptural treasures now have "Christ the Sun of Righteousness" shining upon them; and they can now perceive His power, and are able to embrace Him. Yet

---

3. Ibid., CO 9:831. With a few exceptions, I have made use of McIndoe's translation, "Preface to the Homilies of Chrysostom," 19–26.

there is something equally important as access to Scripture; one must also know what to look for in the sacred writings:[4]

Verum ut tantopere nostra refert doctrina hac salutari non defraudari, qua in vitam aeternam animae pascuntur, ita, ubi eam sumus assequuti, non minus necesse est, scire quid illic quaerere oporteat, scopumque aliquem habere ad quem dirigamur. Quod si non fiat contingat profecto nobis multum diuque sine magno fructu vagari.	But just as it is of the utmost importance for us not to be deprived of this saving doctrine by which souls are nourished unto life eternal, so when we have achieved access to Scripture it is equally necessary to know what we ought to look for in it, and to have some kind of goal towards which to direct ourselves. Failing this, we may very well find ourselves wandering long and far afield without much fruit for our labor.

To be sure, it is the Spirit of God that is our best guide, indeed the only guide that enables us to grasp heavenly wisdom. Yet God has not left us without other instruments whose function it is to assist us toward the truth:[5]

Quum tamen Dominus eadem, qua nos per spiritum suum illuminat, benignitate adminicula quoque nobis contulerit, quibus voluit studium nostrum in veritatis suae investigatione adiuvari, non est cur ea vel negligamus quasi supervacua, vel etiam quasi non adeo necessaria minus curemus. Obversari enim animis nostris debet quod ait Paulus, omnia nostra esse, nos autem Christi. Serviant ergo nobis quae in usum nostrum Dominus destinavit.	Nevertheless, since the Lord by the same bountifulness by which He illumines us through His Spirit, has bestowed upon us aids (*adminicula*) which He intended should be of assistance to our study in the investigation of His truth, there is no reason why we should either regard them as superfluous or even pay less attention to them as if they were not necessary; for we ought to bear in mind what Paul says, that all things are ours and we are Christ's. Let us then make free use of what the Lord intended for our use.

4. *Praef. in Chry. Hom.*, CO 9:832.
5. Ibid.

Here at heart is the basis for Calvin's intention to publish Chrysostom. The same Lord who, by the operation of his Spirit, applies the teaching of Scripture to our hearts has seen fit to give us aids and instruments that prove useful in our search for truth. If it is a right that ordinary Christian people (*plebem christianam*) should not be robbed of the Word of God, they should not be robbed of the aids God has provided for them. Ordinary people do not have the training or accomplishments that are of such assistance in dealing with the Scriptures. Therefore they should be helped by the work of interpreters who have "advanced in the knowledge of God" to the point that they can lead others also to the truth.

Calvin is aware of one further objection that might be raised against his intended publication of Chrysostom:[6]

Equidem non me fugit quid hic obiectari mihi queat: Chrysostomum, quem vulgo hominum publicare instituo, doctis tantum et literarum peritis lucubrationes suas destinasse.	Now I am not unaware of an objection that can be raised against me at this point: that Chrysostom, whom I am on the point of making available to the common people, intended his studies only for the learned and the educated.

Against such an opinion Calvin observes that Chrysostom intended the homilies for the people at large (*universum populum*), a goal that Calvin himself identifies with his own intention:[7]

At vero, nisi et titulus et orationis compositio mentitur, quos ad universum populum sermones habuit hic complexus est. Ita certe et rerum tractationem et dictionem attemperat quasi hominum multitudinem instituere velit.	But on the contrary, unless both the title and style of his oratory are lying, this man composed sermons which he delivered to the people at large. Thus without doubt he modifies both his methods of treatment and language as though wishing to instruct the general run of men.

6. Ibid., CO 9:833.
7. Ibid.

Proinde frustra quis conten-
dat, eum inter doctos recon-
ditum esse oportere, quum
data opera studuerit esse
popularis. Certe haec mihi
plus satis iusta excusatio est,
quod causam habeo cum
Chrysostomo coniunctam,
quia nihil aliud quam cum
plebe communico quae ille
plebi nominatim inscripsit.

Accordingly, anyone who maintains
that he ought to be hidden away
among the learned is quite wrong,
seeing that he has taken pains
specifically to be popular. At least
I myself am more than sufficiently
justified in that I have a common
cause with Chrysostom, because I
am doing nothing else than communicate to the people the things
which he addressed specifically to
the people.

There is one further goal that Calvin hopes his publication of Chrysostom will attain. Calvin has in mind, as his intended readers, not only
the common people of the church, but pastors as well. They too should
have an acquaintance with the ancient forms of the church. Those who
hold the teaching office should be familiar with this kind of literature:[8]

Quantopere autem referat,
ecclesiasticum pastorem tenere
qualis fuerit vetusta ecclesiae
facies, et aliqua saltem antiq-
uitatis notitia esse praeditum,
palam esse existimo. Itaque
hac quoque parte fructuosus
esse poterit meus iste labor,
vel omnium confessione, quia
nemo negat utile esse versari
in hoc scripti genere omnes
eos qui docendi provinciam in
christiano populo sustinent.

I think it is obvious that it is of
great importance for the pastor
of a church to grasp what the ancient form of the Church was like
and to be furnished with at least
some knowledge of antiquity;
and so this work of mine might
well prove fruitful in this respect
also, as all will agree, because no
one denies that it is useful for all
who carry out the teaching office
among Christian people to be
familiar with this kind of writing.

Why, out of all the Fathers, does Calvin choose Chrysostom? In answer
to that question Calvin submits an impressive series of names, comparing
them with Chrysostom:[9]

8. Ibid.
9. Ibid., CO 9:834.

He then moves from a consideration of the "Greeks" to the "Latins":[10]

Quantum ad Latinos attinet, Tertulliani, Cypriani labores istius generis exciderunt. Nec Hilarii multa habentur. Commentarii in Psalterium parum ad intelligendam prophetae mentem faciunt. Canones in Matthaeum plus quidem momenti habent. Sed illic quoque deest praecipua interpretis virtus, perspicuitas.	As far as the Latins are concerned, works of the kind we are considering are lost in the case of Tertullian and Cyprian, and not many of Hilary's survive. The latter's commentaries on the Psalter have little value for understanding the mind of the prophet. The Canons of Matthew do indeed have more importance, but there too is lacking that outstanding quality of the interpreter, clarity.

Jerome does not fare well in Calvin's estimation:[11]

Quae in vetus testamentum scripsit Hieronymus merito exiguam laudem inter doctos habent. Est enim totus fere in allegoriis demersus, quibus nimium licentiose scripturam contorquet. Commentarii in evangelium Matthaei et duas Pauli epistolas tolerabiles, nisi quod hominem non satis in rebus ecclesiasticis exercitatum sapiunt.	Jerome's writings on the Old Testament have deservedly little recognition among the learned; for he is almost completely sunk in allegories in which he twists Scripture in far too free a manner. His commentaries on the Gospel of Matthew and two epistles of Paul are tolerably good except that they smack of one who is not sufficiently experienced in affairs of the Church.

And on Ambrose:[12]

Melior ac uberior ipso Ambrosius, tametsi verbis brevissimus est. . . .	Better and richer than he [Jerome] is Ambrose, despite his extreme brevity. . . .

10. Ibid.
11. Ibid.
12. Ibid.

While Augustine is given his due credit, as an interpreter of Scripture he falls short of Chrysostom:[13]

Augustinus citra controversiam in fidei dogmatibus omnes superat. Religiosus quoque imprimis scripturae interpres, sed ultra modum argutus. Quo fit ut minus firmus sit ac solidus.	Augustine is beyond question the greatest of all in the dogmas of faith; he is also outstanding as a devotional interpreter of Scripture; but he is oversubtle, with the result that he is less solid and dependable.

Then follows the basis of Calvin's estimate and appreciation of Chrysostom:[14]

Chrysostomi autem nostri haec prima laus est quod ubique illi summo studio fuit a germana scripturae sinceritate ne minimum quidem deflectere, ac nullam sibi licentiam sumere in simplici verborum sensu contorquendo.	The outstanding merit of our author, Chrysostom, is that it was his supreme concern always not to turn aside even to the slightest degree from the genuine, simple sense of Scripture and to allow himself no liberties by twisting the plain meaning of the words.

Of all the Fathers, Calvin thus awards to Chrysostom first place in the exposition of Scripture. Therefore, let us enjoy the generosity of the Lord! The homilies of Chrysostom belong to all people. On these grounds Calvin projects his translation and publication of the celebrated homilies.

That Calvin intended to publish Chrysostom at all offers demonstrable evidence of Calvin's magnanimity, for there are major disagreements between the two authors on critical theological issues. In the *Preface*, Calvin takes pains to single out those *loci* in which Chrysostom seems to be less than satisfactory, that readers might be duly forewarned. According to Calvin, Chrysostom, in his excessive tendency to preach the free-will of man and the granting of rewards for works, obscures the grace of God in man's election. Chrysostom strives to work into the idea of election some reference to our own efforts; although for Calvin, Scripture

13. Ibid., CO 9:835.
14. Ibid.

demonstrates that there is nothing by which God may be urged into elect-
ing us. Chrysostom divides the responsibility for our calling between
God and ourselves, while Calvin wishes to ascribe the full responsibility
for our calling and election to God alone. Chrysostom is emphatic that
free-will is necessary for the pursuit of virtue and the observance of the
divine law. For Calvin, however, all capacity to do good is a gift, and no
merit or virtue is ascribed to man. Calvin is afraid that Chrysostom makes
our righteousness before God to some degree dependent on good works;
while Scripture, Calvin insists, demands that our justification is grounded
on faith in Jesus Christ. Given such major theological differences, Calvin
still intends to publish Chrysostom's homilies!

Yet there must be good reasons why so skilled an interpreter as
Chrysostom does not clearly emphasize both the wretched condition of
man and the sole remedy for this wretchedness, the grace of God. Calvin
now reaches across the centuries to exonerate the patriarch-preacher, ex-
plaining why Chrysostom failed to ascribe all honor to God alone. Calvin
observes how little agreement there is between the pronouncements of the
philosophers and the doctrine handed down in the Scriptures concerning
the blindness of the human intellect and the perversity of the heart. Calvin
allows that in Chrysostom's day there were philosophers who dabbled in
religion with the object of alienating others. Now Chrysostom, according
to Calvin, saw it as his duty to meet their quibbles and malicious tech-
niques. The only manner in which he might accomplish this goal was to
modify his standpoint to avoid revolting too strongly from the common
opinion of people. Chrysostom thus had at least good intentions:[15]

Haec ergo prima ratio esse videtur cur et de praedestinatione obscurius loquutus sit, et tantum concesserit voluntatis nostrae arbitrio, ut scilicet sophistarum calumniis ansam praecideret, qui erant in hoc ipsum intenti ut in odium invidiamque traherent, quae simpliciter de iis rebus secundum Dei verbum dicerentur.	So then, it seems to us that the first reason why he not only spoke somewhat obscurely about predestination but also made such large concessions to the sovereignty of our own will was undoubtedly to cut the ground from under the slanders of the sophists whose direct aim was to bring odium and dislike upon every clear statement of these themes recorded in the Word of God.

15. Ibid., CO 9:836.

Non fuit quidem, fateor, illa satis idonea causa cur a scripturae
simplicitate deflecteret. Neque
enim aequum est, ut humano
iudicio cedat Dei veritas, cui
omnes hominum cogitationes
velut captivae debent subiugari,
et in cuius obedientiam redigi
debent mentes omnes cum sua
intelligentia. Sed quum certum
sit, nihil aliud quaesisse quam
ut se expediret ab inimicis
crucis Christi, haec certe tam
pia affectio, utcunque successu
careat, excusationem tamen
aliquam meretur.

This, I grant, was no adequate reason for him to turn away from the
plain sense of Scripture, for it is not
right that the truth of God to which
all the thoughts of men should be
subjected like prisoners, and in
obedience to which all minds ought
to be brought with full awareness,
should give way to human judgment. But, since it is certain that his
sole objective was to deliver himself
from the enemies of the cross of
Christ, a motive as scrupulous as
this deserves some excuse, however
devoid of success it might be.

Calvin stretches every nerve to exonerate Chrysostom's theological deficiencies. Calvin feels that Chrysostom had to contend not only with "philosophers" but also with those within the church living impure lives, who excused their slovenliness on the grounds that they were simply living a life according to the disposition of their corrupt nature. They justified their licentious lives with the excuse that since they had not received assistance from the grace of God, it was not within their power to fight off inexorable necessity. People thereby transferred the blame for their sins from themselves to God. Against such nuisances Chrysostom fought. Yet Calvin realized that the method of direct attack (*expugnandi ratio*) did not suit the saintly man, and on that basis denied that a person was prepared for good works by the grace of God. While, for Calvin, this theological stance is not in harmony with the tenor of Scripture, "lapses" of this kind are easily forgivable in such a great man. Calvin therefore concludes:[16]

... dixi fidelem Christi
servum, quum ad optimum
finem spectaret, a via non-
nihil deflexisse.

... I maintain that he has in no
sense turned the faithful servant of
Christ from the way, since he always kept the highest end in view.

16. Ibid., CO 9:836–37.

Such magnanimity with which Calvin attempted to understand Chrysostom is not usually accorded the personality of the Reformer! Calvin invites his readers to one final enjoyment. In the homilies of Chrysostom, one will find, apart from the straightforward interpretation of Scripture, "many reminders of the old way of things." Calvin catalogues, as if in a spirit of historical nostalgia, the disciplined beauty of the ancient church. The homilies will reveal the function and authority bishops had; the nature of the laws by which the people were kept within the bounds of duty; the kind of discipline that prevailed in the priestly order; the discipline that prevailed among the people themselves; the degree to which restraint was practiced in the priestly order, which prevented them from misusing, for self-gratifying ends, the power granted to priests; the sobriety among the people that prevented them from scorning the responsibility entrusted to them; the character of the sacred communities and the quality of the godly lives for which they were famous; the nature of their rites and the purpose for which they were instituted.

The last sentence of Calvin's unfinished *Preface* to the Homilies of Chrysostom summarizes in a few words the goal toward which Calvin's entire life was directed, the good estate of the church based on a standard of discipline that reaches back into antiquity:[17]

Nam si volumus ecclesiae saluti bene consultum, nulla reperietur magis idonea ratio, mea quidem opinione, quam si disciplinae normam a veteri ecclesia petamus.	For if we wish the good estate of the church to be upheld, no more suitable method will be found, as I at least believe, than to go back and seek a standard of discipline from the ancient Church.

Even though the homilies of Chrysostom contained theological *loci* that Calvin could not accept, the Reformer wished to make the writings of the patriarch-preacher known to people of sixteenth-century Geneva. In these ancient homilies Calvin had found a clear explanation of Scripture. In Chrysostom Calvin found an interpreter who kept closely to the meaning of the words, refusing to turn either to the right or left of their clear intent. Calvin had found in Chrysostom a servant of the church with whose intentions Calvin himself could identify. Among the Fathers of the

17. Ibid., CO 9:838.

church East and West, Calvin assigned first place as an exegete to the Preacher of Antioch. For such reasons Calvin intended to publish for all people these ancient homilies.

3

Chrysostom in the Light of Calvin's Assessment

CALVIN'S *PREFACE TO THE* intended French translation of Chrysostom's homilies offers, in its broadest outline, a tripartite evaluation of the Antiochene. First and foremost, Calvin assigns to Chrysostom top honors as an interpreter of Scripture. Beyond all else, that is the reason Calvin intends to publish Chrysostom in French. Second, despite the lengths to which Calvin goes in order to exonerate Chrysostom for "speaking obscurely about predestination," Calvin understands the preacher-patriarch to be deficient in doctrine. Yet "he in no sense turned the faithful servant of Christ from the way since he always kept the highest end in view."[1] This is truly an amazing statement from the pen of one who thought Chrysostom worked into the doctrine of election man's own efforts; taught the importance of free-will; and made man's righteousness before God, to some degree, dependent on good works! Third, Chrysostom reveals in his writings matters of historical importance that are not only interesting but most useful information. It remains now to draw out this threefold estimate of Chrysostom from the homilies themselves. Examining the homilies as well as other writings of Chrysostom, we hope to demonstrate how Calvin may have come to his threefold evaluation of Chrysostom's writings. Our intention is to see Chrysostom through the eyes of Calvin, thereby clarifying the Reformer's estimate of the fifth-century exegete as

1. *Praef. in Chry. Hom.*, CO 9:836.

Calvin presented him in the *Preface*. Since the focus of our study is Calvin, it should be clear that we do not intend to present here a biography of Chrysostom. Neither shall we attempt a theological or exegetical analysis of Chrysostom. We wish simply to expand Calvin's estimate of Chrysostom from the standpoint of the latter's homilies and related writings. Let us take Calvin's appraisal in reverse order, beginning with the observation that Chrysostom's writings reveal matters of historical importance. and interest.

It is true, indeed, that Chrysostom's writings allow us many insights into "the old way of things." Undoubtedly the document that brings us most closely in contact with Chrysostom's own life and times is his treatise *On the Priesthood*.[2] We are here introduced to Anthusa, Chrysostom's mother, that woman who combined strength of character, a striking Christian piety, and a wise practical turn of mind. When the young John was contemplating entering the monastic life with his friend Basil, Chrysostom tells us in this treatise how the continual lamentations of his mother entreated him to remain at her side:

> For when she perceived that I was meditating this step, she took me into her own private chamber, and, sitting near me on the bed where she had given birth to me, she shed torrents of tears, to which she added words yet more pitiable than her weeping . . . "My child, it was not the will of Heaven that I should long enjoy the benefit of your father's virtue. For his death soon followed the pangs which I endured at your birth, leaving you an orphan and me a widow before my time to face all the horrors of widowhood, which only those who have experienced them can fairly understand. . . . My foremost help indeed was the grace from above; but it was no small consolation to me under those terrible trials to look continually on your face and to preserve in you a living image of him who had gone, an image indeed which was a fairly exact likeness. . . . I spared no expense which was necessary to give you an honorable position, spending for this purpose some of my own fortune, and my marriage dowry. Yet do not think that I say these things by way of reproaching you; only in return for all these benefits I beg one favor: do not plunge me into a second widowhood; nor revive the grief which is now laid to rest. Wait for my death; it may be in a little while I shall depart. . . . When, then, you shall have committed my body to the ground, and mingled my bones with your father's, embark for a long voyage, and set sail on any sea you will; then

2. *De sacerdotio*, PG 68:623-92; trans. Stephens, NPNF 9:33-83.

there will be no one to hinder you; but as long as my life lasts, be content to live with me. . . . "[3]

Perhaps Chrysostom has this bittersweet experience in his mind when, in the seventy-seventh homily on Matthew, he admonishes husbands and wives to seek stability and reverence in the household:

> Each of us has a sheep; let him lead that sheep to the proper pastures. Let the man, as soon as he has risen from his bed, seek nothing else but how he may do and say something whereby he may render this whole house more reverent. And the woman, let her be indeed a good housekeeper. But before attending to this, let her have another more important concern, that the whole household may work the works of Heaven. For if in worldly matters, attending to the affairs of our households, we labor diligently to pay public dues, that we may not for our undutifulness in these matters be beaten and dragged to the market places, and suffer ten thousand unpleasant things, how much more should we pay the same attention to spiritual matters, rendering to God the King what is his due, that we may not come to that place where there is gnashing of teeth.[4]

From the writings of Chrysostom, Calvin observed in his *Preface*, we learn "the character of the sacred communities and the quality of the godly lives for which they were famous." However appealingly the mother of Chrysostom may have spoken to her son, John removed himself to a mountain solitude near Antioch, where he spent four years in ascetic exercises and two further years in a cave. His writings reveal the anxiety he experienced as he faced the rigorous life:

> As I determined to abandon the city and seek the habitation of the monks, a great doubt harassed my soul. How and from where was I to obtain for myself the necessities of life? Would I be able to eat freshly baked bread there? Could one use the same oil for lamps and meals? Would they compel me to eat a dish of miserable beans, do hard labor, dig, carry wood or water, or perform similar tasks? I was greatly concerned about the quiet life.[5]

While young John traveled with hesitant steps toward the mountain retreat, his later descriptions of the sacred communities are full of praise

---

3. *On the Priesthood* 1.5, NPNF 9:34.

4. *Hom. in Matt.* 77, PG 58:709–10.

5. *De compunctione, ad Demetrium*, 1.6, PG 47:403.

and bespeak their strength and glory. In his homily on Matthew he speaks with enthusiasm of Egyptian monasticism:

> Come out to the desert of Egypt and you will see this desert become better than any paradise. There you will find ten thousand choirs of angels in human forms, and nations of martyrs, and companies of virgins, and all the devil's tyranny put down, while Christ's kingdom shines forth in its brightness. . . .[6]

One can only imagine, nine hundred years later, the exaltation that must have overcome Calvin as he read these words! The rules of the monastic communities, Chrysostom further observes, were kept not only among men, but also by women:

> Yes, they, not less than men, practice that search for wisdom, not taking the shield and mounting the horse, as the Grecians' grave lawgivers and philosophers direct, but another and far more severe fight they are undertaking. For the war against the devil and his powers is common to them and to the men, and in no respect does the delicacy of their nature become an impediment in such conflicts, for not by bodily constitution, but by mental choice, are such struggles decided. Women in many cases have actually been more forward in the contest than men, and have set up more brilliant trophies. Heaven is not so glorious with the varied choir of the stars, as the wilderness of Egypt, exhibiting to us all around the tents of the monks![7]

Chrysostom wrote a lengthy defense against those who attacked the monastic communities,[8] in which the life and discipline of the communities are depicted, echoes of which abound throughout the homilies. Chrysostom understood the advantage of monastic over secular life as the absence of hindrances in the "ways of God." Thus the apostles "left everything to follow Christ, and they could follow Him more easily because they had left all things."[9] Commenting on Paul's words in 1 Corinthians 7:35–36, where Paul says, "I say this only to help you, not to put a halter round your necks, but simply to make sure that everything is as it should be and that you give your undivided attention to the Lord," Chrysostom remarks:

---

6. *Hom. in Matt.* 8, PG 57:87.

7. Ibid.

8. *Adversus oppugnatores eorum qui ad monasticam vitam inducunt*, PG 47:319–86.

9. *Hom. in Matt.* 64, PG 58:609.

As St. Paul explained the difference between a virgin and a married woman, he did not mention either marriage or chastity, but rather a life of freedom from care as opposed to one harassed by care. For marriage in itself is not evil, but it is a hindrance to strictness of life.[10]

We learn also from the homilies the "function and authority bishops had, and the discipline that prevailed in the priestly order." The need of medical treatment brought Chrysostom back from his ascetic exercises to the city of Antioch, where he was ordained, first as a deacon and later as a priest. The six books *On the Priesthood* reveal what Chrysostom himself thought of the priestly office:

The priestly office is indeed discharged on earth, but it ranks among heavenly ordinances; and very naturally so; for neither man, nor angel, nor archangel, nor any other created power, but the Paraclete Himself instituted this vocation, and persuaded men while still abiding in the flesh to represent the ministry of angels. Therefore the consecrated priest ought to be as pure as if he were standing in the heavens themselves in the midst of those powers.[11]

The priesthood in the old dispensation was noble and awe-inspiring, making use of bells, pomegranates, stones on the breastplate and ephod, girdle, miter, long robe, plates of gold, and the deep silence within the holy of holies. But in the new dispensation, the priest stands before the altar and sees the Lord himself sacrificed. Therefore no priest can say that he is just a man among men, standing upon the earth. On the contrary, the priest is translated to heaven, and, having cast out every carnal thought from the soul, contemplates with disembodied spirit the pure reason of the things that are in heaven.

One could hardly speak higher of the divine office. The priest's preeminent duty is to act as "spiritual father" (πνευματικός πατήρ),[12] ruler and chief (ὁ ἄρκων)[13] to his congregation. The dignity of the priest stands higher than that of a king, because he possesses a higher authority, originating in God himself:

10. *Hom. in 1 Cor.* 19, PG 61:160.

11. *On the Priesthood* 3.5, NPNF 9:46.

12. Hom. 2.5 in *Salutate Priscillam et Aquilam*, PG 51:204.

13. Ibid., PG 51:203.

> If you wish to see the difference between king and priest, only
> think of the difference in the power entrusted to each, and you will
> understand that the priest stands much higher than the king . . .
> the king has power only over earthly things; beyond these his arm
> does not reach. The throne of the priesthood, on the other hand, is
> erected in heaven, and to him is entrusted what is of heaven. That
> which is lower receives the blessing of that which stands higher.[14]

Yet no one spoke with greater urgency on the necessity of humility as a
distinctive mark of the priesthood:

> Do not misuse your priestly dignity, nor become haughty or ar-
> rogant, but consider yourself small and insignificant. For if God
> spoke, for the sake of the people, by an ass, and by Balaam, a most
> wicked man, how much more will He speak through the mouth
> of a priest![15]

Chrysostom was an untiring reformer of the priesthood. One of his
first acts upon his consecration as patriarch of Constantinople was the introduction of strict ascetic habits among the priests. He drove out "spiritual
sisters" with whom many of the priests were living in "spiritual marriage,"
and checked the parasitic habits of others who were mere "hangers-on"
to the rich. Throughout the homilies one gains the impression of a man
who understood the priesthood as at once the highest calling to which was
owed all honor, and at the same time a calling that demanded the most rigorous application of discipline and the constant pursuit of humility in all
aspects of the calling. To be sure, one finds in the writings of Chrysostom
"many reminders of the old way of things," the discipline that prevailed in
the priestly order, and the quality of godly lives that were the product of
sacred communities.

We turn now to the second major assessment of Chrysostom offered by Calvin in his *Preface*, namely, certain doctrinal areas in which
Chrysostom is inferior to other writers. For Calvin this deficiency focuses
on the working into the doctrine of election, man's works; free-will and
its importance for the pursuit of virtue; the place of works in achieving
righteousness before God.

Before we appraise Calvin's warning, some general observations
on Chrysostom as a theologian are in order. The dominant impression

---

14. Hom. 5.1 in *Vidi dominum*, PG 56:130–31. On the honor due to a priest, cf. *Hom. Hom. in 2 Tim*, 2.

15. *In Ep. 2 ad Tim.*, PG 62:610.

one receives, after reading a sizable number of Chrysostom's homilies, polemical works such as *On the Incomprehensible Nature of God*, moral discourses such as *Against the Circus Games and the Theatre*, and treatises such as *On the Priesthood* and *On Monastic Life*, is that Chrysostom is not primarily a theologian in the Reformation sense of the word. Neither is he inclined to systematic speculation on the theological formulations of the Greek world. The emphasis however, is on the word "systematic," as will presently be seen. One does not find in the writings of Chrysostom the themes that were trumpeted by the Western church either through Augustine in Chrysostom's own time, or by the Reformers in another age. Chrysostom does not present us with delineated doctrines of predestination, justification by grace through faith, total depravity, or irresistible grace. On the subject of original sin, for example, Chrysostom affirms confidently that the consequences of Adam's sin affect not only our first parents, but also their descendants. On the other hand, he never states explicitly that sin itself was inherited by their posterity and is inherent in their nature. While Adam's posterity inherit Adam's *nature* and *punishment*, they do not share in Adam's *sin* and *guilt*. When Chrysostom comments on Paul's words in Romans 5:19, "For as by one man's disobedience many were made sinners, so by the obedience of One shall many be made righteous," Chrysostom says:

> What he says seems indeed to involve no small question; but if any one attends to it diligently, this too will admit of an easy solution. What then is the question? It is the saying that through the offence of one many were made sinners. For the fact that when he had sinned and become mortal, it is not unlikely that those who were of him should also become mortal. But how does it follow that from his disobedience another would become a sinner? For at this rate, a man of this sort will not even deserve punishment if, that is, it was not from his own self that he became a sinner. What then does the word "sinners" mean here? To me it seems to mean "liable to punishment and condemned to death."[16]

For Chrysostom, nature may be inherited but not sin. Thus the heart of Calvin's theology is rejected.

But if Chrysostom does not penetrate to the depths of man's depravity, his writings may not be dismissed as devoid of theological insight. The homilies mirror the traditional faith as given by the Nicene formulations.

16. *In Ep. ad Rom.* 10, PG 60:477.

He distinguishes clearly between *ousia* or *physis* as terms for nature, and *hypostasis* or *prosopon* as terms for person. He teaches that the Son is of the same essence as the Father, using the Nicene formula *homoousios* to characterize the relation of the Son to the Father.[17]

The *Homilies on John* present a decidedly controversial tone because Chrysostom continually meets there the texts which the Arians, especially the Anomoeans, perverted into evidence that the Son is not of like substance with the Father. In the sixth homily, Chrysostom introduces Christ with these words:

> As though he [Christ] had said: "I am God, and the only Begotten [γνήσιος] Son of God, and am of that Simple and Blessed Essence; I need none to witness to Me. Even if no one were to witness to Me, yet I am not diminished in my Essence; but because I care for the salvation of many, I have descended to such humility as to commit my witness to a man."[18]

He returns to this theme on many occasions. Commenting on John 1:14, "And the Word was made Flesh, and dwelt among us," Chrysostom states:

> For He became Son of man, who was God's own Son, in order that He might make the sons of men to be children of God. For the high when it associates with the low changes not at all its own honor, but it raises up the other from excessive lowness; that was how it was with the Lord. His own Nature is not diminished by this condescension; but He raised us who had always sat in disgrace and darkness to glory unspeakable.[19]

Chrysostom engages in battle with the Docetists in his commentary on the words "was made":

> Why then does he use the expression "was made"? To stop the mouths of the heretics. For since there are some who say that all the circumstances of the Dispensation were an appearance, a piece of acting, an allegory, in order to remove beforehand this blasphemy, he says "was made." By that expression he desires to show not a change of substance, (away with that thought), but the assumption of real flesh.[20]

17. *Hom. in Matt.* 1, PG 57:17; cf. also *Hom.* 52, 3. and 64, 1, in *Hom. in Joannem*, PG 59:290 and 298.

18. *Hom. in Joannem* 6, PG 59:61.

19. *Hom. in Joannem* 11, PG 59:79.

20. Ibid., PG 59:79.

Chrysostom was certainly not unaware of theological issues that were the focus of attention in his own day. Although *loci* were not developed in systematic form by Chrysostom, they receive constant attention in his writings. If we examine the homilies for Christological statements, we find that he stresses the complete and perfect divinity of Christ against the Arians, and the complete and perfect humanity against the Apollinarists. He insists on the reality and integrity of the two natures in Christ. Christ is of the same nature as the Father, τῆς αὐτῆς οὐσίας τῷ Πατρί,[21] and also is a human body, not sinful like ours, but identical with ours in nature.[22] Chrysostom's homilies are replete with exhaustive statements bearing on Christological formulations. No one could read his *Homilies on Philippians* and conclude, as does Baur, that Chrysostom's "spiritual make-up did not incline him to philosophical speculation, but rather to asceticism, ethics, and homiletics."[23] The seventh homily on Philippians, for example, presents an exhaustive Christological statement, which reads only in part:

> Thus so much for the heretics. I must now speak against those that deny that He took a soul [that is, against the Apollinarian heresy]. If the "form of God" is "perfect God," then the "form of a servant" is "a perfect servant." Again, against the Arians. Here concerning His divinity, we no longer find "He became," or "He took," but "He emptied Himself, taking the form of a servant, being made in the likeness of men"; here concerning his humanity we find "He took, He became." He became the latter, He was the former. Let us not then confound nor divide the natures. There is one God, there is one Christ, the Son of God. When I say "one," I mean a union, not a confusion ἔνωσιν λέγω, οὐ σύγχυσιν; the one Nature did not degenerate into the other, but was united with that other.[24]

Chrysostom consistently takes his stand against heretical positions, and develops theologically the orthodox stance in the homilies.

Calvin's objection to Chrysostom on theological grounds is based on Chrysostom's "working into the idea of election man's own efforts."[25] "Chrysostom spoke somewhat obscurely about predestination."[26] Let

21. *Hom. in Matt.* 1, PG 57:17.

22. *Hom. in Rom.* 13, PG 60:519.

23. Baur, *John Chrysostom and His Time*, 1:355.

24. *Hom. in Phil.* 7, PG 62:232.

25. *Praef. in Chry. Hom.*, CO 9:835.

26. Ibid., CO 9:836.

us examine the commentary of Chrysostom on two texts of Paul that clearly state the themes of predestination and election: "For those whom he foreknew, he also predestined to be conformed to the image of His Son" (Rom 8:28); and, "He chose us in him before the foundation of the world, that we should be holy and without blemish before him in love" (Eph 1:4). On Romans:

> See what superb honor! For what the Only-begotten was by nature, we have become by grace. And still he was not satisfied with this calling of them conformed to the image of his Son, and even adds another point, "that He might be the first born." And even here he does not come to a pause, but after this he proceeds to mention another point, "among many brethren." So, you see, he wishes to use all means of setting the relationship (συγγένειν) in a clear light. Now all these things you are to take as spoken of in the Incarnation. For according to the Godhead, He is the Only begotten. See, what great things He has given to us! Doubt not then about the future. For he shows even on other grounds his concern for us by saying, that things were fore-ordered in this way from the beginning. For we men have to derive from things our conceptions about them, but to God these things have been long determined, and from of old God bestowed his good-will upon us.[27]

And on Ephesians:

> His meaning is this: Through whom He has blessed us, through Him he has also chosen us. And He, then, it is that shall bestow upon us all those rewards hereafter. He is the very judge that shall say, "Come, ye blessed of my Father, inherit the kingdom prepared for you from the foundation of the world." And again, "I will that where I am you may be also." And this is a point which he is anxious to prove in almost all his Epistles, that ours is no novel system, but that it had thus been figured from the very first, that it is not the result of any change of purpose, but had been in fact a divine dispensation and fore-ordained. And this is a mark of great solicitude. And what is meant by, "He chose us in him"? By means of the faith which is in him, Christ, he means, happily ordered this for us before we were born; even more, before the foundation of the world.[28]

Clearly thus far the assurance and confidence that "election" and "predestination" convey are sounded. But then in the Ephesians homily,

---

27. *In Ep. ad Rom.* 1, PG 60:541.

28. *In Ep. ad Eph.* 1, PG 62:12.

Chrysostom quickly swings to the ethical injunctions and balances election with moral acts:

> But why had He chosen us? "That we should be holy and without blemish before Him." That you may not then, when you hear that "He has chosen us," imagine that faith alone is sufficient, he proceeds to add life and conduct. To this end, he says, has He chosen us, and on this condition "that we should be holy and without blemish."[29]

Here Chrysostom introduces into the idea of election the efforts of man. For Chrysostom, "faith alone is not sufficient," and therefore he adds the importance of life and conduct. It is just here that Calvin's disagreement with Chrysostom is crystallized. This becomes clear when we hear Calvin's comment on the words, "that we should be holy and without blemish before him":

> He indicates the immediate, but not the chief design. For there is no absurdity in supposing that one thing may have two objects. The design of building is that there should be a house. This is the immediate aim. But the convenience of dwelling in it is the ultimate aim. It was necessary to mention this in passing; for Paul at once mentions another aim, the glory of God. But there is no contradiction here. The glory of God is the highest end, to which our sanctification is subordinate. From this we infer that holiness, innocence, and every virtue in men, are the fruit of election. And so once more Paul expressly puts aside every consideration of merit. If God has foreseen in us everything worthy of election, the very opposite would have been said. For he means that all our holiness and innocence of life flow from the election of God. Why is it then that some men are godly, and live in the fear of the Lord, while others give themselves up without reserve to all manner of wickedness? If Paul may be believed, the only reason is, that the latter retain their natural disposition, and the former have been chosen to holiness. The cause certainly does not depend on the righteousness of works, of which Paul here declares that is the cause.[30]

The Antiochene exegete was most certainly not without theological acumen. The themes of election and predestination, without reference

---

29. Ibid.

30. *Ep. ad Eph.*, CO 51:147.

to man's works, were not accented in the writings of Chrysostom as the Reformer wished.

We turn now to Calvin's third major assessment of Chrysostom. "The outstanding merit of our author, Chrysostom, is that it was his supreme concern always not to turn aside even to the slightest degree from the genuine, simple sense of Scripture, and to allow himself no liberties by twisting the plain meaning of the words."[31] Among the ancient exegetes, Chrysostom is given first place as an interpreter of Scripture. Jerome's writings on the Old Testament are given little recognition, for Jerome is almost completely sunk in allegories in which he twists Scripture in far too free a manner. Origen is also singled out as an interpreter who obscures the straightforward sense of Scripture by endless allegories. Clearly the basis for Calvin's appreciation of Chrysostom is the degree to which the Antiochene's writings are free from excessive allegory and exhibit rigid adherence to the straightforward meaning of the words in their immediate context.

Chrysostom's homilies reveal a decided inclination to sober rather than fanciful exegesis. On a number of occasions he states his preference for the exposition of Scripture in a nonallegorical manner. While he did not reject the allegorical interpretation of Scripture, he severely limited the application of allegory as a means toward understanding the meaning of Scripture. Commenting on Isaiah 1:22, "your silver has become dross, your wine mixed with water," Chrysostom observes:

> Some do not understand the ineffable wisdom of God, for they have taken the words allegorically (κατ ἀναγώγην). They say the great and sublime Isaiah would not have discoursed about the craftiness of moneychangers and the corruption of taverners. They say by "silver" he means the oracles of God, and by "wine" doctrine which the people were contaminating by the addition of their own private teachings. My attitude to this kind of exegesis is not to scorn it completely, but I affirm that another exegesis is sounder.[32]

The "other kind of exegesis" to which Chrysostom refers has been called "typological exegesis."[33] What is a type? According to Woollcombe, Chrysostom understands a type as an outline sketch that a painter makes

---

31. *Praef. in Chry. Hom.*, CO 9:835.

32. *Interpretatio in Isaiam Prophetam* 1, PG 56:23.

33. Cf. the essay by Woollcombe, "The Biblical Origins and Patristic Development of Typology," 39–75.

for a portrait before he fills in the colors. Every type therefore must have some resemblance to that which it is said to typify.[34] John McIndoe makes the same point, summarily describing Chrysostom's use of "type":

> The cumulative definition will have three clauses: first, the historicity of the original event is fully acknowledged; second, its value as type depends upon some interior quality which is perceived through the historical pattern of the event; third, this interior quality of the past event must be discernible in the present event also, before there is a correlation between type and antitype.[35]

When Chrysostom comments on Galatians 4:23–24, "But the son of the slave was born according to the flesh, the son of the free woman, through the promise; now these things contain an allegory," Chrysostom allows us an insight into his meaning of the word "type":

> Contrary to usage he calls a type an allegory. What he means is: this piece of history does not declare only the obvious fact, but proclaims some other meaning too. Therefore it is called an allegory.[36]

If a type proclaims another meaning, however, Chrysostom insists that no arbitrary or fanciful meaning be derived from what the type is intended to typify. Thus he requires:

> Here we learn an important and relevant lesson, concerning when and what passages of Scripture we are to interpret spiritually. We have no right to give a merely arbitrary interpretation but must follow the sense of Scripture itself and in this way employ the spiritual method of interpretation.[37]

Perhaps Chrysostom most definitively set down the rules by which Scripture is to be interpreted in his commentary on Psalm 9:7, "The Lord remains for ever." Here he remarks that the meaning intended by the prophet is the unchanging nature of God. He continues:

> But if you feel it necessary to give in addition some kind of figurative interpretation we have no objection. For some passages it is possible to interpret figuratively as well as literally. Others, however, are to be understood solely according to a strictly literal in-

---

34. Ibid., 73.

35. McIndoe, "Chrysostom on St. Matthew," 62.

36. *In Ep. ad Gal.* 4, PG 61:662.

37. *In Isaiam* 5, PG 56:60.

terpretation, e.g., "God made heaven and earth." Others however are to be interpreted in a sense different from the actual words, e.g., "a lovely hind, a graceful doe, let her affection delight you," or, "let what you have be for your own sole use and let no stranger share it with you." Take another example: "Let your fount of water be for yourself alone" (Prov. 5:17–19). Now if you paid rigid attention to what is written here and did not seek any meaning beyond the literal sense the meaning of this passage would be downright inhuman: not even to share a drink of water with someone! But of course what this passage is talking about is a wife. A man is to rejoice in his wife with due moderation. She is called a "fountain" and a "doe" because of the purity of the marriage relationship. That is how this passage is to be taken. In other passages, however, it is necessary to accept both the sense of the words as they stand and the meaning that plainly arises from them, as in the following instance: "Just as Moses lifted up the serpent" (John 3:14). Here you must believe the actual fact, for there is no doubt that it is a fact, and in addition, the sense that was signified by the fact, namely, the type that was fulfilled in Christ.[38]

For Chrysostom, Scripture is capable of two basic senses, the literal and the typical. A decided emphasis is placed on the literal and straightforward meaning of the words. If allegorical or typical interpretations are allowed, there must be both clear resemblance and historical continuity between type and antitype.

Chrysostom will always adopt a literal interpretation if at all possible. Arguing for the historicity of the Genesis account of Paradise in Genesis 2:8, he maintains that Paradise is an actual geographic location, and not, as some "allegorists affirm, something heavenly."[39] In the same passage he puts his finger on the danger, as he sees it, implicit in the allegorical method of interpretation. "The practice of importing into Holy Scripture alien ideas of one's own imagination instead of accepting what stands written in the text, in my opinion, carries great danger for those who have the hardihood to follow it."[40] In the homilies on Matthew Chrysostom pointedly reacts to figurative interpretations. When he comments on Matthew 5:5, "Blessed are the meek, for they shall inherit the earth," he begins asking, "Tell me, what kind of earth? Some say a figurative earth, but it is not this; for nowhere in Scripture do we find any mention of an

38. *Expositio in Psalmum 9*, PG 55:126–27.
39. *Hom. in Gen.* 13, PG 53:108.
40. Ibid., PG 53:109.

earth that is merely figurative (νοητήν)."[41] Chrysostom then goes on to insist that Jesus in this verse means "earth" as a sensible object, just as Paul interprets "earth" when he says, "Honor your father and your mother" (Eph 6:2), and added, "for so shall you live long upon the earth."

Another instance of Chrysostom's understanding a word, which might lend itself to allegory, in concrete historical terms is given in his interpretation of the word διάβολον in Matthew 5:25. "Some say," Chrysostom observes, "that He [Christ] obscurely signifies the devil himself, under the name of the adversary, and bids us have nothing to do with him, for this, they say, is to agree with him."[42] For Chrysostom, however, διάβολον refers not to the devil, but to judges in this world, and concretely, the manner in which the courts of justice operate, and refers also to prisons.

Calvin's appreciation of Chrysostom as an exegete is based on the Antiochene's refusal to engage in flights of fanciful exegesis. Chrysostom insists that typological or allegorical exegesis demonstrate clear resemblance and historical continuity between what the Antiochene called type and that to which the type points. When Scripture was preached to the common people of Antioch, they heard the Word interpreted with singular force and clarity. When, nine hundred years later, Scripture was to be published for the common people, they were to read it, Calvin proposed, interpreted by the ancient preacher of Antioch whose "supreme concern was not to turn aside even to the slightest degree from the genuine, simple sense of Scripture."

41. *Hom. in Matt. 15*, PG 57:226.
42. *Hom. in Matt. 16*, PG 57:253.

PART II

Chrysostom as an Exegetical Source

4

John Chrysostom in Calvin's Commentary on 1 Corinthians

IN PART 1 WE have reviewed the publication of Calvin's commentaries, examining some of the motives, the intentions, and the historical factors that elicited his many-volumed work. We endeavored to demonstrate that the biblical commentaries were of great importance in Calvin's own view of his work and that early in his literary career he saw the necessity of, and determined to produce, commentaries on Scripture.

We then turned to Calvin's intended publication of the homilies of Chrysostom, and saw that this projected work was directly related to Calvin's own goal, namely, offering to people an aid in the study of Scripture. Examining the content of the Preface to the proposed French translation of the homilies, we reviewed Calvin's appraisal of Chrysostom. Finally, we saw from Chrysostom's homilies that Calvin's appraisal of that which may be garnered from the homilies, namely, historical conditions of the church and its disciplined communities, a peculiar doctrinal stance representative of the Antiochene school, and an exegetical tradition that stood opposed to the allegorical method of interpretation, are in fact components of the homilies.

In part 2 we turn to a specific and detailed examination of Calvin's use of Chrysostom as an exegetical source. If Calvin gave to Chrysostom, among the fathers of the church, first place as an expositor of Scripture, we should expect that Chrysostom was a major source for Calvin as the

Reformer wrote his own commentaries. If we examine the number of references to Chrysostom in the commentaries on the Old Testament and New Testament, we can ascertain, at least quantitatively, the number of times Calvin made explicit reference to Chrysostom. Further, we can examine the number of references to other exegetes whom Calvin, in the Preface, cites favorably or even to some extent favorably. We have totaled all the references in the index to the Corpus Reformatorum (vols. 48, 50, 87 = CO 20, 22, 59) to determine the number of times Chrysostom, Augustine, Jerome, and Ambrose are cited in each book of the Bible. The results are given in table 4.1.

TABLE 4.1

Number of Citations to Chrysostom, Augustine, Jerome, and Ambrose in the Biblical Commentaries of Calvin[1]

OLD TESTAMENT

Books	Citations to			
	Chrysostom	Augustine	Jerome	Ambrose
Genesis	1	16	19	2
Harmony: Exod–Deut	–	18	4	–
Joshua	–	–	–	–
Psalms	–	14	9	–
Isaiah	1	1	3	–
Jeremiah	–	3	4	–
Ezekiel	–	–	6	–
Daniel	–	3	2	–
Twelve Minor Prophets	–	3	23	–
Zechariah & Malachi	–	2	21	–
TOTAL	2	60	91	2

1. Statistics represent only a raw count as taken from the *Index* in the *Corpus Reformatorum*. Therefore the evidence must be used with caution.

TABLE 4.1 (CONT.)

NEW TESTAMENT

Books	Citations to			
	Chrysostom	Augustine	Jerome	Ambrose
Harmony	5	13	6	2
John & 1 John	10	34	6	–
Acts	1	3	6	1
Romans	12	16	1	3
1 Corinthians	25	11	5	5
2 Cor, Tim, Titus & Philemon	32	10	–	6
Gal, Eph, Phil, Col	15	10	10	4
Hebrews, 1–2 Peter	4	4	3	–
1–2 Thessalonians	1	–	–	2
James	–	–	1	–
Jude	–	–	–	–
TOTAL	105	101	38	23

What are the results of our tabulations? First, it may be seen that references to Chrysostom in the Old Testament are negligible. One would expect few references to Chrysostom in the Old Testament commentaries, given Calvin's verdict: "his unfamiliarity with the Hebrew language prevented him from showing such skill in the Old Testament."[2] In the Old Testament, Jerome and Augustine are overwhelmingly the most-cited Fathers. In the New Testament as a whole, Chrysostom and Augustine are cited with about even frequency. But in the Pauline letters Calvin refers to Chrysostom more than to the other three Fathers. While many of these references represent points of difference, it is apparent that Calvin is in touch with Chrysostom's homilies on the letters of Paul at nearly every point.

The single book in the New Testament in which Calvin most frequently quotes Chrysostom is 1 Corinthians. In this chapter of our study, therefore, every reference to Chrysostom cited by Calvin in his 1 Corinthians commentary, explicit or implicit, is examined. The chapter is presented in the form of a running commentary, which has at least two advantages. First, in this way, we tried to let comparative analysis speak

2. *Praef. in Chry. Hom.*, CO 9:834.

for itself, without forcing Calvin's use of Chrysostom into any preconceived mold. Secondly, reference may be made to Calvin's use of Chrysostom on any chapter and verse in 1 Corinthians simply by locating the chapter and verse in chronological sequence. At each point where Calvin alludes to or mentions Chrysostom, we sought to draw out the manner in which Calvin employed Chrysostom with reference to the text in question. Tentative conclusions are drawn as the commentary proceeds and the findings become evident.

> 1 Corinthians 1:2.
>
> τῇ ἐκκλησίᾳ τοῦ θεοῦ τῇ οὔσῃ ἐν Κορίνθῳ, ἡγιασμένοις ἐν Χριστῷ Ἰησοῦ, κλητοῖς ἁγίοις, σὺν πᾶσιν τοῖς ἐπικαλουμένοις τὸ ὄνομα τοῦ κυρίου ἡμῶν Ἰησοῦ Χριστοῦ ἐν παντὶ τόπῳ, αὐτῶν καὶ ἡμῶν·

Calvin notes that the words αὐτῶν and ἡμῶν can either refer to Christ or be understood as referring to place. He prefers the former translation, and, in doing so, acknowledges that he here follows Chrysostom:[3]

Iam vero quod istas particulas nostri et sui in genitivo posui, ut ad Christum referantur, quas alii ad locum referentes, per ablativum reddunt: in eo Chrysostomum sum sequutus.	I have placed the little words nostri (ours) and sui (theirs) in the genitive, understanding them as referring to Christ. Others, understanding them as referring to place, render them in the ablative. In doing so, I have followed Chrysostom.

Chrysostom, however, does not understand the words αὐτῶν and ἡμῶν as referring to Christ, but to the faithful who are located in diverse places. It was the intention of Paul, according to Chrysostom, to unite those scattered in various places by adding "both theirs and ours." Chrysostom's words are as follows:[4]

---

3. *Comm. ad Cor. 1*, CO 49:309.
4. *In Ep. ad Cor. 1*, Hom. 1, PG 61:13.

Ἐν παντὶ τόπῳ αὐτῶν τε καὶ ἡμῶν. Εἰ γὰρ καὶ πρὸς Κορινθίους τὰ γράμματά ἐστι γεγραμμένα μόνον, ἀλλὰ καὶ πάντων τῶν ἐν πάσῃ τῇ γῇ μέμνηται πιστῶν, δεικνὺς, ὅτι τὴν ἐπὶ τῆς οἰκουμένης μίαν δεῖ εἶναι Ἐκκλησίαν, καίτοι τόποις πολλοῖς κεχωρισμένην, καὶ πολλῷ μᾶλλον τὴν ἐν Κορίνθῳ. Εἰ δε ὁ τόπος χωρίζει, ἀλλ ὁ Κύριος αὐτοὺς συνάπτει κοινὸς ὤν· διὸ καὶ ἑνῶν αὐτοὺς ἐπήγαγε τὸ, Ἡμῶν τε καὶ αὐτῶν.

"In every place, both theirs and ours." For while the letter is written to the Corinthians only, yet he makes mention of all the believers that are in the entire earth; showing that the Church throughout the world must be one, however separate in diverse places; and much more, than in Corinth. And though the place be separate, the Lord binds them together, being common to all. Therefore uniting them, he adds, "both theirs and ours."

Calvin has consulted Chrysostom for a grammatical interpretation, acknowledging that he follows Chrysostom, but in fact, adopts an alternative reading. One wants to ask the question, why? It is hardly conceivable that Calvin has misunderstood Chrysostom, the latter being so clear and straightforward in his interpretation and exposition. At this point, all we can say is that perhaps Calvin had in mind the view of another exegete with whom Calvin did agree on this particular text.

1 Corinthians 1:4–6.

4. Εὐξαριστῶ τῷ θεῷ μου πάντοτε περὶ ὑμῶν ἐπὶ τῇ χάριτι τοῦ θεοῦ τῇ δοθείσῃ ὑμῖν ἐν Χριστῷ Ἰησοῦ, 5. ὅτι ἐν παντὶ ἐπλουτίσθητε ἐν αὐτῷ, ἐν παντὶ λόγῳ καὶ πάσῃ γνώσει, 6. καθὼς τὸ μαρτύριον τοῦ Χριστοῦ ἐβεβαιώθη ἐν ὑμῖν...

The question with which Calvin here wrestles may be stated in the following manner: does Paul mean that the testimony of Christ was confirmed in the minds and hearts of the Corinthians by means of "speech" and "knowledge," or, does Paul mean that the Corinthians were enriched in "speech" and "knowledge" as (or to the degree that) the testimony of Christ was confirmed in them? Calvin, against Erasmus, prefers the latter interpretation:[5]

5. *Comm. ad Cor. 1*, CO 49:310.

Secus vertit Erasmus: nempe, his rebus confirmatum in illis fuisse testimonium Christi, cognitione scilicet ac verbo. Sed aliter sonant verba: quae si non torqueantur, facilem habent sensum: nempe quod evangelii sui veritatem Deus consignaverit inter Corinthios, ut certior foret.

Erasmus gives a different rendering, to this effect, "that by these things the testimony of Christ was confirmed in them"; that is, by knowledge and by the word. The words, however, convey another meaning, and if they are not wrested, the meaning is easy—that God has sealed the truth of his gospel among the Corinthians, for the purpose of confirming it.

Calvin then goes on to ask how or in what manner the truth of the gospel becomes confirmed among the Corinthians, responding that such truth may be established either through miracles or by the inner testimony of the Holy Spirit. While Chrysostom, Calvin feels, understands miracles as the cause or confirmation of the gospel's truth, it is the "internal witness of the Spirit" that is the first and primary cause:[6]

Dupliciter autem id fieri potuit, vel per miracula, vel per interius spiritus sancti testimonium. Videtur Chrysostomus de miraculis accipere, sed ego latius extendo: ac primo quidem certum est, confirmari proprie evangelium apud nos fide: quia dum fide recipitur a nobis, tunc demum signamus Deum esse veracem.

Now this might be done in two ways, either by miracles, or by the inward testimony of the Holy Spirit. Chrysostom seems to understand it of miracles, but I take it in a larger sense; and first of all, it is certain that the gospel is properly confirmed in our experience by faith, because it is only when we receive it by faith that we "set to our seal that God is true."

Calvin will agree with Chrysostom that miracles have their place in the confirmation of the gospel in the heart of a person; a higher source must nevertheless be sought: nempe quod Dei spiritus arrha et sigillum est.[7]

---

6. Ibid., CO 49:310–11.

7. Ibid., CO 49:310–11; trans. "namely, that the Spirit of God is the earnest and seal."

1 Corinthians 1:11.

ἐδηλώθη γάρ μοι περὶ ὑμῶν, ἀδελφοί μου, ὑπὸ τῶν Χλόης,
ὅτι ἔριδες ἐν ὑμῖν εἰσιν.

Throughout his homilies, Chrysostom constantly takes note of Paul's gentle and gradual manner of rebuking the Corinthians. When Paul reports to the Corinthians that he has been informed by Chloe's people that there is strife in the church, Chrysostom again notes Paul's prudence. Paul is careful not to mention any one person as the informer; rather, he refers to the entire family of Chloe. Such restraint is, for Chrysostom, a highly admirable trait of Paul:[8]

Σκόπει δὲ τὴν σύνεσιν, πῶς οὐ κεχωρισμένον ἔθηκε τὸ πρόσωπον, ἀλλ ὁλόκληρον οἰκίαν, ὥστε μὴ ἐκπολεμῶσαι αὐτοὺς πρὸς τον εἰρηκότα· οὕτω γὰρ καὶ περιέστειλεν ἐκεῖνον, καὶ τὴν κατηγορίαν ἀδεῶς ἐξεκάλυψεν.	Consider also his prudence in not speaking of any distinct person, but of the entire family; so as not to make them hostile towards the informer. For in this way he both protects him, and fearlessly opens the accusation.

While in Chrysostom's view, one person has informed Paul of the strife present in Corinth, and, in order to avoid casting aspersions on the informer, Paul uses a collective term, in Calvin's view the whole family made known the information to Paul. Calvin therefore finds Chrysostom's view "absurd":[9]

---

8. *Hom. ad Cor. 1*, Hom. 3, PG 61:23.
9. *Comm. ad Cor. 1*, CO 49:315.

Existimo igitur familiam fuisse bene institutam, quae morbum hunc Paulo indicaverit ecclesiae Corinthiacae, quem ab eo curari optabat. Quod autem post Chrysostomum sentiunt plerique, ideo abstinuisse nominibus, ne ipsos gravaret invidia, mihi absurdum videtur. Nam non quosdam ex familia dicit hoc sibi nuntiasse, sed potius omnes designat: neque vero dubium est quin se nominari libenter sustinuerint.

I am of the opinion, therefore, that it was a well-regulated household that acquainted Paul with the distempered condition of the Corinthian church, being desirous that it might be remedied by him. The idea entertained by many, in accordance with Chrysostom's view, that he refrained from mentioning names, lest he should bring odium upon them, appears to me to be absurd. For he does not say that some of the household had reported this to him, but, on the contrary, makes mention of them all, and there is no doubt that they would willingly have allowed their names to be made use of.

1 Corinthians 1:17.

Οὐ γὰρ ἀπέστειλέν με Χριστὸς βαπτίζειν, ἀλλὰ εὐαγγελίζεσθαι, οὐκ ἐν σοφίᾳ λόγου, ἵνα μὴ κενωθῇ ὁ σταυρὸς τοῦ Χριστοῦ.

On the basis of this text, Chrysostom places great emphasis on the task of preaching and instructing. Once an unbeliever is instructed and convinced of the truth of the gospel, anyone endowed with the priesthood might baptize the newcomer. But "great labor," and "great wisdom" are demanded of the teacher. It is the evangelist who must "change the deliberate will, alter the turn of mind, tear up error by the roots, and plant truth in the place of error." Much toil and a soul of iron are needed to preach the gospel:[10]

10. *Hom. ad Cor. 1*, Hom. 3, PG 61:26.

Οὐ γὰρ ἀπέστειλέ με Χριστὸς βαπτίζειν, ἀλλὰ εὐαγγελίζεσθαι. Τὸ γὰρ ἐπιπονώτερον καὶ πολλοῦ δεόμενον μόχθου καὶ ψυχῆς σιδηρᾶς, καὶ ὃ πάντα συνεῖχε, τοῦτο ἦν. Διὸ καὶ Παῦλος αὐτὸ ἐνεκεχειρίζετο. Καὶ τίνος ἕνεκεν μὴ ἀποσταλεὶς βαπτίζειν, ἐβάπτιζεν; Οὐ μαχόμενος τῷ ἀποστείλαντι, ἀλλ' ἐκ περιουσίας τοῦτο ποιῶν. Οὐ γὰρ εἶπεν, ὅτι Ἐκωλύθην, ἀλλ' ὅτι Οὐκ ἀπεστάλην ἐπὶ τούτῳ, ἀλλ' ἐπὶ τῷ ἀναγκαιοτάτῳ. Τὸ μὲν γὰρ εὐαγγελίζεσθαι ἑνός που καὶ δευτέρου, τὸ δὲ βαπτίζειν παντὸς ἂν εἴη τοῦ τὴν ἱερωσύνην ἔχοντος.

"Christ sent me not to baptize, but to preach the gospel." For this was the more laborious part, and that which needed much toil and a soul of iron, and that on which all depended. And therefore Paul had it put into his hand. And why, not being sent to baptize, did he baptize? Not in contention with Him that sent him, but in this instance, laboring beyond his task. For he did not say, "I was forbidden," but, "I was not sent for this, but for that which was of the greatest necessity." For preaching the gospel is a work perhaps for one or two, but baptizing, for everyone endowed with the priesthood.

Chrysostom clearly emphasizes the importance of preaching as compared to the administration of baptism. Drawing upon the analogy of wrestling, he compares the teacher of the wrestlers with the preacher, and the one who places the crown on the victor's head with the one who administers baptism:[11]

Ὥσπερ γὰρ τὸ μὲν διδάξαι τοὺς παλαίοντας, ἀνδρός ἐστι γενναίου καὶ παιδοτρίβου σοφοῦ, τὸ δὲ ἐπιθεῖνα τὸν στέφανον τῷ νικήσαντι καὶ τοῦ μὴ δυναμένου παλαίειν ἐστί, καίτοι γε ὁ στέφανος λαμπρότερον ποιεῖ τὸν νικήσαντα. οὕτω καὶ ἐπὶ τοῦ βαπτίσματος.

For, to teach wrestlers in the games is the part of a spirited and wise trainer, but to place the crown on the conqueror's head may be that of one who cannot even wrestle, even though it is the crown which adds splendor to the conqueror. So it is with baptism.

11. Ibid.

Calvin, in his commentary on this verse, does not mention Chrysostom's name. However there is a phrase, that repeatedly occurs when Calvin is comparing or contrasting his view with Chrysostom: quemadmodum quidam putant (just as some think). Calvin is concerned that Paul is, in this text, not detracting from the dignity or utility of the sacrament of baptism. Without direct reference to Chrysostom, Calvin says:[12]

Secundum vero, minime hic sacramenti dignitatem aut fructum extenuari, quemadmodum quidam putant. Neque enim hic de virtute baptismi quaestio est: nec ideo hanc comparationem instituit Paulus, ut quidquam de ea detrahat: sed quum paucorum esset docere, pluribus autem baptizare datum foret.	The second thing is that he does not by any means detract here, as some think, from the dignity or utility of the sacrament. For the question here is, not as to the efficacy of baptism, and Paul does not institute this comparison with the view of detracting in any degree from that. The reason is, it was given to a few to teach, while many could baptize.

Without mentioning Chrysostom by name, does Calvin here seek to correct what he understands to be an under-evaluation of the sacrament of baptism on the part of Chrysostom?

There is one more hint in Calvin's commentary that might support this idea. Calvin feels that to the church in which Paul has worked so industriously certain "masters" came who had won followers to their party by the sprinkling of water. Paul surrenders the title of honor (honoris) to them, and asserts that he is content to have the onerous (onere) work. The imagery Calvin uses to express this thought is strikingly parallel to the "wrestler" being crowned by one who seeks to catch a bit of the glory at the expense of someone else's labor:[13]

---

12. *Comm. ad Cor. 1*, CO 49:319.

13. Ibid.

Imo si propius expendant lectores omnes circumstantias, videbunt subesse tacitam ironiam, qua facete mordentur qui ex labore alieno sub praetextu caeremoniae gloriolam venantur. Incredibiles fuerant labores Pauli in ecclesia illa aedificanda: supervenerant delicati isti magistri, qui aquae adspersione discipulos in suam sectam traxerant: Paulus ergo, titulum honoris illis concedens, se onere contentum esse testatur.

Again, if readers will consider all the circumstances more closely, they will see that tacit irony underlies this, for he wittily bites at those who seek a little glory at the expense of another person's labor, under the pretext of a religious ceremony. For Paul's labor in the building of that church had been incredible. Certain easygoing teachers had come after him, who had drawn disciples into their sects by the sprinkling of water. Paul therefore surrenders the title of honor to them, and asserts that he is content to have the onerous work.

One cannot escape the conclusion that Calvin, without mentioning Chrysostom by name, is offering his commentary on the verse in question. On the one hand, Calvin is correcting what he considers to be an overemphasis on preaching at the expense of the dignity of the sacrament of baptism; and on the other hand, Calvin conveys the meaning of Paul, making use of the imagery employed by the Antiochene exegete.

1 Corinthians 2:3.

κἀγὼ ἐν ἀσθενείᾳ καὶ ἐν φόβῳ καὶ ἐν τρόμῳ πολλῷ ἐγενόμην πρὸς ὑμᾶς . . .

For what reason was Paul ἐν ἀσθενείᾳ, ἐν φόβῳ, καὶ ἐν τρόμῳ? Chrysostom replies that there were many circumstances such as dangers, plots, and being hunted, which threw him into "fear and trembling."[14]

14. *Hom. ad Cor. 1*, Hom. 6, PG 61:49.

ἀλλὰ μετ' αὐτῶν καὶ
ἕτερα κωλύματα ἦν, οἱ
κίνδυνοι καὶ αἱ ἐπιβουλαὶ
καὶ ὁ καθημερινὸς φόβος
καὶ τὸ ἐλαύνεσθαι. Καὶ
γὰρ ἀσθένειαν τοὺς
διωγμοὺς πολλαχοῦ φησι,
καθάπερ καὶ ἀλλαχοῦ.

But with them [the preaching of
the cross and death] there were also
other hindrances, the dangers, and
the plots, and the daily fear, and the
being hunted. For the word "weak-
ness" with him in many places
stands for the persecutions, as also
in several other places.

When Calvin asks the question how the words "fear" and "trembling"
are to be explained, he suggests that Paul was so troubled because of the
magnitude of the office that he sustained or because Paul was surrounded
with great dangers.[15]

Quamquam bifariam pos-
sumus exponere haec duo
nomina: vel quod perpensa
magnitudine negotii, quod
sustinebat, trepidus, nec
sine ingenti sollicitudine
in eo versatus sit: vel quod
multis periculis circumsep-
tus, in perpetuo timore et
anxietate continua fuerit.
Utrumque contextui non
male quadrat: secundum
tamen (meo iudicio) est
simplicius.

There are, however, two ways in
which these two terms may be
explained by us. Either we may understand him to mean, that when he
pondered the magnitude of the office
that he sustained, it was tremblingly,
and not without great anxiety, that he
occupied himself in the office; or, that
being encompassed with many dangers, he was in constant alarm and
incessant anxiety. Either meaning
suits the context sufficiently well. The
second, however, is, in my opinion,
the more simple.

It will be observed that Calvin, again without mentioning Chrysostom's name, follows the interpretation of Chrysostom. This may well be
coincidental, but the final phrase Calvin offers is significant: He says, "the
second (interpretation), however, in my judgment, is the more simple."
Here we have the basis for Calvin's great admiration of Chrysostom as
an exegete. Writing in the Praefatio in Chrysostomi Homilias, Calvin
notes:[16]

15. *Comm. ad Cor. 1*, CO 49:334.
16. *Praef. in Chry. Hom.*, CO 9:835.

Chrysostomi autem nostri haec prima laus est quod ubique illi summo studio fuit a germana scripturae sinceritate ne minimum quidem deflectere, ac nullam sibi licentiam sumere in simplici verborum sensu contorquendo.

The outstanding merit of our author, Chrysostom, is that it was his supreme delight always not to turn aside even to the slightest degree from the genuine, simple sense of Scripture, and to allow himself no liberties by twisting the plain meaning of the words.

Two possible explanations come to Calvin's mind as to why Paul found himself in φόβῳ and τρόμῳ, and of these Calvin adopts the view offered by Chrysostom, which, in this instance, is the most clear, simple and straightforward rendering of the text.

1 Corinthians 2:4.

καὶ ὁ λόγος μου καὶ τὸ κήρυγμά μου οὐκ ἐν πειθοῖς σοφίας λόγοις ἀλλ' ἐν ἀποδείξει πνεύματος καὶ δυνάμεως . . .

One of the major difficulties in tracing the influence of one author on another is the criteria used to establish dependence. Little difficulty is encountered, of course, when Calvin mentions his source by name. Quite a different set of problems ensues at those points when one feels that Calvin has made use of Chrysostom. In such instances, only internal evidence can substantiate the claim that Calvin is writing with Chrysostom close at hand.

In his commentary on this verse, Calvin again does not mention the Antiochene by name, yet there are three reasons for suspecting dependence at this point, the cumulative weight of which strongly supports the thesis that Calvin is writing with Chrysostom clearly in mind.

First, when Calvin makes reference to πειθοῖς σοφίας λόγοις, rather than employing the word πειθοῖς, Calvin renders τὸ πιθανόν:[17]

---

17. *Comm. ad Cor. 1*, CO 49:335.

Vocat persuasoria humanae sapientiae verba exquisitam eloquutionem, quae artificio magis quam veritate nitatur ac pugnet: et simul subtilitatis speciem, quae hominum mentes alliciat. Et merito humanae sapientiae tribuit τὸ πιθανόν.	By the persuasive words of man's wisdom, he means that exquisite oratory which aims and strives rather by artifice than by truth, and also an appearance of refinement, that allures the minds of men. It is not without good reason, too, that he ascribes persuasiveness to human wisdom.

Why this surprising form?

When Chrysostom quotes this passage, on occasion he makes use of the adjective πίθανοις, and in other cases he has πειθοῖς. Is it not possible that Calvin renders the word "persuasive" as τὸ πιθανόν in allusion to those instances in which Chrysostom makes use of the adjective πίθανοις?

Second, again we find Calvin quickly "throwing in" a reference to other interpreters who remain anonymous and unidentified. In this instance the pointing to another source or sources is accomplished virtually with a flick of the wrist, in one Latin word: plerique. But as we have noted before, and will again have occasion to note, either the use of plerique or the words quemadmodum quidam putant frequently point in the direction of Chrysostom.

Third, Calvin inquires into the meaning of the words demonstrationem spiritus et potentiae:[18]

Huic demonstrationem Spiritus et potentiae opponit: quam plerique ad miracula restringunt, ego autem latius accipio, nempe pro manu Dei potenter se modis omnibus per apostolum exserente.	Over against this Paul sets "demonstration of the Spirit and of power," which most interpreters confine to miracles. But I understand it in a wider sense, namely, as the hand of God stretching itself out to act powerfully through the apostle in every way.

18. Ibid.

We must ask, therefore, if Chrysostom understands the words "demonstration of the Spirit and of power" in the sense of *miracula*. That he does may be seen from the following:[19]

Τίς γὰρ, εἰπέ μοι, ὁρῶν νεκροὺς ἀνισταμένους καὶ δαίμονας ἐλαυνομένους, οὐκ ἂν κατεδέξατο.	For who, tell me, after he had seen dead men rising to life and devils cast out, could have helped admitting it?

For Chrysostom, the evidence of the Spirit's operation is "seeing dead men rising to life and devils being cast out." Over against the use of miracles as evidence for the operation of the Spirit, Calvin asserts that he takes demonstrationem spiritus et potentiae in a wider sense, that is, as the hand of God stretching itself out to act powerfully through Paul.

Both on linguistic and theological grounds, therefore it may be fairly asserted that here, as often elsewhere, Calvin is in constant conversation with the Antiochene exegete as Calvin prepares his own commentary.

1 Corinthians 3:1–3.

1. Κἀγώ, ἀδελφοί, οὐκ ἠδυνήθην λαλῆσαι ὑμῖν ὡς πνευματικοῖς ἀλλ' ὡς σαρκίνοις, ὡς νηπίοις ἐν Χριστῷ. 2. γάλα ὑμᾶς ἐπότισα, οὐ βρῶμα. οὔπω γὰρ ἐδύνασθε. ἀλλ' οὐδὲ ἔτι νῦν δύνασθε, 3. ἔτι γὰρ σαρκικοί ἐστε. ὅπου γὰρ ἐν ὑμῖν ζῆλος καὶ ἔρις, οὐχὶ σαρκικοί ἐστε καὶ κατὰ ἄνθρωπον περιπατεῖτε;

The commentaries of our respective authors on this passage demonstrate a major theological difference of approach as they interpret Scripture. One such theological locus concerns the freedom of the will. Calvin, in the Praefatio in Chrysostomi Homilias, warns the reader that Chrysostom is, on this doctrine, "hardly satisfactory":[20]

---

19. *Hom. ad Cor. 1*, Hom. 6, PG 61:49.
20. *Praef. in Chry. Hom.*, CO 9:835.

De libero arbitrio sic loquitur, ac si ad studium virtutis divinaeque legis observationem multum haberet momenti. Atqui ubique Dominus verbi sui testimonio nos omni bene agendi facultate spoliat, nec aliam virtutem reliquam nobis facit, nisi quam ipse spiritu suo subministrat.

He speaks of free-will as if it had great importance for the pursuit of virtue and the observance of the divine law. But everywhere the Lord, by the witness of His word, denies to us all capacity to do good, and leaves to us no virtue except what He supplies by his Spirit.

We shall here see the reason Calvin forms such an opinion.

Why were the Corinthians not able to be addressed as πνευματικοῖς? Why were they not able to receive food (βρῶμα)? The answer, for Chrysostom, lies in the will. Chrysostom is insistent that the lack of ability is equivalent with a lack of will:[21]

Διὰ τί μὴ εἶπεν, Οὐ θέλετε, ἀλλ᾽, Οὐ δύνασθε; Ότι τοῦτο ἀντ᾽ ἐκείνου τέθεικε. Τὸ γὰρ μὴ δύνασθαι, τοῦτο ἀπο τοῦ μὴ θέλειν ἐστίν. . . . Εἰ μὲν γὰρ ἀπὸ φύσεως οὐκ ἠδύναντο, ἴσως ἄν τις συνέγνω· ἐπειδὴ δε ἀπὸ προαιρέσεως, ἀπεστέρηνται τῆς ἀπολογίας.

Why did he not say, "you are not willing," but "you are not able"? Because he places the latter for the former. For as to the want of ability, it arises from the want of the will. . . . For if they had been unable by nature, one might perhaps have forgiven them; but since it was from choice, they were bereft of all excuse.

The fact that Paul calls the Corinthians σαρκίνοις has nothing to do with their permanent nature (φύσις), but is the result of ζῆλος καὶ ἔρις:[22]

---

21. *Hom. ad Cor. 1*, Hom. 6, PG 61:69.
22. *Hom. ad Cor. 1*, Hom. 8, PG 61:69.

Ὅπου γὰρ ἐν ὑμῖν ἔρις καὶ ζῆλος καὶ διχοστασία, οὐχὶ σαρκικοί ἐστε, καὶ κατὰ ἄνθρωπον περιπατεῖτε; Καίτοι καὶ πορνείας καὶ ἀσελγείας ἔχων αὐτῶν εἰπεῖν, ἐκεῖνο μᾶλλον τίθησι τὸ ἁμάρτημα, ὅπερ ἐσπούδασε διορθώσασθαι τέως.

"For whereas there is among you strife, and jealousy, and divisions, are you not carnal and walk as men?" Although he had fornications also, and uncleannesses of theirs to speak of, he sets down rather that offence which he had been a good while endeavoring to correct.

The Corinthians are "carnal" because there are divisions and jealousy and strife among them. In short, for Chrysostom, it is the jealousy and strife that produce the state of "carnality."

Calvin's theological anthropology contrasts markedly to that of Chrysostom. For Calvin, the will is not in need of either stimulation or encouragement. The will, rather, is to be renounced. The will, together with our judgments, is under the influence of humanity's natural corruption:[23]

Quamdiu caro, hoc est, naturalis vitiositas, in homine dominatur, sic occupat ipsius hominis ingenium, ut non sit ingressus sapientiae Dei. Quare si quid proficere volumus in schola Domini, primum est ut nos proprio sensu et propria voluntate abdicemus.

As long as the flesh, that is to say, natural corruption, prevails in a man, it has so completely taken possession of man's mind that the wisdom of God finds no admittance. Hence if we would make proficiency in the Lord's school, we must first of all renounce our own judgment and our will.

Aemulatio and contentio therefore do not cause the state of being carnales, but result from naturalis vitiositas.[24]

---

23. *Comm. ad Cor. 1*, CO 49:348.
24. Ibid.

Probatio est ab effectis: nam quum sint fructus carnis aemulatio, rixae et factiones: ubicunque spectantur, certum est radicem illic vigere. Regnabant haec mala apud Corinthios: hinc ergo convincit eos esse carnales.	The proof is derived from the effects; for as envying, and strifes, and divisions are the fruits of the flesh, wherever they are seen, it is certain that the root is there in its vigor. These evils prevailed among the Corinthians, and accordingly he proves from this that they are carnal.

Calvin warned his readers to be careful of Chrysostom's propensity to overestimate the power of the will, and here we see Calvin, without mentioning Chrysostom's name, correcting what he considered to be an ancient error.

1 Corinthians 4:9.

δοκῶ γὰρ, ὁ θεὸς ἡμᾶς τοὺς ἀποστόλους ἐσχάτους ἀπέ δειξεν ὡς ἐπιθανατίους, ὅτι θέατρον ἐγενήθημεν τῷ κόσμῳ καὶ ἀλλέλοις καὶ ἀνθρώποις.

The word ἐσχάτους is the problem in this text. The meaning for Chrysostom does not have a sequential significance, but is rather tied with the words ἐπιθανατίους and θέατρον. The apostles are set forth as "last of all," doomed to death, a spectacle to the whole world. Being last means being "the most abject of all men, as those who are put forward for continual suffering." Chrysostom notes that Paul includes in his statement not only the fact of being last, but that God made them last:[25]

τούτους ἐσχάτους ἀπέδειξεν, ὡς ἐπιθανατίους, τουτέστιν, ὡς καταδίκους. . . . Βουλόμενος δε εἰς πλείονα ἀτοπίαν ἀπαγαγεῖν τὸν λόγον, καὶ δεῖξαι αὐτὸν ἀπίθανον μεθ' ὑπερβολῆς, οὐκ εἶπεν, ὅτι Ἁπλῶς ἡμεῖς ἐσμεν ἔσχατοι, ἀλλ', Ὁ θεος ἡμᾶς ἐσχάτους ἐποίησε. Καὶ οὐκ ἠρκέσθη τῷ εἰπεῖν. Ἐσχάτους, ἀ λλὰ προσέθηκε καὶ Ἐπιθανατίους . . .	These, "He has set forth last, as doomed to death"; that is, as condemned. . . . And wishing to carry out their reasoning to still greater absurdity, and to exhibit it as incredible in the highest degree, he said not merely "We are 'last'" but "God made us last." Nor was he satisfied with saying "last." But he added also, "doomed to death" . . .

25. *Hom. ad Cor. 1*, Hom. 12, PG 61:99.

This interpretation of the word ἐσχάτους is not agreeable to Calvin. He first inquires whether ἡμᾶς τοὺς ἀποστόλους refers to Apollos and Silvanus as well as Paul himself, allowing here latitude of interpretation, but with the qualification that said apostles were not, "as if for the sake of ignominy," reserved to the last place. Objecting to Chrysostom, Calvin says:[26]

Incertum est, de se ne loquatur solo, an Apollon etiam et Sylvanum comprehendat: nam tales interdum vocat apostolos: malo tamen de ipso solo accipere. Si quis latius extendere volet, facile patiar: modo ne cum Chrysostomo intelligat, omnes apostolos tanquam ignominiae causa in postremum locum reiectos esse. Postremos enim haud dubie vocat, qui in ordinem apostolicum post Christi resurrectionem adsciti fuerant.

It is uncertain if he is speaking about himself alone, or whether he includes Apollos and Silvanus, for he sometimes calls men like them apostles. I prefer however, to take it as referring to himself alone. If anyone wishes to give it wider application, I have no great objection, provided that he does not understand it, like Chrysostom, to mean that all the apostles have been relegated to the least significant place, as if they were in disgrace. For there is no doubt that he means by "last" those who have been admitted to the apostolic order after the resurrection of Christ.

One cannot escape the feeling that the rendering of the word ἐσχάτους as given by Chrysostom is more in line with Paul's thought. If the imagery with which Paul is working is the ancient θέατρον, in which the apostles are presented by God to the world like wretches brought on at the close of a display, wretches who are already condemned to death and sure to perish in combat with each other, then the word ἐσχάτους has more meaning when interpreted in the light of the remaining words in the sentence than as "those admitted to the rank of apostles subsequent to the resurrection of Christ."

We might conjecture what impelled Calvin to interpret the word ἐσχάτους as meaning "those admitted to the apostolic order subsequent to the resurrection." The year 1543 saw the third edition of the *Institutes*, an edition that included, for the first time, the large segment of material

26. *Comm. ad Cor. 1*, CO 49:368–69.

dealing with the scriptural offices of the ministry. Here is explained the "high and necessary functions of the ministry," the prestige of the preaching office, and the several offices in the church according to Scripture. During these years also, following 1541, Calvin is back in Geneva, forging the structure of the Reformed church, devoting his energy to matters of ecclesiastical policy. The question of the government of the church, in particular as it depends upon the primacy of the apostolic office given by Paul (Eph 4:11; cf. *Inst.* 4.3.4) is in the forefront of Calvin's thinking.

The dedicatory preface to the First Corinthians commentary is dated January 1546. The years immediately preceding 1546 would have found Calvin wrestling with the questions of ecclesiastical policy; the same years in which Calvin was working on the commentary. Given this set of circumstances, Calvin could not tolerate the notion that apostles, who are placed in first rank by Paul, could be reduced by God to last place, for the sake of ignominiae.

What is inferred in our conjecture is that historical circumstances and current issues color the interpretation of any exegete. As we continue through the commentary, we shall have other occasions to note instances where Calvin brings overarching issues to the interpretation of a passage.

> 1 Corinthians 5:1-5.
>
> 1. Ὅλως ἀκούεται ἐν ὑμῖν πορνεία, καὶ τοιαύτη πορνεία ἥτις οὐδὲ ἐν τοῖς ἔθνεσιν, ὥστε γυναῖκά τινα τοῦ πατρὸς ἔχειν. 2. καὶ ὑμεῖς πεφυσιωμένοι ἐστέ, καὶ οὐχὶ μᾶλλον ἐπενθήσατε, ἵνα ἀρθῇ ἐκ μέσου ὑμῶν ὁ τὸ ἔργον τοῦτο ποιήσας; 3. ἐγὼ μὲν γάρ, ἀπὼν τῷ σώματι παρὼν δὲ τῷ πνεύματι, ἤδη κέ κρικα ὡς παρὼν τὸν οὕτως τοῦτο κατεργασάμενον 4. ἐν τῷ ὀνόματι τοῦ κυρίου Ἰησοῦ, συναχθέντων ὑμῶν καὶ τοῦ ἐμοῦ πνεύματος σὺν τῇ δυνάμει τοῦ κυρίου ἡμῶν Ἰησοῦ, 5. παραδοῦναι τὸν τοιοῦτον τῷ Σατανᾷ εἰς ὄλεθρον τῆς σαρκός, ἵνα τὸ πνεῦμα σωθῇ ἐν τῇ ἡμέρᾳ τοῦ κυρίου.

This section is interesting in that we find here an outstanding example of the hermeneutical methodology employed by each of our commentators. Throughout his commentary, Chrysostom endeavors to "get inside Paul's skin," as it were. At times, we hardly know if Paul is speaking or if Chrysostom is commentating. Chrysostom repeatedly notes how Paul introduces a subject. The manner of Paul's speaking, his approach to a problem, is as important as the content of the problem. Chrysostom is always concerned to demonstrate where Paul uses utmost tact, where

Paul is "gentle," where Paul seeks first to gain the favor of the Corinthians before making an accusation.

While Calvin, here and throughout his commentaries, is concerned with philology, grammar, and historical inquiry, one cannot escape the fact that Calvin's commentaries are written with sixteenth-century problems in mind. This is not to imply that Calvin jumps too quickly to the "application" of Scripture. What we are suggesting, however, is that the Reformer's commentaries are written with one foot in the first century and one foot in the sixteenth century. For Chrysostom, these five verses are a paradigm for pastoral correction and reproof. For Calvin, these five verses are the springboard for church discipline, government and organization, authority, the power of the keys, and the right to excommunicate members.

But Calvin has not come to his conclusions lightly. He has agonized over the words in verse five: παραδοῦναι τὸν τοιοῦτον τῷ Σατανᾷ εἰς ὄλεθρον τῆς σαρκός. At one time he agreed with Chrysostom, considering these words to mean the infliction of severe punishment upon the body. But further considerations changed his mind, and Calvin came to understand these words as referring to excommunication:[27]

Quoniam ista virtute inter alias praediti erant apostoli, ut malos et contumaces Satanae subiicerent, eoque tanquam flagello uterentur ad eos corrigendos: Chrysostomus et qui eum sequuntur ista Pauli verba referunt ad tale genus castigationis, quemadmodum exponi solet alter locus de Alexandro et Hymenaeo, ad Timotheum. Tradere ergo Satanae, nihil aliud esse sentiunt quam gravem aliquam corporis poenam infligere.	Since, among other powers, the apostles were endowed with that of giving over the wicked and the obstinate to Satan, and using him as a scourge for correcting them, Chrysostom, and those who follow him, take these words of Paul as referring to punishment of that sort. And this is in accordance with the exposition usually given of another passage, 1 Timothy 1:20, concerning Alexander and Hymenaeus. Thus they think that "delivering to Satan" is nothing else than the infliction of some severe physical punishment.

27. Ibid., CO 49:380–81.

Sed ego dum totum contextum propius intueor, et simul confero quae in posteriore epistola habentur: omissa illa interpretatione tanquam co-acta et a sensu Pauli aliena, de excommunicatione simpliciter accipio. Est enim apta loquutio tradere Satanae pro excom-municare: quia sicut in ecclesia regnat Christus, ita Satan extra ecclesiam.

For myself, when I look more closely at the whole context, and at the same time compare it with what is said in the next epistle, I turn that interpretation down as forced and not in line with what Paul means, and take it to mean simply excommunication. For "to deliver to Satan" is fitting to describe ex-communication, for, while Christ reigns within, Satan reigns outside the Church.

Calvin has apparently rejected the interpretation of Chrysostom for that of Augustine, for Calvin adds:[28]

quemadmodum etiam an-notavit Augustinus, sermone De verbis apostoli 68, ubi locum hunc exponit.

Augustine also has a similar com-ment in his 68th Sermon on the Words of the Apostle, where he is expounding this passage.

Here it may significantly be noted that Calvin had at one time agreed with Chrysostom's "simple and straightforward" meaning of the words, but Calvin appeals to Augustine when doctrinal and ecclesiastical impli-cations result.

The conclusion Calvin reaches in the fifth verse seems to color his interpretation of the preceding four verses. Reading the commentary, one has the distinct impression that Paul is angry at the Corinthians, not so much because an act of fornication has taken place in the Corinthian community, but because the Corinthian church has been lax in disciplin-ing the offender. The basic problem to which Paul is addressing himself is not πορνεία, but ignavia. Commenting on the second verse, ut e medio vestri removeretur, Calvin notes:[29]

28. Ibid., CO 49:381.
29. Ibid., CO 49:379.

Hic iam clarius exprimit quid in Corinthiis accuset: nempe ignaviam, quod ad tantam abominationem conniverent. Unde etiam apparet, hac potestate praeditas esse ecclesias, ut si quid est intus vitii, disciplinae severitate corrigant vel eiiciant: neque posse excusari, quae non advigilant ut a sordibus repurgentur. Damnat enim hic Corinthios Paulus. Cur? quod in puniendo unius scelere fuerint negligentes. Atqui immerito reos ageret, si deficeret eos facultas. Excommunicationis ergo potestas hoc loco stabilitur.

He now brings out more distinctly what he finds fault with in the Corinthians—remissness, in closing their eyes to so great an abomination. From which it also appears that churches are provided with this power, that they can correct or remove by strict discipline any fault that there may be in them; and those which are not vigilant about clearing away filth cannot be excused. For Paul condemns the Corinthians here. Why? Because they had been quite unconcerned about punishing one man for his crime. But his charge against them would have been unjust, if they did not possess this power. Therefore the power of excommunication is established by this passage.

Deriving the power of excommunication from this passage, Calvin has apparently understood the ἵνα of verse two as an imperatival ἵνα, rather than as a subjunctive result clause following καὶ οὐχὶ μᾶλλον ἐπενθήσατε. It is significant that Calvin here differs from Chrysostom again, although Calvin does not indicate that this represents, as in verse five, a change of mind. For Chrysostom, the Corinthians are to mourn, producing the result that the offender would be thereby removed from among them. For Calvin, the Corinthians ought to mourn because the lapse of one person affects the whole church. Hence, for Calvin, the mourning process is seen as the proper result of an offence, while for Chrysostom, the mourning process is to be the cause of the person's being removed. For Calvin, mourning does not remove the offender; rather, it is an official act of excommunication that accomplishes the desired result.

Thus we see Calvin developing an ecclesiastical program based on Scripture. In doing so, however, he turns for his interpretation, not to Chrysostom, but to Augustine. For the words "to deliver over to Satan," to mean excommunication, Calvin must employ a theological construct whereby Satan reigns outside the church, and has been defeated within the Christian community.

1 Corinthians 5:9-11.

9. Ἔγραψα ὑμῖν ἐν τῇ ἐπιστολῇ μὴ συναναμίγνυσθαι πόρνοις, 10. οὐ πάντως τοῖς πόρνοις τοῦ κόσμου τούτου ἢ τοῖς πλεονέκταις καὶ ἅρπαξιν ἢ εἰδωλολάτραις, ἐπεὶ ὠθείλετε ἄρα ἐκ τοῦ κόσμου ἐξελθεῖν. 11. νῦν δὲ ἔγραψα ὑμῖν μὴ συναναμίγνυσθαι ἐάν τις ἀδελφὸς ὀνομαζόμενος ᾖ πόρνος ἢ πλεονέκτης ἢ εἰδωλολάτρης ἢ λοίδορος ἢ μέθυσος ἢ ἅρπαξ, τῷ τοιούτῳ μηδὲ συνεσθίειν.

When Paul, in his Vorbrief, instructed the Corinthians not to associate intimately with the πόρνοις, his counsel had been interpreted by the Corinthians to mean any and all immoral persons, wherever they might be found. Paul now corrects the misunderstanding, suggesting that they should not try to separate themselves from the πόρνοις τοῦ κόσμου τούτου, for to do so they would have to ἐκ τοῦ κόσμου ἐξελθεῖν. Paul's intention is that the Corinthians should not associate intimately with any immoral person who ἀδελφὸς ὀνομαζόμενος.

Three observations may be noted when one examines the commentaries of our two authors. First, let us note how each author perceives the issue that Paul is addressing. For Chrysostom, Paul is making it easier for the Corinthians to follow the advice given in a former letter. To avoid contact with the immoral of the world is an impossibility, but this injunction can be adhered to if it applies to a brother in the church. One would have to "go out of the world" to follow the advice completely; however, applied to a brother, the legislation can be easily accomplished:[30]

30. *Hom. ad Cor. 1*, Hom. 16, PG 61:129–30.

Εἶδες πῶς ἐστιν ἀνεπαχθής, καὶ πανταχοῦ οὐ τὸ δυνατὸν μόνον, ἀλλὰ καὶ τὸ εὔκολον τῆς νομοθεσίας σκοπεῖ; Πῶς γὰρ ἔνι ἄνθρωπον ὄντα, φησί, καὶ οἰκίας καὶ παίδων προϊστάμενον, καὶ τὰ τῆς πόλεως πράττοντα, ἢ χειροτέχνην ὄντα, ἢ στρατευόμενον, τῶν πλειόνων ὄντων Ἑλλήνων, τοὺς πανταχοῦ πόρνους φεύγειν; πόρνους γὰρ κόσμου τοὺς παρὰ τοῖς Ἕλλησι λέγει. Νῦν δὲ ἔγραψα ὑμῖν, ἐάν τις ἀδελφὸς ᾖ τοιοῦτος, τῷ τουούτῳ μηδὲ συνεσθίειν.

Do you see that he is not a hard master, and that in his legislation he constantly regards not only what may be easily done. For how is it possible says he, for a man having care of a house and children, and engaged in the affairs of the city, or who is an artisan or a soldier (the greater part of mankind being Greeks) to avoid the unclean who are to be found everywhere? For by "the fornicators of the world," he means those who are among the Greeks. "But now I write to you, if any brother be of this kind, with such a one do not eat."

If, for Chrysostom, Paul is accommodating himself to the exigencies of the situation, for Calvin, Paul is reminding the Corinthians that they should not have relations with anyone who is wicked. Paul is not altering a previous injunction, he is exposing the dilatory behavior of the Corinthians:[31]

Reducit Corinthiis in memoriam quid illis iam praeceperit: nempe ut ab improborum consuetudine abstinerent. Hoc enim est commisceri, familiariter versari cum aliquo et eius consuetudine implicari. Porro commemoratio ista ad exprobrandam segnitiem valet, quod admoniti cessaverant.

He reminds the Corinthians of what he has already advised them: to refrain from having relations with the wicked. For the meaning of the word, "to have company with" is to live on friendly terms with someone, and to be intimately involved with him. Moreover, his reminder has the effect of showing up their remissness, because, despite his admonition, they have done nothing.

What has become of the idea that Paul has transferred rejection of the worldly immoral people to rejection of the immoral within the church?

31. *Comm. ad Cor. 1*, CO 49:383–84.

For Calvin, Paul has not changed his idea or accommodated himself to the situation; rather, Paul singles out the "brother" in order to demonstrate that rejection of relations with immoral people, while applying to everyone, applies particularly to those that belong to the church. The idea of the "brother," for Calvin, is added by Paul, as an *exceptio*:[32]

Addit exceptionem, quo melius intelligant, ad ecclesiae domesticos id proprie spectare: quum de mundo fugiendo non sint admonendi.	He adds an exception, so that they might understand better that what he says refers particularly to those within the Church.

We observe therefore, first of all, that the reason why Paul said νῦν δὲ ἔγραψα ὑμῖν μὴ συναναμίγνυσθαι ἐάν τις ἀδελφὸς ὀνομαζόμενος ἦ πόρνος, is seen in contrasting light by each of our authors. For Chrysostom, Paul said this because it is impossible to avoid contact with everyone in the world. For Calvin, Paul said this because he was singling out an exceptional example, a church member, among all people, immoral in behavior, whom the Corinthians should avoid.

Our first observation makes the second all the more interesting, for here we find Calvin supporting the contention of Chrysostom as the best of the several interpretations of the phrase ἐπεὶ ὠθείλετε ἄρα ἐκ τοῦ κόσμου ἐξελθεῖν. To be sure, Calvin favors an interpretation differing even from that of Chrysostom, consistent with what we found Calvin saying in our first observation. Concerning the phrase, Calvin notes:[33]

Dicunt enim aliqui: citius e Graecia migrare vos oportet. Ambrosius autem: Potius vobis est moriendum. Erasmus resolvit in optativum, ac si Paulus diceret: Utinam quidem e mundo liceret penitus exire: sed quia id non potestis, saltem ab iis exeatis, qui falso Christianos se vocant et pessimo interea exemplo vivunt.	Some say: "you must rather emigrate from Greece." Ambrose says, "you must rather die." Erasmus puts it into the optative, as if Paul should mean, "Indeed I wish that it were possible for you to leave the world altogether; but because you cannot do that, you may at least give up relations with those who falsely call themselves Christians, and whose lives, at the same time, give very bad examples."

32. Ibid., CO 49:384.
33. Ibid.

Propius aliquanto ad verisimilitudinem accedit Chrysostomi expositio, secundum quem hic est sensus: Quum iubeo vos a scortatoribus fugere, non quoslibet intelligo: alioqui alium mundum quaerere oporteat. Vivendum enim nobis est inter spinas, quamdiu in terra peregrinamur: sed hoc tantum exigo, ne vos commisceatis cum scortatoribus, qui fratres censeri volunt: ne videamini eorum nequitiam tolerando, probare.

Chrysostom's explanation comes somewhat nearer to the truth. According to him the meaning is this: "When I tell you to avoid fornicators, I do not mean all in that category, otherwise you would need to seek another world. For we are required to live among thorns so long as we are sojourners on the earth. The only stipulation I make is that you do not mix with fornicators who wish to be regarded as brethren, in case, by tolerating their wickedness, you may give the impression of approving it.

But Calvin is insistent. Paul intends the Corinthians to avoid contact with the fornicators both within and outside the church. Calvin does not want to "twist the meaning of words to make them suit an interpretation." He adds:[34]

Ego quia non libenter interpretationes recipio, quae aliter accommodari verbis nequeunt quam si verba ad ipsas torqueantur, aliam ab his omnibus diversam magis amplector, ut "exire" pro segregari sumatur; "mundus" pro mundi inquinamentis. Quasi diceret: Quid opus est vobis praecipere de filiis saeculi, quando ut semel renuntiastis mundo, ita oportet vos ab eorum consortio subducere? totus enim mundus in maligno positus est.

I do not find it easy to accept interpretations which can only be made to fit in with the words if the words are twisted to suit them, and so I favor one that is rather different from all these. I take "to go out" to mean "to be separated"; and "world" to mean "the filthy things of the world." It is as if Paul said: "What need is there to warn you about the sons of this world, for seeing that you have once and for all renounced the world, you ought to be keeping away from their company." For "the whole world is in the power of the evil one."

34. Ibid., CO 49:384–85.

Si cui ea non placet, est haec quoque altera probabilis: Non scribo vobis in universum ut fugiatis societatem scortatorum huius saeculi: quamquam id sponte facere debetis, etiamsi non admoneam. Mihi tamen magis probatur illa superior: nec vero eam primus excogitavi, sed ab aliis prius adductam melius (ni fallor) aptavi contextui paulino.

If anyone is not satisfied with that explanation, this is another probable one: "I do not write to make a general appeal to you to avoid the company of the fornicators of this world; nevertheless you ought to be doing that on your own initiative, without any warning from me." However, I prefer the one I have given above. Indeed, I am not the first to think of it, but what others have suggested before, I have brought more into line with Paul's argument, if I am not mistaken.

Let us paraphrase the passage now, as Calvin would have us interpret it: "I wrote to you in the previous letter not to associate intimately with the fornicators. I am not talking about fornicators of this world. Since you have already renounced the pollutions of this world, there is no need to mention such people. You ought to have done that without any reminder from me. You have already gone out of the world. Now I am writing to you not to associate intimately with a brother in the faith who is a fornicator."

While such an interpretation may well be consonant with what Paul might say, it is extremely difficult to derive such a meaning from Paul's Greek and the context of Paul's argument. One has the feeling here that Calvin is guilty of that which he says he wants to avoid, namely, accepting an interpretation which can only be made to fit in with the words if the words are twisted to suit that interpretation. Calvin bases his interpretation on taking ἐξελθεῖν as meaning segregari sumatur and κόσμου as meaning mundi inquinamentis. But it is by no means clear how Calvin derives from his definition of these two words Paul's intention that the Corinthians were to avoid contact with any and all fornicators.

We may conclude, therefore, as our second observation, that while Calvin sets for himself the admirable goal of staying as close as possible to the "clear and straightforward meaning of Scripture," in this instance he has produced an interpretation that is wide of the mark.

Third, we can observe in this section that while Calvin offers his own preferred interpretation of the passage, he not only allows the reader to follow Chrysostom, but actually comes to the defense of Chrysostom's exegesis. If one wants to follow Chrysostom, notes Calvin, then the legitimate question may be raised as to what is to be done "in our own" day when everyone at least nominally acknowledges the name of Christ. When there are no insiders and outsiders, how is one to avoid contamination by association with the wicked "in our own day"? Calvin responds to the question with the doctrine of excommunication:[35]

Si cui Chrysostomum sequi libeat, huic non difficilis erit responsio, Paulum hic pro confesso sumpsisse quod verum est, ubi ius est excommunicandi, facile remedium esse quo segregentur mali a bonis, si ecclesiae officium suum faciant. Adversus extraneos nulla erat Christianis iurisdictio Corinthi, nec coercere dissolutam eorum vitam poterant: necesse ergo illis fuisset mundum relinquere, si malos, quorum vitiis mederi non poterant, fugere voluissent.	If anyone is willing to follow Chrysostom, it will not be difficult for him to answer: Paul has taken for granted the truth that, where the right of excommunication exists, it is a simple remedy for separating the evil from the good if the churches do their duty. The Christians in Corinth had no jurisdiction over those outside, and they had no power to control their dissolute lives. Therefore, it was necessary for them to leave the world, if they wanted to avoid the wicked, whose vices they could not cure.

Here we have, for the first time, an explicit reference to the contemporary situation in sixteenth-century Geneva. One has the feeling that Calvin is strongly attracted to Chrysostom's interpretation of the passage, but here notes that the setting of Chrysostom's day and Calvin's day has changed. In Chrysostom's day, as Calvin understands it, the lines were more clearly drawn between those on the inside and those on the outside. In Calvin's own day, everyone has enlisted under Christ's banner. Do we have here a clue as to why Calvin prefers his own rendering of the passage rather than that of Chrysostom? The import of Calvin's interpretation is Paul's insistence that all immoral people are to be avoided, an interpretation more nearly suited to the situation in Geneva. We may conjecture at this point that while, when Calvin does his commentary work, the historical setting of the passage is all important, the final interpretation adopted is one that is applicable to his own day.

35. Ibid., CO 49:384.

1 Corinthians 5:13b.

ἐξάρατε τὸν πονηρὸν ἐξ ὑμῶν αὐτῶν.

On occasion, Calvin will brush off with a sentence or two an inter-pretation rendered by Chrysostom. Yet, when one examines Chrysostom's commentary, one discovers that Calvin has not been entirely fair to the Antiochene. While such a procedure may reflect sixteenth-century meth-ods of citation, in which the task of an interpreter does not include full reproduction of an author's views, it is worth observing that when Calvin represents a position taken by Chrysostom, the total impact of what Chrysostom has said is not included in Calvin's treatment.

Commenting on this verse, Calvin notes:[36]

Cur autem Chrysostomus rigorem legis cum evangelii clementia comparet, quia Paulus excommunicatione contentus fuit in eo scelere, de quo lex capitis poenam exigeret, nulla est ratio. Neque enim iudices gladio armatos Paulus alloquitur, sed inermem turmam, cui tantum fraterna correctio permissa erat.	Chrysostom compares the rigor of the Law with the mildness of the Gospel, inasmuch as Paul was satisfied with excommunication in the instance of an offence for which the law required the punishment of death. But there is no justifica-tion for this. For Paul is not here addressing judges that were armed with the sword, but an unarmed group, able to make brotherly correction.

The impression one receives from such a statement is that Chrysostom contrasts the two dispensations: the old, which is severe, and the new, which is tolerant, producing two quite different covenants. The old cov-enant is characterized by the infliction of death on the adulterer, but in the new covenant the adulterer is "let off" with excommunication. Chrysostom, however, goes to considerable length to demonstrate that such a division to which Calvin alludes is not acceptable. He shows that in the Old Testament instances of less punishment are found; while in the New Testament one finds examples of heavy punishment:[37]

36. Ibid., CO 49:387.
37. Hom. ad Cor. 1, Hom. 16, PG 61:131.

Καὶ γὰρ ἐν τῇ Παλαιᾷ
μοιχεύσας καὶ φονεύσας
ὁ Δαυὶδ, διὰ μετανοίας
ἐσώθη, καὶ ἐν τῇ Καινῇ
μικρὰ ἀπὸ χωρίου τιμῆς
ὑφελόμενος ὁ Ἀνανίας μετὰ
τῆς γυναικὸς ἀπώλετο. Εἰ
δὲ πλεονάζει ταῦτα ἐν τῷ
Παλαιᾷ, τὰ δὲ ἐναντία ἐν
τῇ Καινῇ, ἡ διαφορὰ τῶν
προσώπων τὴν διαφορὰν
τῆς τοιαύτης οἰκονομίας
ἐργάζεται.

Thus in the Old Testament, David, who had committed adultery and murder, was saved by means of repentance. In the New Testament Ananias, who withdrew but a small portion of the price of the land, perished together with his wife. Now if these instances are more frequent in the Old Testament, and those of the contrary kind in the New, the difference of the persons produces the differences in the treatment of the two dispensations.

Chrysostom gives particular emphasis to the fact that the covenants themselves do not determine the severity of the punishment, but the difference of persons determines the discipline adopted.

Calvin does not accept Chrysostom's interpretation because, as Calvin understands him, Chrysostom associates severity with the old dispensation, but leniency with the new, a position Calvin was manifestly not willing to entertain.

1 Corinthians 6:3.

οὐκ οἴδατε ὅτι ἀγγέλους κρινοῦμεν, μήτιγε βιωτικά;

The interpretation of the word ἀγγέλους is the issue here. Here again we have an example of the very loose manner of citation employed by Calvin. Calvin observes that Chrysostom reports the word ἀγγέλους as referring to "priests," but nowhere in the body of Calvin's commentary do we discover if Chrysostom agrees with such an interpretation. Calvin simply calls the idea far-fetched:[38]

Chrysostomus refert, a quibus- dam de sacerdotibus intelligi, sed illud est nimis coactum.

Chrysostom reports that some understand it as referring to priests, but this is forced indeed.

---

38. *Comm. ad Cor. 1*, CO 49:389.

When we turn to Chrysostom, we discover that as soon as he notes such an interpretation has been brought forth by others, the notion is immediately rejected:[39]

Τινὲς ἐνταῦθά φασι τοὺς ἱερέας αἰνίττεσθαι· ἀλλ' ἄπαγε· περὶ γὰρ δαιμόνων ὁ λόγος αὐτῷ.

Some say that here the priests are hinted at, but away with this. His speech is about demons.

Paul, for Chrysostom, is not alluding to priests, but demons, those "angels" of whom Christ speaks:[40]

Ἀλλὰ περὶ ἐκεινων λέγει τῶν ἀγγέλων, περὶ ὧ φησιν ὁ Χριστός. Πορεύεσθε εἰς τὸ πῦρ τὸ ἡτοιμασμένον τῷ διαβόλῳ καὶ τοῖς ἀγγέλοις αὐτοῦ· καὶ ὁ Παῦλος, ὅτι Οἱ ἄγγελοι αὐτοῦ μετασχηματίζονται ὡς διάκονοι δικαιοσύνης. Ὅταν γὰρ αἱ ἀσώματοι δυνάμεις αὗται ἔλαττον ἡμῶν εὑρεθῶσιν ἔχουσαι τῶν σάρκα περιβεβλημένων, χαλεπωτέραν δώσουσι δίκην.

But he speaks concerning those angels about whom Christ says, "Depart into the fire which is prepared for the devil and his angels. And Paul says, "his angels fashion themselves as ministers of righteousness." For when the very incorporeal powers shall be found inferior to us who are clothed with flesh, they shall suffer heavier punishment.

It is precisely this interpretation of the word ἀγγέλους to which Calvin subscribes. He allows that "heavenly angels" would not be out of line with Paul's meaning, but finally settles for "apostate angels."[41]

---

39. *Hom. ad Cor. 1*, Hom. 16, PG 61:133.
40. Ibid.
41. *Comm. ad Cor. 1*, CO 49:389.

Neque enim minus quadrabi targumentum, hoc modo: daemones, qui ex origine adeo nobili orti sunt, et nunc quoque postquam exciderunt suo principatu creaturae sunt immortales et corruptibili mundo superiores, iudicabimus.	For the argument will be no less conclusive in this way: "Devils, who sprang from so illustrious an origin, and even now, when they have fallen from their high estate, are immortal creatures, and superior to this corruptible world, shall be judged by us.

Thus, Calvin's interpretation of the word ἀγγέλους, far from being a rejection of the "far-fetched" meaning noted in association with Chrysostom's name, turns out to be in total harmony with Chrysostom's rendering of the word.

1 Corinthians 6:4.

βιωτικὰ μὲν οὖν κριτήρια ἐὰν ἔχητε, τοὺς ἐξουθενημένους ἐν τῇ ἐκκλησίᾳ τούτους καθίζετε.

There are several possible renderings of this text, the final resolution being determined by whether Paul is here asking a question or making an exclamation, whether καθίζετε is indicative and interrogative, or imperative. To place the issue before us, let us state the possible translations:

a. "So, if you have cases concerning affairs of this life, do you appoint as judges those who have no standing in the church (i.e., Roman judges)?"

b. "If you have cases dealing with affairs of this life, (show your contempt for the Roman and hence profane judges) by appointing the most despised members of the church as judges."

c. "If you have cases concerning everyday affairs, why do you lay them before those who are least esteemed by the church?"

d. "If you have to judge things pertaining to this life, set those to judge who are of least account in the church."

Both Chrysostom and Calvin understand Paul as making a directive statement (d), but without the irony implied in (b). For Chrysostom, Paul is instructing the Corinthians as forcibly as possible that they ought not to commit themselves to any judges outside the church, no matter what the issue may be. Chrysostom has proposed a previous question, to which

Paul here is giving an answer. The question would be: "Suppose there is no one among us (the Corinthians) who is competent to adjudicate a case; then what do we do?" In response, Paul says, "even though there is no one competent, you are still to entrust things to those who are of least weight." Chrysostom is clear that in no case are the Corinthians to go outside the church:[42]

Μεθ' ὑπερβολῆς ἡμᾶς διδάξαι βουλόμενος, ὅτι, οὐδ' ἂν ὁτιοῦν ᾖ, τοῖς ἔξωθεν ἑαυτοὺς διδόναι χρὴ, τὴν δοκοῦσαν εἶναι ἀντίθεσιν κινήσας, προηγουμένως ταύτην ἔλυσεν. Ὁ γὰρ λέγει, τοιοῦτόν ἐστιν·῎Ισως ἐρεῖ τις, ὅτι οὐδεὶς ἐν ὑμῖν σοφὸς οὐδὲ ἱκανὸς διακρῖναι, ἀλλ' εὐκαταφρόνητοι πάντες. Καὶ τί τοῦτο; Κᾂν γὰρ μηδεὶς ᾖ σοφός, φησί, τοῖς ἐλαχίστοις ἐπιτρέπετε.	Wishing to instruct us as forcibly as possible that they ought not to commit themselves to those without, whatever the matter might be, and having raised what appeared to be an objection, he answers it in the first instance. For what he says is something like this: Perhaps someone will say, "no one among you is wise, nor competent, to pass sentence; all are contemptible." Now what follows? "Even though none be wise," he says, "I bid you to entrust things to those who are of the least weight.

With one major exception, Calvin's interpretation is in agreement with Chrysostom's. Paul is making a directive, and ἐξουθενημένους refers not to profane Roman judges, but to those in the church who are held in lowest standing. Calvin also feels that Paul is here responding to the hypothetical question, "suppose there is no one in the church suitable, then what is our course of action?" Paul's response, for Calvin, is "Even the lowest in the church is competent to discharge this office:[43]

42. *Hom. ad Cor. 1*, Hom. 16, PG 61:133.

43. *Comm. ad Cor. 1*, CO 49:389.

Ac ne causentur, se destitui meliore remedio, iubet ex ecclesia deligere arbitros, qui placide et ex aequitate causas decidant: ne vero idoneos sibi negent suppetere, dicit infimum quemque sustinere posse istas partes.	And in case they might plead that they were being deprived of a better remedy, he tells them to choose judges from the church, to settle the cases peacefully and fairly. In case they should say that they have no suitable men for this, he says that the lowest is able to discharge this office.

But there is one major difference between the interpretation of our two authors. Calvin acknowledges that Chrysostom nearly agrees with him, although "Chrysostom adds something to it":[44]

Ad hunc sensum prope accedit Chrysostomus, tametsi aliquid praeterea adiungit: putat enim apostolum voluisse dicere, etiamsi inter Corinthios nemo inveniretur, qui satis haberet prudentiae ad iudicandum, eligendos tamen esse qualescunque essent.	Chrysostom comes near this interpretation, though he appends to it something additional. For he is of the opinion, that the Apostle meant to say that even though the Corinthians should find no one among themselves who had sufficient wisdom for judging, they must nevertheless make a choice of some, no matter what they were like.

Now what is it that Chrysostom has added? Both authors are in agreement that the Corinthians are to have a case adjudicated by even the lowest of the believers, rather than place the issue before a court of unbelievers. When Calvin summarizes his interpretation in one sentence, he says:[45]

Ego mihi videor apostoli mentem fideliter expressisse, quod postremos fidelium praetulerit infidelibus in iudicandi facultate.	I think I have faithfully brought out the apostle's intention, that the lowest among believers was preferred by him to unbelievers, as to the capacity of judging.

44. Ibid.
45. Ibid., CO 49:389–90.

But this is exactly the import of Chrysostom's interpretation. Thus one asks, what is the basis of Calvin's objection to Chrysostom? What is it that, in Calvin's mind, Chrysostom has added to the clear interpretation of the text?

The answer is found in Calvin's own commentary. Calvin is anxious to assert that Paul has in mind particular kinds of cases. Paul, for Calvin, is not talking about public trials, but private matters. Public trials do not fall within the province of the church, but private matters may be settled without the magistrate. Then Calvin states what is uppermost in his mind: "Therefore we do not detract from the authority of the magistrate":[46]

Non ergo hic elevatur magistratus dignitas, dum eorum munus contemptis hominibus mandari praecipit.	Therefore the authority of the magistrate is not impaired here, when he directs that their function should be handed over to people who are looked down upon.

What Calvin is doing here is seeking to harmonize the concept of the authority of the magistrate with Paul's injunction never to take a legal dispute before the secular authority. Calvin therefore makes a distinction between public and private disputes, the former coming under the authority of the civil authority, the latter under the authority of the church. This explains why Calvin cannot fully accept Chrysostom's interpretation, or why Calvin feels that Chrysostom has "added" something to the text. What, for Calvin, Chrysostom has added is Chrysostom's notion that Paul intends the Corinthians to settle the issue within the church, οὐδ᾽ ἂν ὁτισοῦν ᾖ (whatever the matter might be)!

What conclusion may be drawn? One is inclined to agree with Calvin's final position on the matter of Christians bringing cases before civil authorities; however, sympathy for Calvin's position is based not so much on his exegesis of this particular text, but on what Calvin says elsewhere (Inst. 4.20.19). There, for instance, Calvin argues persuasively that Paul himself claimed in court the privilege of Roman citizenship, and even appealed from the unjust judge to the judgment seat of Caesar.

What is Calvin doing then, in his commentary? He is exegeting a text, the results of which, however, must be in harmony with what is found elsewhere in Scripture. It is Scripture that must interpret Scripture.

46. Ibid., CO 49:389.

From this passage alone, one may conclude that Paul nowhere makes mention of a distinction of cases. From this text alone, Chrysostom's οὐδ᾽ ἂν ὁτισοῦν ᾖ applies. Calvin's commentary, his final interpretation, however, is not complete in itself. It must be seen and understood in the light of other portions of Scripture. Some therefore may find Calvin taking excessive liberties with a text; but, as Calvin himself affirms, he has "faithfully brought out the Apostle's intention."

1 Corinthians 9:24.

Οὐκ οἴδατε ὅτι οἱ ἐν σταδίῳ τρέχοντες πάντες μὲν τρέχουσιν, εἷς δὲ λαμβάνει τὸ βραβεῖον; οὕτως τρέχετε ἵνα καταλάβητε.

Calvin frequently consults Chrysostom for an interpretation that involves a principle of Greek grammar. He, in addition, does not fail to point out a possibility that Chrysostom might have missed!

Here Calvin raises the observation that the particle οὕτως may be taken in two ways:[47]

Particula οὕτως, dupliciter potest accipi. Chrysostomus superioribus coniungit, hoc modo: Ut cursores illi non desinunt currere donec ad metam pertigerint: sic etiam perseverate, nec facite finem currendi quamdiu vivitis. Sed neque inepte cohaerebit sequentibus, ac si diceret: Non est ita currendum ut deficiatis in medio stadio, sed ita ut palmam adipiscamini.

The particle "so" can be taken two ways. Chrysostom joins it to what goes before, in this manner: "As those runners do not stop running until they have reached the goal, so you must persevere, and not stop running as long as you live." It will, however, correspond not ineptly with what follows: "You must not run so as to fall out in the middle of the race, but so that you may obtain the prize.

Chrysostom adopts the straightforward sense, using the word οὕτως as a demonstrative adverb with a preceding antecedent, while Calvin uses the word οὕτως as an adverbial correlative with ἵνα.

1 Corinthians 11:19.

δεῖ γὰρ καὶ αἱρέσεις ἐν ὑμῖν εἶναι, ἵνα καὶ οἱ δόκιμοι φανεροὶ γένωνται ἐν ὑμῖν.

47. Ibid., CO 49:449.

In his *Praefatio in Chrysostomi Homilias,* Calvin warns his readers against Chrysostom's excessive tendency to preach the free-will of man. Such large concessions to the sovereignty of man's will Calvin, of course, could not accept:[48]

In praedicando hominis libero arbitrio, in meritis operum efferendis immodicus, gratiam Dei in electione ac vocatione nostra, gratuitam deinde misericordiam, qua nos a vocatione ad mortem usque prosequitur, sic nonnihil obscurat. Primum electionem cum aliquo operum nostrorum respectu implicare nititur: quum scriptura passim reclamet nihil esse quo ad nos eligendos provocetur Deus nisi extremam miseriam, nec aliunde ipsum sumere quo nobis opem ferat, quam a sua ipsius bonitate. Deinde laudem vocationis nostrae inter Deum et nos quodammodo partitur, quum scriptura constanter solidum eius complementum Deo assignet. De libero arbitrio sic loquitur, ac si ad studium virtutis divinaeque legis observationem multum haberet momenti. Atqui ubique Dominus verbi sui testimonio nos omni bene agendi facultate spoliat, nec aliam virtutem reliquam nobis facit, nisi quam ipse spiritu suo subministrat.	In his excessive tendency to preach the free-will of man, and in holding out rewards for works, he obscures to a considerable degree the grace of God in our election and calling and the gracious mercy that follows us from our calling to the very moment of death. First, he strives to work into the idea of election some reference to our own efforts, although Scripture everywhere proclaims that there is nothing by which God may be urged into electing us except our utter wretchedness, and no other source upon which He could draw except His own goodness. Second, he divides the responsibility for our calling between God and ourselves, although Scripture invariably ascribes the full responsibility for it to God alone. He speaks of free-will as if it had great importance for the pursuit of virtue and the observance of the divine law. But everywhere the Lord, by the witness of His Word, denies to us all capacity to do good and leaves to us no virtue except what He supplies by His Spirit.

Calvin's reaction against Chrysostom's position on the liberty of the will is well illustrated in the commentaries on this text. Chrysostom, directly

48. *Praef. in Chry. Hom.,* CO 9:835.

at the outset of his observations on the text, makes clear his aversion to any fatalistic rendering of δεῖ γὰρ καὶ (for there must indeed be . . .). As an example, he cites the words of Jesus in Matthew 18:7: Οὐαὶ τῷ κόσμῳ ἀπὸ τῶν σκανδάλων. ἀνάγκη γὰρ ἐλθεῖν τὰ σκάνδαλα. . . . But when Christ said "it is necessary" (ἀνάγκη) that offences come, he is not, according to Chrysostom, destroying the liberty of the will, nor is he appointing any necessity and compulsion, but simply foretelling what would certainly come from the evil mind of men. Furthermore, σκάνδαλα would arise, not because Christ predicted them, but because the "incurably disposed" are so minded. They were about to happen in the natural course of events, and therefore Christ foretold them. If the occasions of stumbling were of necessity and not of the mind of them that bring them in, Chrysostom observes that Christ would never have said, "Woe to that man through whom the offence comes."

Hence, the latter phrase in 1 Corinthians 11:19, does not mean that αἱρέσεις (factions) come into being in order that the approved may be made manifest; but, these factions taking place, such and such was the result. Chrysostom understands ἵνα here as indicating not cause but result.

For Calvin, δεῖ γὰρ καὶ αἱρέσεις ἐν ὑμῖν εἶναι means that this situation does not arise by chance, but by the *certa Dei providentia*. By trials like these, the Lord is putting the perseverance of his own people to the test. Rather than be disturbed by the presence of factions, the Corinthians should understand them as an opportunity to give clear evidence of their steadfastness and sincerity.

But if there is "necessity" or "fate" here, Calvin does not understand God as the source of that necessity. He instead applies it to Satan, who "leaves no stone unturned in order to break up the unity of the Church." If we ask Calvin how the rise of factions, which are the work of Satan, are related to the "sure providence of God," he answers: "It is God who, in His wisdom, turns the pernicious contrivances of Satan to the salvation of the faithful."

Hence, Calvin sees no difficulty in understanding the ἵνα as causative; and, in that connection, raises his objection to Chrysostom:[49]

---

49. *Comm. ad Cor. 1*, CO 49:481–82.

Quod autem Chrysostomus particulam ἵνα non causam sed eventum indicare conten- dit: non est tanti momenti. Causa enim est, arcanum Dei consilium, quo sic attemper- antur mala ut in bonum finem cedant.	Now Chrysostom maintains that the particle ἵνα indicates not cause, but result. That is not of much importance. For the cause is the secret purpose of God, by which evil things are manipulated in such a way that everything turns out well.

As if to polish off those who are contending for the free-will of man, Calvin concludes that even the ungodly are impelled by Satan in such a way that they are acted upon and act by the prompting of their will:[50]

Scimus postremo impios sic impelli a Satana, ut voluntario motu agantur simul et agant. Quare sublata illis est excusatio.	Finally, we know that the ungodly are pressed by Satan in such a way that they, by the prompting of their will, at one and the same time are acted upon and act. Therefore they are left without excuse.

1 Corinthians 11:20–21.

20. Συνερχομένων οὖν ὑμῶν ἐπὶ τὸ αὐτὸ οὐκ ἔστιν κυριακὸν δεῖπνον φαγεῖν, 21. ἕκαστος γὰρ τὸ ἴδιον δεῖπνον προλαμβάνει ἐν τῷ φαγεῖν, καὶ ὃς μὲν πεινᾷ, ὃς δὲ μεθύει.

Paul is here reproving the Corinthians. Several questions arise from a consideration of Calvin's and Chrysostom's commentaries on these two verses. The first question centers on the object of Paul's reproof and may be stated as follows: Is Paul seeking to correct the misconduct of the Corinthians at (a) an Agape feast, at (b) the Lord's Supper, or at (c) an event in which these divisions are indistinguishable? Second, if the conclusion is reached that Paul has in mind two distinguishable parts, which came first? Did the Corinthians first observe a "sacred institution" which was followed by a common meal, or was the "sacred institution" (Calvin), or the "Holy Mysteries" part and parcel of a common meal? Third, is Paul correcting the Corinthians, saying that their conduct at the meal precluded the possibility of the meal being the Lord's Supper, or is Paul correcting the Corinthians because they were mixing a profane

50. Ibid., CO 49:482.

banquet with what should be a sacred observance? With these questions in mind we turn to the commentaries of Calvin and Chrysostom.

For Calvin, the heart of the problem to which Paul is addressing himself lies in the fact that the Corinthians were mixing two events that should be kept distinct from each other. They were mixing profane banquets with a sacred and spiritual feast:[51]

Nunc taxat abusum, qui in coenam Domini obrepserat apud Corinthios: quod sacro et spirituali epulo profana symposia permiscerent, idque cum pauperum contumelia.	He now reproves the abuse that had crept in among the Corinthians' observance of the Lord's Supper. They were mixing up ordinary banquets with the feast that is holy and spiritual; and that with contempt for the poor.

The problem of "contempt for the poor" is not given as much emphasis as the profanation of the "most sacred institution of Christ." The reason the Corinthians were not "eating the Lord's Supper" lies not so much in misconduct, but in the admixture of *profana symposia* with the *sacro et spirituali epulo*. This confusion of what should be two separate events marks a deviation from the original Lord's Supper, and Calvin marvels that such a profanation should have been accomplished in so short a time.[52]

Mirum est sane et fere portenti instar, Satanam tam exiguo temporis spatio tantum potuisse. Sed hoc exemplo admonemur quid valeat sine ratione antiquitas: hoc est, quantum habeat autoritatis longa consuetudo nullo verbi Dei testimonio probata.	It is truly amazing, and almost like a miracle that Satan was able to do so much in such a short time. This serves as an example to warn us, what something that is old can do when it is unsupported by any reason. In other words, how much weight a well-established custom has, when the Word of God itself provides not a thread of evidence to justify it.

For Calvin, then, Paul is arguing for the purity of the sacrament. Paul does not want the *sacrum mysterium* to be mixed up with ordinary feasts.

51. Ibid.
52. Ibid.

Let us turn now to Chrysostom's description of the event. For him, we learn that the Corinthians first gathered in an "assembly," (σύνοδος), at which all people, rich and poor, came together. This assembly was followed by a banquet (τράπεζα), and it is the conduct of the Corinthians at the banquet to which Paul is addressing his admonitions. The conduct of the Corinthians at the banquet bears no relation to the brotherly affection characteristic of the assembly; and therefore, at the banquet, "it is not possible to eat the Lord's Supper," or, "the supper that you eat there is certainly not the Lord's Supper":[53]

Τὸ μὲν γὰρ σχῆμα τῆς συνόδου, φησὶν, ἄλλο· ἀγάπης γάρ ἐστι καὶ φιλαδελφίας· εἰς γοῦν ὑμᾶς ἅπαντας δέχεται τόπος, καὶ ὁμοῦ συναγελάζεσθε· ἡ δε τράπεζα λοιπὸν οὐχ ὁμοία τῇ συνόδῳ. Καὶ οὐκ εἶπε, Συνερχομένων ὑμῶν οὐκ ἔστι κοινῇ φαγεῖν, οὐκ ἔστι μετ᾽ ἀλλήλων ἐστιαθῆναι, ἀλλὰ πάλιν ἑτέρως καὶ πολλῷ φοβερώτερον αὐτῶν καθάπτεται, λέγων, Οὐκ ἔστι Κυριακὸν δεῖπνον φαγεῖν, ἐκείνη παραπέμπων αὐτοὺς ἐντεῦθεν ἤδη τῇ ἑσπέρα, καφ᾽ ἥν τὰ φρικτὰ μυστήρια παρέδωκεν ὁ Χριστός.

"For the appearance of your assembly" he said, "is different." "It is one of love and brotherly affection. At least one place receives you all, and you are together in one flock. But the Banquet, when you come to that bears no resemblance to the assembly of worshippers." And he did not say, "When you come together, do not eat in common," or, "do not feast with one another," but in another vein and much more drastically, he reprimands them, saying, "it is not possible to eat the Lord's Supper," sending them away from this point to that evening on which Christ delivered the awful Mysteries.

Then Chrysostom gives the reason "it is not the Lord's Supper" that they were eating: The supper that the Corinthians were eating lacked the very essence and distinctive mark of the Lord's Supper, namely, commonality. By making the supper a private matter, they deprived the table of its greatest prerogative; it must be κοινός.[54]

---

53. *Hom. ad Cor. 1*, Hom. 27, PG 61:227.
54. Ibid.

Ὅτι τὸ Κυριακὸν δεῖπνον, τουτέστι, τὸ Δεσποτικὸν, ὀφείλει κοινὸν εἶναι. Τὰ γὰρ τοῦ δεσπότου οὐχὶ τοῦδε μὲν ἐστι τοῦ οἰκέτου, τοῦδε δὲ οὐκ ἐστιν, ἀλλὰ κοινῇ πάντων.

For the Lord's Supper, that is the Master's, ought to be common. For the property of the master belongs not to this servant without belonging to that, but must be in common to all.

For Chrysostom, the Lord's Supper is synonymous with the "community" of the feast:[55]

Τὸ οὖν Κυριακὸν τοῦτό φησι τὸ κοινόν. Εἰ γὰρ τοῦ Δεσπότου σοῦ ἐστιν, ὥσπερ οὖν καὶ ἐστιν, οὐκ ὀφείλεις ὡς ἴδια ἀποσπᾶν, ἀλλ' ὡς τοῦ Κυρίου καὶ τοῦ Δεσπότου ὄντα, κοινῇ πᾶσι προτιθέναι. Τοῦτο γὰρ ἐστι Κυριακόν.

Thus, by "the Lord's Supper," he expresses this, the community of the feast. If it is the Master's, as assuredly it is, you ought not to withdraw it as private, but since it belongs to your Lord and Master, you ought to set it in common before all. For this is the meaning of "the Lord's."

We may now compare our findings. For Calvin, Paul is primarily admonishing the Corinthians to preserve the Lord's Supper in its original form, prior to its being abused. The sacred and spiritual feast was being polluted by mixing it with a common and profane meal. When Paul says, "it is not the Supper of the Lord that you eat," he means that the sacred institution of Christ cannot be observed by those who were not prepared (nempe Corinthios non esse comparatos ad coenam Domini edendam). Profane banquets should not be mixed with what belongs to Christ.

For Chrysostom, Paul is admonishing the Corinthians to be more inclusive. When Paul says, "it is not the Supper of the Lord that you eat," he means that the Corinthians were separating themselves off, making a supper that ought to be common to all into a private matter. Private banquets should not be mixed with what belongs to Christ.

When Calvin inquires into the origin of the "abuse" by which the sacred meal became profaned, he appeals to Chrysostom! Calvin says:[56]

---

55. Ibid.
56. *Comm. ad Cor. 1*, CO 49:482.

Caeterum unde ortus sit hic abusus, aut qua occasione tam cito emerserit, dubium est. Chrysostomus ἀπὸ τῶν ἀγαπῶν fluxisse putat, quod quum divites soliti essent domo afferre unde promiscue cum pauperibus et in commune epularentur: postea exclusis pauperibus soli de suis lautitiis ingurgitare coeperunt. Et certe vetustissimum fuisse illum morem, patet ex Tertulliano. Vocabant autem agapas coenas illas communes, quas inter se agitabant, quod essent fraternae dilectionis symbola et eleemosynis constarent. Nec dubito quin sacrificiorum ritus, tam Iudaeis quam gentibus communes, causam praebuerint.

It is uncertain, however, what was the origin of this abuse, or what was the occasion of its springing up so soon. Chrysostom is of the opinion that it originated in the love feasts, and that, while the rich had been accustomed to bring with them from their houses the means of feasting with the poor indiscriminately and in common, they afterwards began to exclude the poor, and to guzzle over their delicacies by themselves. And certainly, it appears from Tertullian that such a custom was a very ancient one. Now they gave the name "Agape" to those common entertainments, which they contrived among themselves, as being tokens of the eternal affection, and consisted of alms. Nor have I any doubt that it took its rise from sacrificial rites commonly observed both by Jews and Gentiles.

Some conclusions may now be drawn. First of all, Chrysostom is not talking about love feasts at all here. If he has an explanation of love feasts, it does not appear in connection with his interpretation of the eleventh chapter of 1 Corinthians. Nowhere do we find the words ἀπο τῶν ἀγαπῶν as an explanation for what the Corinthians were doing when they came together in the church. Secondly, there is every reason to believe that Chrysostom is describing an actual Lord's Supper, which consisted of an assembly characterized by brotherly affection, and followed by a meal that was understood to be the Lord's Supper. Thirdly, Chrysostom's name is introduced in Calvin's commentary in such a way that it would appear that Chrysostom is in full support of Calvin's analysis of the problem to which Paul is speaking. But from the above it is clear that the "abuse" as Calvin saw it has little to do with the abuse as Chrysostom understood it. For the former the issue was the preservation of a pure, sacred, spiritual sacrament; while for the latter the issue was the inclusion of all people into a common meal that had been desecrated into a private banquet. Finally, since Calvin quotes or cites Chrysostom constantly throughout the 1 Corinthians commentary, takes pains to point out those places where he is in disagreement with Chrysostom over fine points of grammar, and has apparently read Chrysostom's interpretation of these words of Paul, why does Calvin not offer a rebuttal? Why does Calvin not only refrain from offering a challenge to Chrysostom's interpretation of such a crucial issue as the Lord's Supper, but instead appeals to Chrysostom for an understanding of the Supper's abuse? It is this latter question that yet remains to be answered.

1 Corinthians 12:7.

ἑκάστῳ δὲ δίδοται ἡ φανέρωσις τοῦ πνεύματος πρὸς τὸ συμφέρον.

One problem that will have to be settled is the text with which Calvin was working. Did he read Chrysostom in the Greek; or did he use a Latin translation, and if a Latin translation, which one? This problem is raised in the interpretation of 12:7.

In the context of verse 7, Paul is discussing the varieties of gifts that are given to Christians. Christians differ from each other in the spiritual gifts distributed to each. Despite the fact that there are a variety of διακονιῶν (ministries), and varieties of ἐνεργημάτων ("operations"), it is the same Spirit who gives, and to each person is given ἡ φανέρωσις τοῦ πνεύματος (the manifestation of the Spirit).

Let us first observe Chrysostom's comment on this verse:[57]

Φανέρωσιν δὲ Πνεύματος τὰ σημεῖα καλεῖ, εἰκότως. Ἐμοὶ μὲν γὰρ τῷ πιστῷ δῆλος ὁ Πνεῦμα ἔχων ἀπὸ τοῦ βαπτισθῆναι· τῷ δὲ ἀπίστῳ οὐδαμόθεν ἔσται τοῦτο καταφανὲς, ἀλλ' ἢ ἀπὸ τῶν σημείων.	But he calls "signs" a "manifestation of the Spirit," with good reason. For to me, a believer, he that has the Spirit is manifest from his having been baptized. But to the unbeliever, this will in no way be manifest, except from the signs.

Chrysostom appears to be saying that there are certain signs indicative of the fact that a person has a manifestation of the Spirit. For some, the

57. *Hom. ad Cor. 1*, Hom. 29, PG 61:244.

sign is the gift of healing; for others, the gift of prophecy, and so on. Now to me, a believer, it is clear that every Christian has a certain gift of some kind, for every one who is baptized receives some gift. But to those who are unbelievers, it is not clear that every baptized person receives a gift. Unbelievers will only be sure that a person has been given a gift by the Spirit when they witness some sign of the gift. The point Chrysostom seems to be making is this: the fact that a person has received a gift is a sign that the Spirit has given a gift.

Calvin sees a forced interpretation in the position taken by Chrysostom:[58]

Durius est, quod ait Chrysostomus, et coactius: ideo sic vocari, quoniam infideles nonnisi visibilibus miraculis Deum agnoscant.	The view taken by Chrysostom is rather harsh and forced, viz., that this term is used because unbelievers do not recognize God, except by visible miracles.

Calvin seems to understand Chrysostom as saying that unbelievers will not "recognize" God or "come to" God except by the manifestation of a miracle. Such a statement indeed sounds "forced and harsh," but also very "un-Chrysostomic." Chrysostom rather is saying that an unbelieving person, seeing a gift in another person, will be convinced that such a gift is the result of the operation of the Spirit. The import of Chrysostom's statement is not that unbelievers will become believers only through the working of a miracle.

If this analysis has some validity, the question may be raised whether Calvin came to his understanding of Chrysostom's remark because the text Calvin used translated σημεῖον as miracula rather than signa. Or, it is possible that, if Calvin used the Greek text of Chrysostom, he understood σημεῖον as miracula. This textual question is dealt with at length in chapter 5.

1 Corinthians 12:9.

ἑτέρῳ πίστις ἐν τῷ αὐτῷ πνεύματι . . .

At issue here is the meaning of the word πίστις. Both Chrysostom and Calvin impose a qualification upon the word.

58. *Comm. ad Cor. 1*, CO 49:499.

For Chrysostom, Paul here means not the faith that is concerned with doctrines, but the faith that has to do with the performance of miracles. It is the faith concerning which Christ said: "If you have the faith of a grain of mustard-seed, you shall say to this mountain, 'Move,' and it shall move." Chrysostom holds this kind of faith as superior to the faith that has to do with doctrines. The faith the apostles asked for, when they said, "Increase our faith," is the "faith that is the mother of miracles." It is this faith too, the πίστις τῶν σημείον, and not the πίστις τῶν δογμάτων, that is superior to the gift of healing:[59]

Ὁ μὲν γὰρ ἔχων χάρισμα ἰαμάτων, ἐθεράπευε μόνον· ὁ δὲ ἐνεργήματα δυνάμεων κεκτημένος, καὶ ἐτιμωρεῖτο. Δύναμις γὰρ ἐστιν οὐ τὸ ἰάσασθαι μόνον, ἀλλὰ καὶ τὸ κολάσαι, ὥσπερ ὁ Παῦλος ἐπήρωσεν, ὥσπερ ὁ Πέτρος ἀνεῖλεν.	For he that had a gift of healing used only to do cures. But he that possessed powers for working miracles used to punish also. For a miracle is not the healing only, but the punishing also, even as Paul inflicted blindness, and just as Peter slew.

Calvin also calls πίστις in this verse a particular kind of faith. Likewise, Calvin too refers to this faith as that which deals not with doctrines. But this faith for Calvin is not greater or more salutary, but incomplete:[60]

Fides particularis est, quae non totum Christum in redemptionem, iustitiam et sanctificationem apprehendit: sed quatenus tantum in eius nomine eduntur miracula.	The term faith is employed here to mean a particular kind of faith, as the context will soon make clear. This is the type of faith that does not lay hold of Christ in His wholeness for redemption, justification, and sanctification, but only insofar as miracles are performed in His name.

Even Judas had this kind of faith![61]

---

59. *Hom. ad Cor. 1*, Hom. 29, PG 61:245.
60. *Comm. ad Cor. 1*, CO 49:500.
61. Ibid.

| Talem habuit Iudas, et per eam | Judas had faith like that, and even |
| miracula etiam edidit. | he carried out miracles by it. |

Calvin then notes that Chrysostom makes the distinction between fidem signorum and fidem dogmatum, although it is made paulo aliter (somewhat differently!):[62]

Chrysostomus paulo aliter	Chrysostom makes a slightly different
distinguit, fidem appellans	distinction, calling it the "faith of mira-
signorum, non dogmatum:	cles and not dogmatic faith," but there is
quod tamen a priore sensu	not much divergence between that and
non admodum discrepat.	the interpretation that I have given.

Of interest, for our purposes here, is the last clause: quod tamen a priore sensu non admodum discrepat. On what grounds can Calvin say, knowing what Chrysostom means, that there "is not much divergence between that [Chrysostom's rendering]" and what Calvin has just said? While it is true that the distinction is similar between "the faith of miracles" and the "faith of dogmas," as given by both Chrysostom and Calvin, there is a world of divergence between the interpretations offered by the two authors.

Here again we observe that the uncritical reader of Calvin's commentary would conclude that Chrysostom is in total agreement with Calvin, whereas in fact the conclusions drawn by each commentator are diametric to each other.

1 Corinthians 12:27.

Ὑμεῖς δέ ἐστε σῶμα Χριστοῦ καὶ μέλη ἐκ μέρους.

Calvin here is not in agreement with Chrysostom's interpretation of the phrase καὶ μέλη ἐκ μέρους. Finding it rather forced, Calvin notes:[63]

62. Ibid.
63. Ibid., CO 49:505.

Chrysostomus hanc particulam additam putat, quia non essent Corinthii universalis ecclesia: qui sensus mihi videtur coactior. Aliquando putavi notam esse improprietatis: sicuti Latini dicunt quodammodo: sed dum propius omnia expendo, potius refero ad illam membrorum divisionem cuius meminerat. Membra igitur ex parte sunt, sicut cuique attributa est sua portio et finitum officium. Ad hunc sensum contextus ipse nos ducit: ita ex parte et in solidum erunt inter se opposita.

Chrysostom thinks that this phrase was added because the Corinthians were not the Church Universal. That interpretation is, to my mind, forced. I once thought that it was an indication of some impropriety; "after a fashion," to use the Latin term. But when I take everything into closer consideration, I rather think it refers to the differences among the members, which Paul had mentioned. Therefore, they are members "in part," inasmuch as each one has had allocated to him his own share and his precise duties. The context itself leads us to that meaning. So, "in part," or "individually," and "as a whole," will be correlatives.

Chrysostom does understand the words Ἐκ μέρους as meaning "part of the Church which exists in every part of the world":[64]

Ἐπειδὴ γὰρ εἶπε, Σῶμα, τὸ δὲ πᾶν σῶμα ἦν, οὐχὶ ἡ παρὰ Κορινθίοις Ἐκκλησία, ἀλλ᾽ ἡ πανταχοῦ τῆς οἰκουμένης, διὰ τοῦτο ἔφησεν, Ἐκ μέρους.

For since Paul had said, "the body," whereas the whole body was not the Corinthian church, but the Church in every part of the world, therefore he said, "in part."

The church at Corinth, Chrysostom affirms, is a part of the church existing everywhere, and part of the body that is made up of all the churches.

It should be noted, however, that this observation of Chrysostom is added to a larger discourse on the nature of the body as a composite entity, in which "the many comprise the one, and the one is in the many":[65]

---

64. *Hom. ad Cor. 1*, Hom. 32, PG 61:264.
65. Ibid., PG 61:263–64.

Καὶ μέλη ἐκ μέρους. Οὐ γὰρ δὴ σῶμα μόνον, φησὶν, ἀλλὰ καὶ μέλη ἐσμέν. Περὶ γὰρ ἀμφοτέρων τούτων ἀνωτέρω διελέχφη, τοὺς πολλοὺς εἰς ἕν συνάγων, καὶ δεικνὺς ἅπαντας ἕν τι κατὰ τὴν τοῦ σώματος εἰκόνα γινομένους, καὶ τὸ ἕν τοῦτο διὰ τῶν πολλῶν συνιστάμενον, καὶ ἐν τοῖς πολλοῖς ὄν, καὶ τὰ πολλὰ ἐκ τούτου συνεχόμενα καὶ δυνάμενα εἶναι πολλά.

"And several members." That is, "not only," he said, "are we a body, but members also." For of both these he had before discoursed, bringing the many together into one, and implying that all become some one thing after the image of the body, and that this one thing is made up of the many and is in the many, and that the many by this are held together and are capable of being many.

The major thrust of Chrysostom's interpretation of this verse, combined with Paul's whole analogy of the body, lies in the complex nature of the Body, of which there are members "in part."

1 Corinthians 12:28.

Καὶ οὓς μὲν ἔθετο ὁ θεὸς ἐν τῇ ἐκκλησίᾳ πρῶτον ἀποστόλους, δεύτερον προφήτας, τρίτον διδασκάλους, ἔπειτα δυνάμεις, ἔπειτα χαρίσματα ἰαμάτων, ἀντιλήμψεις, κυβερνήσεις, γένη γλωσσῶν.

The question here is the interpretation of the word ἀντιλήμψεις. Chrysostom asks what is the meaning of this word, and responds as follows:[66]

---

66. Ibid., PG 61:266.

῞Ωστε ἀντέχεσθαι τῶν ἀσθενῶν.
Τοῦτο οὖν χάρισμα; εἰπέ μοι.
Μάλιστα μὲν καὶ τοῦτο τῆς τοῦ
Θεοῦ δωρεᾶς, τὸ προστατικὸν
εἶναι, τὸ πράγματα οἰκονομεῖν
πνευματικά. ἄλλως τε δὲ
πολλα καὶ τῶν ἡμετέρων
κατορθωμάτων χαρίσματα
καλεῖ, οὐκ ἀναπίπτειν ἡμᾶς
βουλόμενος, ἀλλὰ δεικνὺς ὅτι
πανταχοῦ τῆς τοῦ Θεοῦ δεόμεθα
βοηθείας, καὶ παρασκευάζων
εὐχαρίστους εἶναι, καὶ
προθυμοτέρους ταύτῃ ποιῶν καὶ
διεγείρων αὐτων τὰ φρονήματα.

So as to support the weak:
Is this then a gift, tell me?
In the first place, this too is
a gift of God, suitable for a
great leader. It means the
dispensing of spiritual things.
In addition, he calls many of
our own good deeds, "gifts,"
not meaning us to lose heart,
but showing that in every
case we need God's help,
and preparing them to be
thankful, and thereby making them more forward and
stirring up their minds.

Calvin does not accept Chrysostom's view, on the grounds that Paul, in this section, is detailing offices, rather than gifts:[67]

Quoniam hic officia recenset apostolus, non recipio quod ait Chrysostomus, ἀντιλήψεις, hoc est, subsidia vel opitulationes, consistere in sustinendis infirmis. Quid igitur? aut certe tam munus quam donum olim fuit, quod nobis hodie est incognitum: aut ad diaconiam pertinet, hoc est, curam pauperum. Atque hoc secundum mihi magis arridet.

Because the Apostle is enumerating offices here, I do not approve of what Chrysostom says, that ἀντιλήψεις, that is "helps" or "supports" means supporting the weak. What does it mean, then? Surely, either it refers to an office, as well as a gift, that was exercised in the church in ancient times, but of which we have no knowledge now; or, it is connected with the office of the Deacon; that is to say, the care of the poor. I prefer the second explanation.

Here we have a clear-cut example of the basis upon which Calvin rejects the interpretation of Chrysostom. Chrysostom's interpretation, for Calvin, does not conform to the intention of Paul in this section, where Paul is detailing offices and not gifts. Paul, in verses 28–29, is speak-

---

67. *Comm. ad Cor. 1*, CO 49:507.

ing about the administration of gifts, rather than the gifts themselves. Moreover, it is crucial that this separation of gifts and administration of gifts be observed for the "right ordering of things." The Lord does not appoint ministers without first endowing them with the requisite gifts, qualifying them for the discharge of their duties. Just so, Paul first speaks of gifts, and then offices:[68]

Atqui hic est ordo naturalis, ut dona ministerium ipsum praecedant.	In reality, the natural order is that the gifts come before the office.

We may conclude, therefore, that the reason Calvin rejects Chrysostom at this point is that Chrysostom's designation of the word ἀντιλήψεις as a "gift," does not correspond with the "inner meaning" of Paul's order, from which Calvin infers that "those who force themselves upon the church, who boast of a secret call from God, and who are un-learned and utterly ignorant and destitute of the necessary qualifications, are fanatics." The ordo naturalis, rather, requires first the gift and then the administration of the office. In calling ἀντιλήψεις a "gift," Chrysostom has destroyed a crucial distinction or division that must be maintained.

1 Corinthians 13:2.

καὶ ἐὰν ἔχω προφητείαν καὶ εἰδῶ τὰ μυστήρια πάντα καὶ πᾶσαν τὴν γνῶσιν, κἂν ἔχω πᾶσαν τὴν πίστιν ὥστε ὄρη μεθιστάναι, ἀγάπην δὲ μὴ ἔχω, οὐθέν εἰμι.

The same observation regarding the word πίστις is made here as in 12:10. Calvin notes that the word "faith" is here used in a special sense, limited by that faith which works miracles. It does not apprehend the "whole" Christ. By adding, "so as to remove mountains," Paul, for Calvin, means to restrict faith to miracles.

The opposite, as we previously observed, is true for Chrysostom. The faith that is able to remove mountains is the greatest faith. Paul is con-trasting "love" not with limited gifts, but with the greatest of all gifts:[69]

68. Ibid., CO 49:506.
69. *Hom. ad Cor. 1*, Hom. 32, PG 61:269.

Καὶ οὐδὲ ἠρκέσθε τουτῳ, ἀλλὰ
καὶ, ὅπερ ὡς μέγιστον εἶπεν ὁ
Χριστός, καὶ τοῦτο προσέθηκεν
εἰπών· Ωστε ὄρη μεθιστάνειν,
ἀγάπην δὲ μὲ ἔχω, οὐδέν εἰμι.

He was not content with that,
but added that which Christ
spoke of as greatest, saying, "so
as to remove mountains, and
have not love, I am nothing."

1 Corinthians 14:2.

ὁ γὰρ λαλῶν γλώσσῃ οὐκ ἀνθρώποις λαλεῖ ἀλλὰ θεῷ,
οὐδεὶς γὰρ ἀκούει, πνεύματι δὲ λαλεῖ μυστήρια·

Whatever else one may observe concerning the interaction between
Calvin and Chrysostom, by now it is abundantly clear that exegetically
Calvin is his own man with little slavish dependence upon Chrysostom.
In this text Calvin will agree with Chrysostom's interpretation of πνεύ
ματι δὲ λαλεῖ, and disagree with the interpretation of the very next
word, μυστήρια.

Let us first see what Calvin understands by πνεύματι δὲ λαλεῖ.[70]

loquitur spiritu: hoc est,
dono spirituali (sic enim
cum Chrysostomo interpre-
tor) mysteria et res occultas,
ideoque nullius utilitatis.
Mysteria hic Chrysostomus
accipit honorifice pro eximiis
Dei revelationibus: ego vero in
malam partem, pro aenigmatibus obscuris et involutis: quasi
diceret, loquitur quod nemo
percipiat.

He speaks in the spirit: that is, by
a spiritual gift (for that is the way
I interpret it, with Chrysostom),
mysteries and hidden things,
therefore that are of no profit.
Chrysostom takes mysteries in a
good sense, as meaning extraordinary revelations from God. But I
interpret in a bad sense as unintel-
ligible, baffling, enigmatic sayings;
as if he had said, "He speaks what
nobody understands."

Before we address a question to Calvin, let us hear Chrysostom on the
verse:[71]

---

70. *Comm. ad Cor. 1*, CO 49:517.

71. *Hom. ad Cor. 1*, Hom. 35, PG 61:296.

῞Ορα τοίνυν πῶς αὐτὸ καὶ καθαιρεῖ καὶ ἐπαίρει. Τῷ μὲν γὰρ εἰπεῖν,Ὁ λαλῶν γλώσσαις, οὐκ ἀνθρώποις λαλεῖ, ἀλλὰ Θεῷ· οὐδεὶς γὰρ ἀκούει, καθεῖλε, δείξας οὐ πολὺ τὸ χρήσιμον ὄν· τῷ δὲ ἐπάγειν, ὅτι Πνεύματι λαλεῖ μυστήρια, πάλιν ἐπῆρεν, ἵνα μὴ περιττὸν εἶναι δόξῃ καὶ ἄχρηστον καὶ εἰκῆ δεδομένον.

See accordingly how he both depresses and then elevates the "speaking in tongues." Thus, by saying, "He that speaks with tongues, speaks not to men, but to God, for no man understands," he depresses it, implying that the profit of it was not great. But by adding, "but in the Spirit he speaks mysteries," he again elevated it, that it might not seem to be superfluous and useless and given in vain.

The question to Calvin is this: does Calvin want the reader to understand that πνεύματι δὲ λαλεῖ is a positive attribute or a negative attribute? For Calvin, speaking in the spirit is of nullius utilitatis. Yet, quoting Chrysostom, it is a "spiritual gift." How, then, can that which is a spiritual gift be of little value? Let us rephrase the question. Does Calvin want the reader to understand that Chrysostom agrees with him on the point that "speaking in the spirit" is a "spiritual gift," or does Calvin want the reader to understand that Chrysostom agrees with him on the point that "speaking in the spirit" produces no profit? Clearly, from Chrysostom's statement, "speaking in the spirit" is a positive attribute, for by saying this Paul "elevated" the gift, in order that "it might not appear to be superfluous and useless and given in vain."

But our only observation here is this: by placing in the middle of the sentence sic enim cum Chrysostomo interpretor, the reader might easily understand Calvin to be saying that Chrysostom is in full support of the notion that speaking in the spirit is fruitless; whereas in fact, Chrysostom understands πνεύματι δὲ λαλεῖ as both a positive attribute and a counterbalance to ὁ γὰρ λαλῶν γλώσσῃ οὐκ ἀνθρώποις λαλεῖ ἀλλὰ θεῷ, οὐδεὶς γὰρ ἀκούει.

To be sure, Calvin does acknowledge that Chrysostom understands the word μυστήρια "in a good sense," while Calvin himself interprets it in malam partem, pro aenigmatibus obscuris. The point, however, is that Chrysostom also understands πνεύματι δὲ λαλεῖ positively, while Calvin interprets it negatively in the same sentence in which Calvin says Chrysostom agrees with him.

1 Corinthians 14:14.

ἐὰν γὰρ προσεύχωμαι γλώσσῃ, τὸ πνεῦμά μου προσεύχεται,
ὁ δὲ νοῦς μου ἄκαρπός ἐστιν.

In attempting to explain the words τὸ πνεῦμά μου, Calvin offers four possible interpretations: those of Augustine, Ambrose, Chrysostom, and yet a fourth. Of the four, Calvin accepts the position taken by Chrysostom, and rejects the other three. On what grounds does he make this decision?

When Paul says, "For if I pray in a tongue, my spirit prays but my mind is unfruitful," the meaning of "in a tongue" is, for Calvin, clear. The word γλώσσῃ means simply a foreign language. It is interesting to note that both Calvin and Chrysostom, throughout their commentaries, consistently understand "tongues" as a foreign language, rather than an ecstatic utterance.

The meaning of τὸ πνεῦμά μου, however, is not immediately clear. The position taken by Ambrose is without foundation, Augustine is too subtle, and those who hold that the words refer to the "breathings of the throat" conflict with the way Paul uses the phrase:[72]

Omni non ratione tantum caret, sed etiam colore, quod Ambrosius ad spiritum refert, quem accepimus in baptismo. Augustinus subtilius pro apprehensione accipit, quae ideas concipit et signa rerum: ut sit animae facultas inferior mentis intelligentia. Probabilior est eorum opinio qui spiritum gutturis interpretantur, hoc est, flatum. Verum huic interpretationi repugnat perpetua in hac Pauli disputatione verbi significatio.	Ambrose's reference to the Spirit which we receive in baptism has no foundation at all, or anything resembling a foundation. Augustine, in a more subtle way, takes it to mean the apprehension which grasps ideas and the signs of realities, so that it is a faculty of the soul inferior to mental intelligence. Those who understand it as the breathing of the throat, that is, the breath, hold a more likely view. But the way that Paul constantly uses the word in this discussion conflicts with that interpretation.

72. *Comm. ad Cor. 1*, CO 49:521.

Calvin then goes on to explain why he accepts Chrysostom's understanding of τὸ πνεῦμά μου as a spirituale donum:[73]

Quin etiam apparet repetitum saepius fuisse per concessionem. Superbiebant enim honorifico isto titulo, quem Paulus illis quidem permittit: sed rursum indicat quam praeposterus sit rei bonae et praeclarae abusus. Ac si diceret: Tu mihi spiritum iactas, quorsum, si est inutilis? Hac ratione adducor ut in sensu huius verbi assentiar Chrysostomo, qui exponit sicuti prius de spirituali dono.	Further than that, indeed, the word appears to have been repeated so often by way of concession. For they were taking pride in that honorable description, which Paul certainly allows them to have. But he, on the other hand, is pointing out how dangerous it is to make wrong use of a good and wonderful thing. It is as if said: "you are boasting to me about this spirit of yours. But why, if it is a useless thing? That is why I am led to agree with Chrysostom's understanding of this word, for he gives it the same meaning as it had before, that is, "a spiritual gift."

Is not this last phrase of Calvin, qui exponit sicuti prius, a key to Calvin's appreciation of Chrysostom? Chrysostom gives to the words the same meaning as they previously held, which is another way of saying "the Bible is its own interpreter," or the meaning of any phrase depends upon the total context of the words. Augustine's interpretation of the words—"a faculty of the soul inferior to mental intelligence which grasps ideas and the signs of things [signa rerum]" may well be true, but such an interpretation represents the imposition of a metaphysic upon the words that does not in any way arise out of the words themselves. That is why the interpretation of "breath," is even more likely than Augustine's view, but even "breath" does not arise out of the context. Standing above such interpretations is Chrysostom, who is a continuous expositor, and who derives his meaning from the situation to which Paul himself was speaking.

1 Corinthians 14:23.

Ἐὰν οὖν συνέλθῃ ἡ ἐκκλησία ὅλη ἐπὶ τὸ αὐτὸ καὶ πάντες λαλῶσιν γλώσσαις, εἰσέλθωσιν δὲ ἰδιῶται ἢ ἄπιστοι, οὐκ ἐροῦσιν ὅτι μαίνεσθε;

73. Ibid.

In order to make the following argument as clear as possible, let us first recall Paul's words in verses 22, 23, and 24. The issue centers around the giving of γλῶσσαι and προφητεία as signs for believers and unbelievers. Paul contends that "tongues" are meant to be a sign not for believers but for unbelievers; while "prophecy" is a sign not for unbelievers but for believers (v. 22). If unbelievers come into the church where everyone is speaking in tongues, the unbelievers will conclude that those speaking in tongues are "mad" (v. 23). But if unbelievers come into a church where people are speaking edifying words, that is, prophecy, the unbelievers would find themselves judged, the secrets of their hearts disclosed, and worship God (v. 24).

Commenting on verse 23, Calvin notes that Chrysostom raises the question of how, if tongues were meant to be a sign to unbelievers, they, at the same time, can be offended and scoff at the sign. Calvin agrees with Chrysostom's answer that as a sign, the function of "tongues" is to fill unbelievers with astonishment, but does not serve to instruct or reform them. Calvin takes issue, however, with Chrysostom's additional comment, that it is because of the sinfulness of the unbelievers that they interpret the sign as madness:[74]

Mihi solutio isthaec non placet: nam utcunque moveatur infidelis aut idiota miraculo donumque Dei revereatur: non tamen ideo ridere desinet ac damnare intempestivum doni abusum, et apud se ita cogitare: Quid isti sibi volunt, se ipsos et alios inaniter fatigando? quorsum pertinet loqui ut nihil dicant?	That explanation does not meet with my approval. Granted that an unbelieving or ignorant person may be moved by the miracle, and stand in awe of this gift of God. That does not make him cease, all the time, from ridiculing and condemning the wrong use of the gift at the wrong time. Further, he will think within himself: "what are these men aiming at, by wearying themselves and others to no purpose? What on earth is the use of speaking and saying nothing?"

The basis for Calvin's objection to Chrysostom's interpretation is that Chrysostom places the fault on the unbeliever. It is his "sinfulness" that, according to Chrysostom, does not allow the unbeliever to understand

74. Ibid., CO 49:526.

the sign. For Calvin, however, Paul contends that the unbeliever will scoff at the sign, not because of any fault in the unbeliever, but because the Corinthians are at fault in their λαλῶσιν γλώσσαις. Calvin sees Paul laying the blame at the feet of the Corinthians, and not at the unbelievers, and therefore concludes:[75]

Itaque significat Paulus, merito damnatum iri insaniae Corinthios ab incredulis et indoctis, utcunque sibi multum placeant.	Paul's meaning therefore is that the Corinthians can be highly pleased with themselves, but the unbelieving and uninformed will be perfectly justified in condemning them for behaving in a senseless way.

For Calvin, Chrysostom has, in an attempt to explain a logical contradiction in Paul, gone beyond the intent of Paul's meaning, and therefore Chrysostom's explanation is rejected. The basis of this rejection is seen even more clearly in the continuation of Chrysostom's argument with respect to "prophecy."

Paul has said that προφητεία is given to believers as a sign, but then adds that if an unbeliever enters a church where the congregation is prophesying, he will be judged, the secrets of his heart will be disclosed, and he will worship God. Thus arises the question, if prophecy is given as a sign for believers, how then can it be suitable for unbelievers? Chrysostom's involved answer can be outlined as follows:

a. Paul did not say that prophecy is not useful for unbelievers, but "it is not given to them for a sign."

b. There are two types of signs: a useful sign that produces good, and a useless sign that does not produce good.

c. To the unbelievers, "tongues" is a useless sign, the proof of which is the result that they respond by saying that those speaking in tongues are "mad."

d. The unbelievers respond in this way, however, not from the nature of the sign, but from their own folly.

e. There are two kinds of unbelievers: those who are incurably diseased and remain uncorrected, and those who can be changed.

75. Ibid.

f. Paul's meaning therefore is this: prophecy avails both the unbelieving and the believing. As to "tongues," when heard by the unbelieving and inconsiderate, instead of profiting by "tongues," they rather deride those speaking as madmen. In this case, it is given as a sign only to astonish them, but those who have understanding can profit by it.[76]

Calvin notes that Chrysostom asks the question, how it is consistent to say that prophecy is effective in influencing unbelievers, when Paul had said that it was not given for them:[77]

Respondet, non esse illis datam ut signum inutile, verum eruditionis causa.	He [Chrysostom] responds: "It is given to them not as a useless sign, but as a means of instructing them.

While Chrysostom can say that prophecy is not given to unbelievers as a sign, and nevertheless can be useful to those with understanding, Calvin is not favorably inclined to the complex argument of Chrysostom and prefers a simpler interpretation:[78]

Ego autem simplicius et ideo aptius fore sentio, si dicamus non esse datam incredulis qui pereunt, quorum Satan corda excaecavit, ne lucem illic fulgentem conspiciant: idque melius conveniet, si cohaereat haec sententia cum vaticinio Iesaiae [28:11]: quia propheta de incredulis loquitur, apud quos nullum usum vel profectum habet prophetia.	I myself feel it would be simpler and therefore more appropriate were we to say that it is not given to unbelievers who are perishing, whose minds Satan has blinded to keep them from seeing the light shining in it. And it will suit better still if this sentence is linked up with the prophecy of Isaiah [28:11], because there the prophet is speaking about unbelievers, in whose case prophecy is futile and unproductive.

Thus, in order to demonstrate that prophecy can have a beneficial result on unbelievers, Chrysostom enters into an extended argument, employing distinctions of signs and distinctions of unbelievers, pointing out what

76. This is my own reconstruction of Chrysostom's argument. His own words may be found in *Hom. ad Cor. 1*, Hom. 36, PG 61:307.

77. *Comm. ad Cor. 1*, CO 49:527.

78. Ibid.

Paul did not say as well as what he did say. Calvin, on the other hand, rests his case with the affirmation that there are unbelievers whose eyes Satan has so blinded that prophecy finds among them no profit or advantage.

What may we conclude from the above? First, for Calvin, Paul is attempting to correct a situation at Corinth in which the Corinthian church has misused a gift. Likewise for Calvin, Chrysostom has, in an attempt to solve a problem imposed on the text, switched the focus of the problem from the Corinthians to the unbelievers, and in the process, altered the meaning of Paul. That is the basis of Calvin's rejection of Chrysostom's interpretation.

Secondly, there is unquestionably a basic orientation toward unbelievers operative in the approach of each commentator to this text. Chrysostom is concerned to allow unbelievers access to the church, granting them the benefit of a sign that, according to Paul, was not designed for unbelievers. Calvin, on the other hand, rejects the idea that prophecy was given to unbelievers, who, he says, are perishing because of their blindness.

For Calvin, Chrysostom has toned down the severity with which Paul criticized the Corinthians, and has not fully appreciated the limitation Paul placed on the gift of tongues.

1 Corinthians 15:5-6.

5. καὶ ὅτι ὤφθη Κηφᾷ, εἶτα τοῖς δώδεκα· 6. ἔπειτα ὤφθη ἐπάνω πεντακοσίοις ἀδελφοῖς ἐφάπαξ, ἐξ ὧν οἱ πλείονες μένουσιν ἕως ἄρτι, τινὲς δὲ ἐκοιμήθησαν·

Calvin raises the question of how the resurrected Christ could appear to the twelve apostles, inasmuch as there were only eleven left after the death of Judas:[79]

Quomodo autem visum ipsis duodecim fuisse dicit, quum iam post mortem Iudae undecim tantum restarent? Chrysostamus putat id fuisse factum subrogato iam Matthia. Alii maluerunt corrigere ac si mendum fuisset.	But how can he say that he appeared to the twelve, when there were only eleven of them left after the death of Judas? Chrysostom thinks that this happened after Matthias had been elected in his place. Others preferred to correct the figure, as if it were a mistake.

79. Ibid., CO 49:539.

Chrysostom writes these words:[80]

Ποίοις δὲ δώδεκα ἐνταῦθα
φησίν ἀποστόλοις; μετὰ γὰρ
τὴν ἀνάληψιν ὁ Ματθίας
κατελέγη, οὐ μετὰ τὴν
ἀνάστασιν εὐθέως. Ἀλλ᾽
εἰκὸς αὐτὸν καὶ μετὰ τὴν
ἀνάληψιν ὦφθαι.

But of what twelve apostles does
he here speak? For after He was
received up, Matthias was taken
into the number, not immediately
after the resurrection. But it is
likely that He appeared even after
He was received up.

Thus for Chrysostom, the "twelve" included Matthias, who was added to
the eleven remaining apostles after the ascension. Calvin is rather of the
opinion that the "twelve" simply refers in a general way to the "apostolic
college," much as the body of men at Rome called the Centumviri actually
contained one hundred two men, rather than one hundred.

Interpreting this text, Calvin refers once again to Chrysostom on the
question of the appearance to "the five hundred." Observing that the time
of the appearance is not defined, Calvin notes Chrysostom's interesting
use of the word ἐπάνω:[81]

Chrysostomus ad adscen-
sionem refert et particulam
ἐπάνω exponit e sublimi.

Chrysostom makes it [the time of the
appearance] refer to the Ascension,
and explains ἐπάνω as "from above."

Chrysostom does mention the possibility that ἐπάνω might be taken to
mean "above," in the sense of "overhead," rather than connecting it with
the numeral five hundred:[82]

---

80. *Hom. ad Cor. 1*, Hom. 38, PG 61:326.
81. *Comm. ad Cor. 1*, CO 49:539.
82. *Hom. ad Cor. 1*, Hom. 38, PG 61:326.

Τινὲς τὸ, Ἐπάνω, ἄνω ἐκ τῶν οὐρανῶν εἶναί φασιν. Οὐ γὰρ επὶ γῆς βαδίζων, ἀλλ᾽ ἄνω, καὶ ὑπὲρ κεφαλῆς αὐτοῖς ὤφθη. Καὶ γὰρ οὐχὶ τὴν ἀνάστασιν πιστώσασθαι ἐβούλετο μόνον, ἀλλὰ καὶ τὴν ἀνάληψιν. Τινὲς δὲ λέγουσι τὸ, Ἐπάνω πεντακοσίοις, τοῖς πλείοσιν ἤ πεντακοσίοις.

Some say that "above" is above from heaven; that is, "not walking upon earth, but above and overhead He appeared to them"; adding that it was Paul's purpose to confirm not the resurrection only but also the ascension. Others say that the expression, "above five hundred," means "more than five hundred."

We may observe that Calvin does not feel compelled to "tell the whole story" regarding Chrysostom's commentary. Calvin simply notes that "Chrysostom explains ἐπάνω as meaning 'from above,'" as if this were Chrysostom's final conclusion. In fact, however, Chrysostom makes the observation that "some render the word ἐπάνω as meaning 'from above,' while others understand the words ἐπάνω πεντακοσίοις as meaning more than five hundred."

1 Corinthians 15:29.

Ἐπεὶ τί ποιήσουσιν οἱ βαπτιζόμενοι ὑπὲρ τῶν νεκρῶν; εἰ ὅλως νεκροὶ οὐκ ἐγείρονται, τί καὶ βαπτίζονται ὑπὲρ αὐτῶν;

Let us first turn to Chrysostom's interpretation of this enigmatic statement that on the surface looks like Paul is speaking of baptism by proxy. Chrysostom first recalls the Marcionite perversion:[83]

---

83. *Hom. ad Cor. 1*, Hom. 40, PG 61:347.

Τί οὖν ἐστιν ὅ φησιν; ἢ βούλεσθε πρῶτον εἴπω, πῶς παραποιοῦσι τὴν ῥῆσιν ταύτην οἱ τὰ Μαρκίωνος νοσοῦντες; Καὶ οἶδα μὲν ὅτι πολὺν κινήσω γέλωτα, πλὴν ἀλλὰ καὶ διὰ τοῦτο μάλιστα ἐρῶ, ἵνα μειζόνως αὐτῶν φύγητε τὴν νόσον. Ἐπειδὰν γάρ τις κατηχούμενος ἀπέλθῃ παρ' αὐτοῖς, τὸν ζῶντα ὑπὸ τὴν κλίνην τοῦ τετελευτηκότος κρύψαντες, προσίασι τῷ νεκρῷ καὶ διαλέγονται καὶ πυνθάνονται, εἰ βούλοιτο λαβεῖν τὸ βάπτισμα· εἶτα ἐκείνου μηδὲν ἀποκρινομένου, ὁ κεκρυμμένος κάτωθεν ἀντ' ἐκείνου φησὶν, ὅτι δὴ βούλοιτο βαπτισθῆναι· καὶ οὕτω βαπτίζουσιν αὐτὸν ἀντὶ τοῦ ἀπελθόντος, καθάπερ ἐπὶ τῆς σκηνῆς παίζοντες· τοσοῦτον ἴσχυσε ταῖς τῶν ῥᾳθύμων ψυχαῖς ὁ διάβολος.

What then is the meaning of Paul? Or, should I first mention how they who are infected with the Marcionite heresy pervert this expression? And I know for sure that I shall excite a great deal of laughter from you. Nevertheless, I will mention it that you may all the more avoid this disease. When any Catechumen departs among them, having concealed the living man under the couch of the dead, they approach the corpse and talk with him, and ask him if he wishes to receive baptism. Then, when he makes no answer, he that is concealed underneath responds in his place that of course he should wish to be baptized. So they baptize him instead of the departed, like men jesting upon the stage. So great power has the devil over the souls of careless sinners.

Chrysostom labels such actions as an extreme perversion of what Paul intends, and then continues to unfold his understanding of Paul's meaning.

For Chrysostom, Paul is speaking here of that baptism that unites us with the death of Christ and consequently the resurrection of Christ. It is as if Paul were saying: "you believe that your dead body will rise from the dead because, by your baptism, you have been joined with the death and resurrection of Christ. How then can you Corinthians say there is no resurrection, if by your baptism you have been baptized for the death and resurrection of your bodies?" "Baptism for the dead" means baptism for the resurrection of the dead body, and has, for Chrysostom, nothing to do whatsoever with baptism for or on behalf of another person. Recalling Paul's statement in Romans 6:4, where baptism signifies the death and resurrection of our bodies, Chrysostom says:[84]

84. Ibid., PG 61:348.

Τὸ γὰρ βαπτίζεσθαι καὶ καταδύεσθαι, εἶτα ἀνανεύειν, τῆς εἰς ᾅδου καταβάσεώς ἐστι σύμβολον καὶ τῆς ἐκεῖθεν ἀνόδου. Διὸ καὶ τάφον τὸ βάπτισμα ὁ Παῦλος καλεῖ λέγων· Συνετάφημεν οὖν αὐτῷ διὰ τοῦ βαπτίσματος εἰς τὸν θάνατον. Ἀπὸ τούτου καὶ τὸ μέλλον ἀξιόπιστον ποιεῖ, τῶν σωμάτων λέγω τὴν ἀνάστασιν.

For being baptized and immersed, and then emerging, is a symbol of the descent into Hades and return. Therefore, Paul calls baptism a burial, saying, "therefore we are buried with Him by baptism into death." [Rom 6:4] By this he makes that which is to come credible, that is, the resurrection of our bodies.

That Chrysostom means baptism for one's own body rather than for the body of another is most clearly stated in another place, in the twenty-third homily. Commenting on Paul's statement in chapter 10, verse 1, "our fathers . . . were all baptized into Moses," Chrysostom observes:[85]

Τί δέ ἐστιν, Εἰς τὸν Μωϋσῆν ἐβαπτίσαντο; Καθάπερ ἡμεῖς τῷ Χριστῷ πιστεύσαντες καὶ τῇ ἀναστάσει αὐτοῦ, βαπτιζόμεθα, ὡς καὶ αὐτοὶ τῶν αὐτῶν μυστηρίων κοινωνήσοντες· Βαπτιζόμεθα γάρ, φησίν, ὑπὲρ τῶν νεκρῶν, τουτέστι, τῶν σωμάτων τῶν ἡμετέρων· οὕτω κἀκεῖνοι θαρρήσαντες τῷ Μωϋσεῖ, τουτέστιν, ἰδόντες αὐτὸν διαβάντα πρῶτον, κατετόλμησαν καὶ αὐτοὶ τῶν ὑδάτων.

But what is, "They were baptized into Moses?" Like as we, on our belief in Christ and His resurrection, are baptized, as being destined in our own persons to partake in the same mysteries. "We are baptized," he said, "for the dead," that is, for our own bodies. Just so, placing their confidence in Moses, and having seen him cross first, they ventured themselves into the waters.

Clearly here, "baptism for the dead" means for the death of our own bodies. By baptism we are destined to partake in the same mysteries of Christ, just as the people of Israel, seeing Moses cross through the waters safely, were baptized into the same "mystery" of which Moses was a participant. What Paul in 15:29 asks is, "how can you say there is no resurrection when you are baptized for the resurrection of the dead body?" For Chrysostom,

85. *Hom. ad Cor. 1*, Hom. 23, PG 61:191.

there is absolutely no hint of Paul using or referring to a superstitious baptism in order to argue for the resurrection of the dead.

Now we turn to Calvin's interpretation of the text. Before he offers his own understanding, Calvin is anxious to set aside a common interpretation resting on the authority of Chrysostom:[86]

Antequam locum hunc exponam, operae pretium est refellere vulgatam expositionem, quae veterum autoritate nititur et omnium fere consensu recepta est. Putant ergo Chrysostomus et Ambrosius, quos alii sequuntur, Corinthios, ubi quempiam subita mors baptismo privasset, solitos fuisse aliquem vivum supponere mortui loco, qui ad sepulcrum eius baptizaretur. Atque hunc morem non negant perversum plenumque superstitionis fuisse: sed Paulum ad redarguendos Corinthios hoc solo fuisse contentum, quod resurrectionem, quam negabant, interea se credere profiterentur. Ego vero ut hoc credam, nullo modo adducor: neque enim credibile est, qui resurrectionem negabant eos simul cum aliis usurpasse eiusmodi ritum.

Before I explain this verse, it is worth while refuting the usual exposition, which is supported by the authority of the Fathers, and to which nearly everyone assents. Thus Chrysostom and Ambrose, followed by others, think that when anyone had been deprived of baptism by sudden death, the Corinthians were in the habit of substituting a living person for the dead one to be baptized at his grave. Indeed, they do not deny that this custom was a perversion, and full of superstition. But they also say that, in order to refute the Corinthians, Paul relied on this one argument, that while they were denying the resurrection, they were yet making it quite plain that they did believe in it. But as far as I am concerned, nothing induces me to give credence to this, for it is hard to believe that people who are denying the resurrection were at one and the same time making use of a rite like this one, along with others.

Calvin is saying here that Chrysostom, along with Ambrose and others, understood Paul to be contented with this one fact or argument (hoc solo fuisse contentum), namely, the substitution of a living person in the place of the deceased, in order to demonstrate that while the Corinthians denied that there was a resurrection, they in fact declared in this way that they believed in it. Calvin is not induced to give credence to such

86. *Comm. ad Cor. 1*, CO 49:550–51.

an interpretation, on the grounds that the Corinthians would not have engaged in a rite of this sort if they denied the resurrection. He then goes on, in opposition to Chrysostom, to give reasons why Paul could not possibly have allowed such a profane practice to continue.

Calvin therefore is affirming that Paul did not have reference to the profanation of the sacrament of baptism. Paul could not possibly have offered an argument or made a reference to a practice which was a pollution of the sacrament, without correcting the gross error:[87]

Obsecro, an verisimile est, sacrilegium, quo baptismus inquinaretur ac traheretur in abusum prorsus magicum, apostolum protulisse vice argumenti, et non uno saltem verbulo notasse vitium?	I ask you, is it likely that the apostle would adduce, as an argument, a sacrilege by which baptism was corrupted and turned into a completely magical abuse, and have not even a single syllable to say in condemnation of its offensiveness?

Now let us observe what has happened here. Calvin alleges that he disagrees with Chrysostom. Calvin cannot accept Chrysostom's interpretation because, as Calvin sees it, Chrysostom allows Paul to content himself with the profanation of the sacrament in order to affirm the reality of the resurrection in the minds of the Corinthians. But where does Calvin derive this understanding? It is nowhere to be found in Chrysostom. Quite to the contrary, Chrysostom goes to extended lengths to demonstrate that Paul did not have "substitutionary baptism" in mind, but rather baptism for the death of one's own body. Chrysostom does point out that this text had been horribly profaned by those of the Marcionite heresy, which for Chrysostom demonstrates the power that the devil holds "over the souls of careless sinners."

What in fact Calvin does is absolutely agree with Chrysostom. Chrysostom has understood Paul's statement on baptism for the dead as a reference not to the substitution of one body for another, but as a reference to that baptism in which dead bodies become participants in the resurrection of Jesus Christ. Most interesting, then, is Calvin's statement that he offers after his extended refutation of the idea that Paul made use of a distortion in order to refute the Corinthians:[88]

87. Ibid., CO 49:551.
88. Ibid.

Ego certe non de tali baptismi corruptela, sed de recto usu mentionem hic fieri interpretor.	I certainly understand Paul to be speaking here about the regular use of baptism, and not a corruption of it like that.

Calvin is sure Paul is speaking of the correct use of baptism, which is exactly Chrysostom's position!

When Calvin embarks on his own interpretation of the text, he indicates that he had changed his mind on the matter:[89]

Nunc sensum quaeramus. Aliquando putavi universalem baptismi finem designatum hic fuisse a Paulo: neque enim baptismi utilitas hac vita continetur: sed quum postea accuratius verba expenderem animadverti Paulum hic aliquid speciale attingere. Non enim de omnibus loquitur, quum dicit, quid facient qui baptizantur? Deinde non amo argutas interpretationes, quae non perinde sint solidae. Quid ergo? Baptizari pro mortuis dico, qui iam mortui censeantur, et qui de vita omnio desperaverint. Atque ita particula ὑπέρ valebit latinum pro: ut quum dicimus, habere pro derelicto. Quae significatio non est coacta. Vel si magis placeat altera significatio, baptizari pro mortuis, erit sic baptizari ut mortuis non vivis prosit.	Now let us discover what the meaning is. I used to think that Paul was pointing out the all-embracing end of baptism here, for the benefit of baptism is not confined to our lives here. But afterwards, when I gave more careful consideration to the words, I saw that Paul is dealing with one particular aspect here. For he is not speaking about everybody, when he says, "what will they do who are baptized . . . etc." I do not like interpretations which are clever rather than sound. What does it mean then? I maintain that the people who are baptized for the dead are those who are thought of as dead already, and who have given up hope of life altogether. And so the preposition ὑπέρ will have the meaning of the Latin pro, for example in the expression habere pro derelicto, to regard as abandoned. That meaning is not forced. Or there is another way of looking at it, which you may prefer. To be baptized for the dead will mean to be baptized so as to receive the benefit when dead, and not when alive.

89. Ibid.

Calvin first considered Paul had reference to the "all-embracing end" (universalem baptismi finem) of baptism, affirming that the "end" is the incorporation of the dead into the living body of Christ. Calvin then alters his position to understand "the dead" as those who are thought of as already dead. People who are baptized "for the dead" would in this interpretation be those people who have given up hope of life altogether. In this case Calvin understands the word ὑπέρ to mean not "on behalf of," but "for" in the sense of "as if" dead or "regarded as" dead. The Greek word ὑπέρ is understood to have the force of the Latin pro, as in the expression habere pro derelicto (to regard as abandoned). This interpretation, says Calvin, is not forced.

Having established this meaning, Calvin proposes yet a third possible interpretation:[90]

Vel si magis placeat altera significatio, baptizari pro mortuis, erit sic baptizari, ut mortuis non vivis prosit. Scitur autem, statim ab initio ecclesiae, eos qui catechumeni adhuc in morbum inciderant, si imminebat certum mortis periculum, baptismum solitos fuisse petere, ne ante migrarent ex hoc mundo quam nomen Christo dedissent: idque ut secum ferrent salutis suae obsignationem.

Or, if you would prefer another meaning, to be baptized for the dead will mean to be baptized so as to profit when dead, and not when alive. For it is well known, that from the early days of the Church, when people who were still unbaptized beginners in the faith had fallen ill, and if they were in imminent danger of death, they were accustomed to ask for baptism, that they might not depart from this world before they had professed Christ, that they might carry the seal of their salvation with them.

Here "baptism for the dead" carries the force of "baptism for death" or "for the time when one is dead." The catechumen who had accepted the Christian faith asked for baptism since, with death imminent, he wished to have the token or proof of his salvation sealed in his own body.

What conclusions may be drawn? It is first to be observed that Chrysostom, in describing the profanation of the sacrament, is describing it as practiced by those of the Marcionite heresy, and not among the Corinthians. Second, Chrysostom nowhere says Paul was making use or

90. Ibid.

contenting himself with the profanation of the sacrament in order to refute the Corinthians. Third, the interpretation rendered by Chrysostom and the interpretations given by Calvin are, for all practical purposes, identical. For both Calvin and Chrysostom "baptism for the dead" does not mean "substitutionary baptism," and "baptism for the dead" does mean baptism so as to benefit the person baptized.

1 Corinthians 16:2.

κατὰ μίαν σαββάτου ἕκαστος ὑμῶν παρ' ἑαυτῷ τιθέτω θη—
σαυρίζων ὅ τι ἐὰν εὐοδῶται, ἵνα μὴ ὅταν ἔλθω τότε λογεῖαι
γίνωνται.

Since Calvin offers two objections to Chrysostom's interpretation of this text, we first examine the latter's remarks:[91]

Κατὰ μίαν σαββάτου, τουτέστι, Κυριακὴν, ἕκαστος ὑμῶν παρ' ἑαυτῷ τιθέτω θησαυρίζων ὅ τι ἂν εὐοδῶται." Ορα πῶς καὶ ἀπὸ τοῦ καιροῦ προτρέπει· καὶ γὰρ ἡ ἡμέρα ἱκανὴ ἦν ἀγαγεῖν εἰς ἐλεημοσύνην. Ἀναμνήσθητε γὰρ, φησὶ, τίνων ἐτύχετε ἐν τῇ ἡμέρᾳ ταύτῃ. Τὰ γὰρ ἀπόρρητα ἀγαθὰ, καὶ ἡ ῥίζα καὶ ἡ ἀρχὴ τῆς ζωῆς τῆς ἡμετέρας ἐν ταύτῃ γέγονεν.	"On the first day of the week," that is, the Lord's Day, "each one of you is to place something aside and store it up, as he may prosper." Notice how he exhorts them even as to the time. For indeed, the day itself was enough to lead them toward the giving of alms. "For remember," he says, "what you attained on this day; how all the unspeakable blessings and that which is the root and beginning of our life took place on this day."

Now let us note Calvin's two objections. He first argues that Chrysostom is wrong in understanding κατὰ μίαν σαββάτου as primo sabbatho:[92]

Particulam hanc κατὰ μίαν σαββάτων exponit Chrysostomus primo sabbatho: cui ego non assentior.	This phrase, κατὰ μίαν σαββάτου, Chrysostom renders as "the first sabbath." With this I do not agree.

91. *Hom. ad Cor. 1*, Hom. 43, PG 61:368.
92. *Comm. ad Cor. 1*, CO 49:566.

Potius enim significat Paulus, ut conferant hic uno sabbatho, alius alio: aut etiam singuli uno-quoque sabbatho si voluerint. Commoditatem enim respicit primum: deinde quod sacer conventus, ubi celebratur sanc-torum communio, addere illis calcar poterat.	Paul means, rather, that they should contribute, one on one Sabbath and another on another: and even each of them every Sabbath, if they choose. For he is thinking, in the first place, in terms of convenience: and secondly that the gathering for worship, where believers rejoice in the communion of the saints, could be an additional incentive to them.

Calvin here is making the observation that Paul has used the cardinal number (μίαν) rather than the ordinal (πρῶτος). Therefore Chrysostom is incorrect, understanding κατὰ μίαν σαββάτου as primo sabbatho (the first sabbath), rather than una sabbathorum (one of the sabbaths).

Calvin's second objection lies with Chrysostom's understanding of κατὰ μίαν σαββάτου as meaning Κυριακὴν (the Lord's Day):[93]

Nihilo magis recipio, quod idem Chrysostomus sab-bathum pro die dominico positum existimat: nam verisimilius est, apostolos diem initio retinuisse iam usitatum: postea iudaica superstitione coactos illo abrogato alium substituisse.	No more do I accept the same Chrysostom's opinion that the term "Sabbath" is employed here to mean the Lord's Day, for the probability is that the apostles, at the beginning, re-tained the day that was already in use, but that afterwards, constrained by the superstition of the Jews, they set aside that day and substituted another.

Calvin undoubtedly has reference to the fact that throughout the New Testament, κατὰ μίαν σαββάτων never means "the Lord's Day," but "the first day of the week."

The above observations raise again the textual question, in particular here the Greek text with which Calvin was working. Apparently Calvin's Greek text employed the words κατὰ μίαν σαββάτων, which Calvin translated into in una sabbathorum (on one of the sabbaths), rather than the idiomatic "on the first day of the week." The textual problems are con-sidered in chapter 5.

93. Ibid.

5

The Textual Problem

IN CHAPTER 4, WE examined in detail all twenty-six references, explicit or implicit, in which Calvin either cites, quotes, or alludes to John Chrysostom. In chapter 6 we shall, with the help of additional data from further New Testament references and citations or quotations included in the *Institutio*, formulate observations and conclusions concerning Calvin's methodology as a biblical commentator.

Before we can come to these observations, however, the material in chapter 4 has raised a fundamental textual question that needs to be answered. Did Calvin in fact have the actual text of Chrysostom's homilies on 1 Corinthians and other Chrysostomic literature before him? If, for instance, Calvin had access only to the observation that Chrysostom designated πίστις in 1 Corinthians 12:9 the *fides miraculorum*, meaning superior to *fides dogmatorum*, then we readily would understand why Calvin notes that there is "not much divergence" between Chrysostom's position and his own; whereas in fact, Calvin's interpretation and Chrysostom's position are diametric to each other. Many of the problems raised in chapter 4 would be clarified if it were demonstrated that Calvin understood Chrysostom primarily through secondary sources rather than through direct access to the Chrysostom text. On the other hand, if it were demonstrated that Calvin had access to either the Greek text or Latin translations, and was familiar with the content of such texts, then our final conclusions concerning Calvin's methodology and principles of interpretation must necessarily arise out of the data and additional supporting data presented in chapter 4.

Therefore, in order to ascertain the extent of Calvin's familiarity with Chrysostomic literature, we shall address three basic questions:

1. To what extent was Chrysostom available to Calvin? In order to answer this question we shall examine the publication of Chrysostom during the first half of the sixteenth century.

2. To what extent did Calvin make use of the published *Opera* of Chrysostom? In order to answer this question, we shall attempt to trace Calvin's use of Chrysostom in his early publications and in the successive editions of the *Institutio*.

3. To what extent can we establish that Calvin was dealing with an actual text of Chrysostom? Here we shall examine the 1530 text of Chrysostom published under Erasmian direction by Froben, making actual textual comparisons of Chrysostom passages quoted by Calvin.

What texts of Chrysostom were available to Calvin? Whether or not it was the element of *caritas* in the writings of Chrysostom that attracted Erasmus to the writings of the fourth-century homiletician,[1] we owe it to Erasmus and the Basel printer Froben, among others, that the writings of Chrysostom were introduced to the early sixteenth century. As early as 1511, Erasmus indicated his interest in Chrysostom when he sent John Colet a copy of the Liturgy of Chrysostom. Writing to Colet, Erasmus begins his letter:[2]

Mitto quae petis, Officium Chrysostomi, et epistolam, in qua, nisi fallor, erunt quae non probabis, propterea quod tu rationem et artem contemnis . . .	I sent what you requested, the Liturgy of Chrysostom, and the Epistle, in which, if I am not mistaken, there are things of which you will not approve, because you have contempt for method and art . . .

In 1519 Erasmus proposed a Greek edition of Chrysostom to Francis Asculanius,[3] but apparently nothing came of the plan. It was not until

---

1. This is the view of Peters in his edition of Erasmus, *Preface to the Fathers*, not paginated.

2. *Opus Epistolarum Desiderius Erasmi*, 1:467.

3. Ibid., 5:252.

1524 that an edition of sixty-two works of Chrysostom was produced by the despised translator Oecolampadius, published by another of the Basel printers, Andreas Cratander. Undoubtedly the publishing of this edition stimulated further work on Chrysostom, and Erasmus published the *De Sacerdotio* in the following year, 1525. The same year saw the publication of Chrysostom's *De Orando Deum*, with Greek text and Latin translation. On January 30, 1526, Erasmus dedicated Chrysostom's *Conciunculae Sex De Fato et Providentia Dei* to John Claymond, first president of Corpus Christi College, Oxford. August of the same year saw the publication of *In Epistolam ad Philippenses Homiliae Duae*, taken from the third book of Chrysostom's Fifteen Homilies on Philippians. In the following year, Erasmus published six groups of Chrysostom's homilies under the title *Chrysostomi Lucubrationes*, and Chrysostom's *Commentarius in Epistolam ad Galatas*.

The publication of Chrysostom's *Libellus de Babyla Martyre* by Erasmus on August 14, 1527, has an interesting background. In his *Preface* to the work, Erasmus notes that the College du Faucon was having some difficulty. He draws an analogy between these difficulties and the sequence of events following on the order by Julian the Apostate for the removal of the remains of Babylas, martyr-bishop of Antioch during the Decian persecution, from the grove at Daphne, near Antioch, where they had been buried. The grove was returned to the worship of Apollo, but the temple at Daphne was destroyed by fire (June 26, 363). Whereupon Libanius, the pagan orator, delivered an oration, only to have it torn to shreds by Chrysostom in a biting verbal attack. For Chrysostom, the whole episode is a proof of the triumph of Christianity over paganism! Erasmus then reminds Varius that as Chrysostom is the "sum of admirable eloquence and piety," so are languages to be used in the service of God. "The danger of contemporary literature," notes Erasmus, "lies in its being unrelated to piety!"[4]

The year 1529 saw the publication of ten letters, homilies, and other short pieces by Chrysostom under the title *Aliquot Opuscula*. Perhaps the culmination of Erasmian work on Chrysostom came in 1530, with the publication of the five-volume *Opera*. This latter work, published by Froben in Latin, contains most of Chrysostom's works, although not the *Homilies on Romans*; for one month following the publication of the

---

4. Erasmus, *Preface to the Fathers*, not paginated.

Opera, we find Erasmus suggesting to Brixius the need for a supplementary volume to include the Romans homilies.[5]

Thus, by 1530, the larger portion of Chrysostom had been published. But what of the 1 Corinthians Commentary? Was this work also in circulation by that date? On October 24, 1529, Erasmus received a letter[6] from Cuthbert Tunstall, writing from London. In the last line of this letter, the Bishop of London notes:[7]

Apud nos est in Academia ingens volumen Homeliarum eiusdem [Chrysostomus] in primam ad Corinthios Epistolam, a Francisco Aretino versum.	Among us in the Academy is the remarkable volume of homilies by the same man [Chrysostom] on 1 Corinthians, translated by Francisco Aretino.

Erasmus printed the first twenty-nine of these homilies on 1 Corinthians as translated by the above-mentioned Francisco Aretino. However, Erasmus was not altogether pleased with the translation of Aretino; for, speaking about the publication of the Chrysostom *Opera*, Erasmus, in a letter to Germanus Brixius dated March 27, 1530, notes:[8]

Homilias in priorem ad Corinthios vertit Franciscus Aretinus, sed infeliciter, usque ad XXX; reliquum alius quidam eruditus absoluit.	Francisco Aretino translated the homilies on 1 Corinthians, although it is an unhappy translation, up to number 30. The remaining should be produced by someone more erudite.

It was someone "more erudite" indeed who completed the task. In the same year, 1530, Simon Grynaeus, professor of Greek at Heidelberg in 1524 and Basel in 1530, completed the homilies numbered thirty through forty-four.[9] It is of interest to note here that nine years later Calvin dedicated his commentary on Paul's Letter to the Romans to this same Simon Grynaeus, whom Calvin calls "a man worthy of all honor."

5. *Opus Epistolarum Desiderius Erasmi*, 9:31.

6. Ibid., 8:290, Ep. 2226.

7. Ibid., 8:292.

8. Ibid., 8:391.

9. See the introduction to the letter of Erasmus to Grynaeus in *Opus Epistolarum Desiderius Erasmi*, 6:245.

In answer to our first question, therefore, by the end of the year 1530, the *Opera* of John Chrysostom, including the commentary on 1 Corinthians, had been published and was at least available to Calvin. In addition, the supplemental volume containing the first eight homilies on Romans appeared in 1533, followed by the Chevallon edition of the *Opera* published in 1536. A second Basel edition was produced in 1539.

Given the availability of the printed works of Chrysostom, we have now to inquire into the second question, the extent of Calvin's use of the published *Opera*.

In Calvin's first published work, the 1532 commentary on Seneca's *De Clementia*, there is not one reference to Chrysostom.[10] In 1534, while he was at Orleans, Calvin wrote his *Psychopannychia*, a work that contains three references to Chrysostom. In the first, Calvin is arguing against the notion that the image of God in man refers to the dominion that was given to man over the brutes; and that in this respect, man has some resemblance to God. Calvin makes the observation that Chrysostom, "in the heat of debate," fell into the position against which Calvin stood:[11]

In quem lapsum Chrysostomus quoque incidit, dum nimia contentione provehitur contra insanos anthropomorphitas.	Into this mistake even Chrysostom fell when he was carried away in the heat of debate against the insane Anthropomorphites.

The second reference to Chrysostom in the *Psychopannychia* concerns the story of the rich man and Lazarus (Luke 16:19–31). Contending that the story is history (*historia*) and not a parable, Calvin summons to his defense such a distinguished gallery as Gregory, Tertullian, Irenaeus, Origen, Cyprian, Jerome, and with some reservation, Augustine. But even if it were a parable, says Calvin, a parable is a similitude founded on reality. Those who insist upon a parabolic interpretation of the story should follow Chrysostom:[12]

10. *Calvin's Commentary on Seneca's De Clementia*, ed. and trans. Battles and Hugo, 413–14.

11. *Psychopannychia*, CO 5:180–81.

12. Ibid., CO 5:188.

Imitentur Chrysostomum, hac in re suum Achillem. Existimavit quidem ille esse parabolam, ex qua tamen veritatem saepe elicit. Ut quum inde probat, mortuorum animas in certis esse locis, ostendit gehennae gravitatem et delitiarum perniciem.

Let them imitate Chrysostom, who is their Achilles in this matter. He thought that it was a parable, though he often extracts a reality from it, as when he proves from it that the dead have certain abodes, and shows the dreadful nature of Gehenna, and the destructive effects of luxury.

An extended quotation comprises the third reference to Chrysostom. Calvin, discussing the souls of the saints following death, calls upon ancient writers, "those who have cautiously and reverently handled the mysteries of God," in support of the conviction that such souls are "with God and live in God," while they wait for the final resurrection to receive their glory and reward. The quotation from Chrysostom is as follows:[13]

Et Chrysostomus: Intelligite quale et quantum est, Abraham sedere, et apostolum Paulum, quando perficiatur, ut possint tunc mercedem recipere. Nisi enim nos illuc venerimus, tunc praedixit eis pater, non se daturum mercedem: sicut bonus pater amator filiorum, et probabilibus filiis et opus perficientibus dicit, se non daturum cibum, nisi venerint alii fratres. Tu autem anxius es, quia necdum accipis? quid autem faciet Abel, qui ante vicit, et adhuc sine corona sedet? Quid Noe? quid caeteri illorum temporum? Quia ecce exspectaverunt, et alios exspectant, qui post te futuri sunt. Paulo post: Praevenerunt nos in certaminibus, sed non praevenient in coronis: quia unum definitum est tempus omnium coronarum.

Chrysostom says, "Understand what and how great a thing it is for Abraham to sit, and the apostle Paul, when he is perfected, that they may then be able to receive their reward. Unless we come to him, the Father has foretold us that he will not give the reward, as a good father who loves his children says to probable children and those finishing their labor, that he will not give food until the other brothers have come. Are you anxious because you do not yet receive? What then will Abel do, who formerly conquered, and still sits without a crown? What will Noah do? What will the others of those times do? They have waited and still wait for others who are to be after you." A little after that, Chrysostom says, "They were before us in the contest, but they will not be before us in the crown; for there is one set time for all the crowns."

13. Ibid., CO 5:215.

We have here only weak evidence that Calvin was beginning to make use of Chrysostom as early as 1534, for our present text of the *Psychopannychia* was not published until 1542.

In 1535 Calvin, published only one work, the *Praefationes Bibliis Gallicis Petri Roberti Olivetani*. In this Latin preface to Olivétan's French translation of the New Testament, Calvin mentions Chrysostom along with Augustine, commending them to lay people for interpretation of Scripture:[14]

Chrysostomus, et Augustinus, quando non plebem hortantur ad haec studia? quam frequenter inculcant, ut domi relegant, quae in ecclesia audierunt?	Chrysostom and Augustine; when have they not encouraged the common people to these studies? How frequently they impress upon us the importance of going over again at home what they have heard in the church?

This evidence, however, is also inconclusive; for both Chrysostom and Augustine are mentioned in the context of a chain of patristic authorities, such lists being in common circulation during Calvin's time.

It is not until we turn our attention to a critical study of the Chrysostomic references in the *Institutio* that our evidence begins to gather weight. In order to demonstrate the extent and nature of Calvin's use of Chrysostom, we have examined every reference to Chrysostom in the successive editions of the *Institutio*, the results of which are given in the statistical tables that follow. Table 5.1 gives the following information for each reference:

1. The location of the reference in the Latin text (Barth, Niesel, *Opera Selecta*)

2. The year in which the Chrysostom reference was added (Stratum)

3. The work of Chrysostom in which the reference appears (where this could be found)

4. Whether the reference is a direct quote or a more general borrowing

5. Whether Calvin cites Chrysostom positively or negatively (The ≠ is employed to indicate that Calvin disagrees with Chrysostom but allows his interpretation)

---

14. *Praefationes Bibliis Gallicis Petri Roberti Olivetani*, CO 9:788.

6. The subject matter Calvin is treating in the context of the Chrysostom reference

Finally, a statistical summary table (table 5.2) draws together the above information.

TABLE 5.1
Chrysostom References in the *Institutes*

#	Location	Stratum	Chrysostom Opera	Quote or General Reference ↓	Positive or Negative ↓	Subject in Calvin
1	1.13.21	1539	*Hom. de incomprehensibili Dei Natura*	G	+	Knowledge of God
2	2.2.4	1539	*De proditione Judaeorum*	Q	–	Freedom of the will
3	2.2.9	1539	*Hom. in adventu*	G	+	Freedom of the will
4	2.2.11	1539	*De profectu evangelii*	G	+	Humility
5	2.3.7	1539	*Hom. in Matt.*	Q	–	Freedom of the will
6	2.3.10	1539	*De ferendis reprehensionibus; Hom. in Jo.*	G	–	Freedom of the will
7	2.5.2	1539	?	G	–	Freedom of the will
8	2.5.3	1539	*Hom. in Gen.*	G	–	Freedom of the will
9	2.5.3	1539	?	G	–	Freedom of the will
10	2.8.57	1539	*De compunctione cordis*	G	+	Law
11	3.4.1	1539	*De poenitentia*	Q	+	Repentance
12	3.4.4	1539	*Hom. de muliere Chananaea*	G	≠	Confession
13	3.4.5	1559	Pseudo-Chry. *Contra Judaeos, Gentiles, et Hareticos*	G	+	Confession
14	3.4.8	1539	Pseudo-Chry. *Sermo de poenitentia et confessione De incomprehensibili Dei Natura c. Anomo. De Lazaro Concio*	Q	+	Confession

#	Location	Stratum	Chrysostom Opera	Quote or General Reference	Positive or Negative	Subject in Calvin
15	3.4.31	1539	Pseudo-Chry. *De fide et lege naturae*	G	+	God's judgments
16	3.4.33	1539	Pseudo-Chry. *Sermo de poenitentia et conf.*	Q	+	God's chastisement
17	3.4.35	1539	*Hom. de providentia ad Stagirium*	Q	+	God's judgments
18	3.4.38	1539	Pseudo-Chry. *Psalm 50*	Q	+	Satisfaction
19	3.4.38	1539	*Hom. in Gen.*	G	+	Satisfaction
20	3.4.39	1536	[Simple listing of his name]	G	+	Satisfaction
21	3.14.15	1539	*In Ep. ad Philemon*	Q	+	Supererogation
22	3.15.2	1539	*Hom. in Gen.*	Q	+	Merit
23	3.24.13	1539	*De ferendis reprehensionibus et de mutatione nominum* Bas. ed. (Pauli)	Q	–	Reprobation
24	4.4.6	1543	[Simple listing of his name]	G	+	Use of church possessions
25	4.8.13	1539	Pseudo-Chry. *Sermo de Sancto Spiritu*	Q	+	Word and Spirit (against infallibility of the church)
26	4.12.5	1543	*Hom. in Matt.*	Q	+	Church discipline
27	4.12.8	1543	*De non anathematizandis vivis atque defunctis*	Q	+	Church discipline
28	4.12.28	1539	*Hom. de inventione crucis*	Q	+	Celibacy
29	4.13.8	1543	*Adv. oppugnatores vitae monisticae*	G	+	Monasticism
30	4.14.3	1543	*Hom. ad populum* Bas. ed.	Q	+	Lord's Supper
31	4.14.19	1539	Chry. *Opera.* 1530 Erasmus ed. 2, 82	G	+	Ordinary Sacraments
32	4.15.7	1539	*Hom. in Matt.*	G	–	Baptism (forgiveness of sins)
33	4.17.6	1543	*Hom. 60.* Basel, 1530 4, 581	Q	+	Lord's Supper

#	Location	Stratum	Chrysostom Opera	Quote or General Reference ↓	Positive or Negative ↓	Subject in Calvin
34	4.17.45	1543	*In Ep. ad Ephes.*	Q	+	Lord's Supper (duty of part.)
35	4.17.46	1543	*In Ep. ad Ephes.*	Q	+	Lord's Supper (against once a year)
36	4.17.48	1543	*In Ep. ad 2 Cor.*	Q	+	Lord's Supper
37	4.18.10	1543	*In Ep. ad Hebr.*	G	+	Lord's Supper (a sacrifice?)
38	4.18.11	1539	*De sacerdotio* *In Ep. ad Rom.* *In Ep. ad 1 Cor.* *In Ep. ad Hebr.*	G	–	Lord's Supper (repeated sacrifice)

TABLE 5.2
Statistical Summary

Total number of references	38
Added in 1536	1
Added in 1539	26
Added in 1543	10
Added in 1559	1
Number of times direct quote is given	19
Number of times general reference is given	19
In agreement with Chrysostom	28
Disagrees with Chrysostom	9
Disagrees but allows Chrysostom's interpretation	1

Subject with which Calvin is dealing when mentioning Chrysostom:

Knowledge of God	1
Freedom of the will	7
Humility	1

Law	1
Repentance	1
Confession	3
God's judgments/chastisement	3
Satisfaction/supererogation/merits	5
Reprobation	1
Use of church possessions	1
Infallibility of the church	1
Discipline	2
Celibacy	1
Monasticism	1
Ordinary Sacraments	1
Baptism	1
Lord's Supper	7

What conclusions may be drawn regarding the extent of Calvin's use of Chrysostom? First, prior to 1536, Calvin had become familiar with the published works of Chrysostom, although there is little evidence that he drew from Chrysostom in support of his positions. If we take the evidence from the *Psychopannychia*, it may be argued that he had brief acquaintance with the homiletical works on Genesis, Matthew, and Hebrews; although the late publication date of this work proves the evidence to be inconclusive. With the publication of the first edition of the *Institutio*, we find only one reference to Chrysostom, and that again in a chain of patristic authorities. This latter fact, however, does not argue either for or against Calvin's growing appreciation of Chrysostom, for extensive patristic or even biblical citation was not characteristic of the 1536 edition; the vast expansion of documentation came with the publication of the successive editions of the *Institutio*. However with the 1539 edition, we find twenty-six references appearing, ten additional in the 1543 edition, and only one more with the 1559 edition. We may therefore conclude, secondly, that between the years 1536 and 1539, Calvin's knowledge of and interest in Chrysostom markedly increased. Exactly when that happened, and who introduced Calvin to the writings of Chrysostom would be interesting to pursue. The fact that Calvin moved from Geneva and settled in Strassburg by September of 1538 gives rise to the distinct possibility that Calvin came to an appreciation of Chrysostom under the tutelage of the Strassburg Reformer, Martin Bucer. It is of interest to note that Calvin, at the conclusion of his *Argumentum* to the *Commentarius in Harmoniam Evangelicam*, speaks of Bucer as his "model," an eminent teacher "who availed himself of the labors of the ancients who had traveled this road before him":[15]

Verum an operae pretium quale spero fecerim necne, iudicium ex suo usu faciant lectores. Certe adeo nullam ex novitate ipsa laudem captavi, ut libenter profitear (sicut homine ingenuo dignum est), hanc methodum ex aliorum imitatione sumptam esse. BUCERUM praesertim sanctae memoriae virum et eximium ecclesiae Dei doctorem sum imitatus, qui prae aliis non poenitendam hac in re operam meo iudicio navavit. Quemadmodum autem ipse veterum labore adiutus fuit, qui in hoc stadio eum praecesserant, ita mihi sua industria et sedulitate non parum levationis attulit. Sicubi autem ab eo dissentio (quod mihi libere, quoties necesse erat, permisi), ne ipse quidem, si superstes ageret in terra, moleste ferret.*

Whether or not I have succeeded to my expectation, the reader must decide by his own experience. So far from claiming the praise of having brought out something new, I readily acknowledge, as becomes an honest man, that I have adopted this method in imitation of others. BUCER, a man of revered memory, and an eminent teacher of the Church of God, who above all others appears to me to have labored successfully in this field, has been especially my model. As he availed himself of the labors of the ancients who had traveled this road before him, so my toils have been not a little alleviated by his industry and application. Where I use the liberty of differing from him (which I have freely done, whenever it was necessary), Bucer himself, if he were still an inhabitant of the earth, would not be displeased.

* *Commentarius in Harmoniam Evangelicam*, CO 45:4. This is Pringle's translation in Calvin, *Commentary on a Harmony of the Evangelists*, xl.

It may well be that Calvin came to his full appreciation of Chrysostom as an exegetical tutor during the Strassburg sojourn. Whether or not it was Bucer who directed Calvin's attention to Chrysostom for documentation to the issues addressed in the 1539 edition of the *Institutio*, we may with considerable justification conclude that by the time the 1 Corinthians

15. *Commentarius in Harmoniam Evangelicam*, CO 45:4.

commentary was completed, in 1546, Calvin had become eminently familiar with the Chrysostom literature.

We turn now to our third and final question: to what extent can we establish that Calvin was dealing with an actual text of Chrysostom? Here we shall attempt actual textual comparisons of Chrysostom passages quoted by Calvin.

If we examine the several references or allusions to Chrysostom made by Calvin in the body of the Corinthian commentary, we discover that Calvin rarely offers a direct quotation. Virtually every reference is a free paraphrase of Chrysostom's position, with the possible exception of the reference found in the commentary on 1 Corinthians 14:23 (chapter 4, p. 102), which at best is a "free-literal" quotation. Hence it is impossible to establish the fact that Calvin was working with an actual text of Chrysostom based on the evidence in the Corinthian commentary alone. When we turn to the *Institutio*, however, much clearer evidence can be found. For this examination, the 1530 Basel five-volume Latin edition that Erasmus prepared for Froben was used. We have chosen, for comparison, passages quoted by Calvin from six authentic works of Chrysostom, and three from spurious works attributed to Chrysostom by Calvin. The results of our findings appear in the Table of Textual Comparisons of Chrysostom Passages Quoted by Calvin (table 5.3), on the following pages. In the right-hand column appears Calvin's quotation of Chrysostom. Numerals refer to book, chapter, section, page, and line, as given in Barth-Niesel *Opera Selecta*. The left-hand column lists Chrysostom's words, following the work in which they are found.

TABLE 5.3

Textual Comparisons of Chrysostom Passages Quoted by Calvin

Chrysostom, Basel Edition, 1530	Calvin, *Institutionis*
1. *In Caput Geneseos Quartum. Homilia* 19.88.	1. *Inst.* 2.2.4. 244.34.
Saepe enim si voluerit, etiam qui malus est, mutatur, & fit bonus: & qui bonus, per ignaviam excidit, & fit malus. Quia liberi arbitrii esse nostram naturam fecit omnium dominus. Ipse enim quae sua sunt, omnia pro sua misericordia semper exhibet.	Saepe qui malus est, si voluerit, in bonum mutatur: et qui bonus, per ignaviam excidit, et fit malus; quia liberi arbitrii esse nostram naturam fecit Dominus: nec imponit necessitatem, sed congruis remediis appositis totum iacere in aegrotantis sententia sinit.

Chrysostom, Basel Edition, 1530	Calvin, *Institutionis*

2. *In Caput Geneseos Septem.*
Homilia 25.

Neque enim possibile est bonum aliquod nos recte agere, non habita superna gratia.

2. *Inst.* 2.2.4. 245.3.

Sicut nisi gratia Dei adiuti, nihil unquam possumus recte agere:

---

3. *In Ep. ad 2 Cor.* Cap. 8, 468.

Non sicut in veteri lege, partem quidem sacerdos comedebat, partem quidem populus . . . sed verum omnibus unum corpus proponitur & poculum unum. . . Ea quae sunt eucharistiae . . . communia sunt omnia.

3. *Inst.* 4.17.48. 415.08.

Non sicut in veteri lege, partem quidem sacerdos comedebat, partem populus vero . . . verum omnibus corpus unum proponitur et poculum unum. Ea quae sunt eucharistiae communia sunt omnia.

---

4. Pseudo-Chry. *In Ps. 50.* Hom. 2.5.

Peccata autem tua dicito, ut deleas illa. Si confunderis alicui dicere, quia peccasti, dicito ea quotidie in anima tua. Non dico ut confitearis conservo tuo, ut exprobret. Dicito deo, qui curat ea.

4. *Inst.* 3.4.8. 94.32.

Peccata, inquit, tua dicito, ut deleas illa; si confunderis alicui dicere quae peccasti, dicito quotidie ea in anima tua. Non dico ut confitearis conservo tuo, qui exprobret: dicito deo qui curat ea.

---

5. Pseudo-Chry. *In Ps. 50.* Hom. 2.2.

Ubi misericordia flagitatur, interrogatio cessat. Ubi misericordia postulatur, iudicium non saevit. Ubi misericordia petitur, poenae locus non est. Ubi misericordia, quaestio nulla. Ubi misericordia, condonata responsio est.

5. *Inst.* 3.4.38. 130.11.

Ubi misericordia flagitatur, interrogatio cessat: ubi misericordia postulatur, iudicium non saevit: ubi misericordia petitur, poenae locus non est: ubi misericordia, quaestio nulla: ubi misericordia, condonata responsio est.

---

6. *In Inventione Sanctae Crucis.*
Hom. 38.130.

Nam primus gradus est castitatis syncera virginitas: secundus, fidele coniugium. Ergo species secunda virginitatis, est matrimonii casta dilectio.

6. *Inst.* 4.12.28. 237.26.

Primus gradus castitatis est, syncera virginitas: secundus, fidele coniugium. Ergo species secunda virginitatis, est matrimonii casta dilectio.

---

7. *Dominica I. Adventus Domini*;
Incerto Interprete. Hom. 35.124.

Omnis enim homo naturaliter non solum peccator est, sed etiam totus peccatum.

7. *Inst.* 2.2.9. 252.05.

Quod omnis homo non modo naturaliter peccator, sed totus peccatum est.

Chrysostom, Basel Edition, 1530	Calvin, *Institutionis*
8. *De Sumentibus Indigne Divine et Sancta Mysteria.* Hom. 60, Ex Matthaeo. [Christum] non fide tantum, verum & ipsa re nos suum efficit corpus.	8. *Inst.* 4.17.6. 348.16. Christum non fide tantum, sed re ipsa nos suum efficere corpus.
9. *De Lazaro Concio.* 4.4. Cave enim homini dixeris, ne tibi opprobret. Neque enim conservo confiteris, ut in publicum proferat, sed ei qui dominus est, ei qui tui curam gerit, ei qui medicus est ostendis vulnera. . . . Non cogo te in medium prodire theatrum, ac multos adhibere testes. Mihi soli dic peccatum privatim, ut sanem ulcus.	9. *Inst.* 3.4.8. 95.14. Certe ne homini dixeris, ne tibi opprobret; neque enim conservo est confitendum, qui in publicum proferat: sed Domino qui tui curam gerit, et qui humanus est, et medicus ostende vulnera. . . . Non cogo te in medium prodire theatrum, ac multos adhibere testes: mihi soli dic peccatum tuum privatim, ut sanem ulcus.

It will be seen that of the nine comparisons shown, number five is identical. Numbers four, six, seven, eight, and nine are identical with the exceptions of either a change in the word order or the addition of just a few words by Calvin. Passage number one is not clearly parallel, although the second and third selections are close enough to suggest a Calvinian paraphrase of the Chrysostom material.

Our evidence strongly suggests that Calvin had the 1530 Basel edition of the Chrysostom *Opera* before him as he entered into his *Institutio* Chrysostomic selections. The evidence further suggests that Calvin made use of the Latin translations of Chrysostom, since Calvin's quotations of Chrysostom so closely parallel the Latin 1530 edition.

In answer to the three questions that we posed at the beginning of the chapter, we may draw together our findings with the following conclusions:

1. Through the work of Erasmus and assisting translators such as Brixius and Grynaeus, together with the publishing efforts of Froben at Basel, Calvin gained access to the *Opera* of Chrysostom, including the text of Chrysostom's Homilies on 1 Corinthians.

2. Calvin's familiarity with Chrysostom was probably not extensive prior to 1538. Following that date, Calvin's interest in and use of Chrysostom increased rapidly, perhaps under the tutelage of Bucer in Strassburg.

3. The text of Chrysostom that Calvin used was undoubtedly the 1530 Latin edition of Erasmus published by Froben at Basel.

6

Calvin's Use of Sources in the
Biblical Commentaries

T HE READER OF CHAPTER 4, in which we critically examined every
reference, implicit and explicit, that Calvin made to Chrysostom in
the 1 Corinthians commentary, may well draw conclusions regarding
Calvin as an exegete and biblical commentator that are not very compli-
mentary. Since, in chapter 5 we have established that Calvin unquestionably had access to and made use of the 1530 Basel Latin translation of the
Chrysostom *Opera*, one is prompted to ask how John Calvin, a meticulous
scholar, an indefatigable man of research, a Latinist whose competence
with the language is unquestioned, and, above all, a Reformer who celebrated antiquity, could have so inadequately represented the full import
of Chrysostom's thought on so many occasions.

For fear that the question itself appear excessively harsh, one has only
to review the results of our comparative readings of Calvin's and Chrysostom's commentaries on such verses as 5:13, 6:3, 11:20–21, 12:9, 13:2, 14:2,
and 15:29 to be assured that there are legitimate grounds for asking the
question. Indeed, such a review will prompt even further questions: Did
Calvin read Chrysostom too hastily? Did he leap to conclusions that, under scrutiny, seem unwarranted? Did Calvin make use of an intermediary
source whose representation of Chrysostom's position was considerably
less than accurate?

We shall attempt in this chapter to offer a concrete explanation for such questions. In order to do so, however, we must step back from the actual commentaries themselves and inquire into Calvin's own concept of methodological procedure as he set out to write his commentaries. An answer to this prior question of method shall throw considerable light on the many problems raised in chapter 4, Having delineated Calvin's methodology, we shall then subject a few of the more difficult problems to reexamination, in order to clarify Calvin's use of Chrysostom as the most-quoted source in the biblical commentaries.

1. Calvin's Approach to the Writing of Biblical Commentaries

One of the difficulties in attempting to elucidate Calvin's methodological approach to the task of writing commentaries is his reluctance to offer us anything resembling "prolegomena to exegesis." Just as the person attempting to write a biography of Calvin from Calvin's own autobiographical statements must consult diverse sources, so the person attempting to explicate Calvin's methodology must do so from scattered references. From such references, nevertheless, we do have clear indications informing us of the manner in which Calvin planned to proceed, what Calvin attempted to accomplish, and, equally important, what he planned to avoid. We first examine the dedicatory preface to the commentary on Paul's Letter to the Romans.

Calvin dedicated his Romans commentary to his friend Simon Grynaeus, professor of Greek first at Heidelberg and subsequently at Basel, the same Grynaeus who translated the Chrysostom homilies numbered thirty through forty-four from Greek to Latin for the Froben 1530 Chrysostom *Opera*. Calvin's preface contains much interesting material, not the least of which is Calvin's own recollection of friendly discussions between himself and Grynaeus on the subject of the best way to write biblical commentaries. Here Calvin reveals fundamental principles upon which he approached the task:[1]

---

1. *Calvinus Grynaeo*, Ep. 191, CO 10:402–3.

Memini, quum ante triennium de optimo enarrandae scripturae genere inter nos familiariter commentaremur, eam quae plurimum tibi placebat rationem mihi quoque prae aliis probatam tunc fuisse. Sentiebat enim uterque nostrum praecipuam interpretis virtutem in perspicua brevitate esse positam. Et sane, quum hoc sit prope unicum illius officium mentem scriptoris quem explicandum sumpsit patefacere, quantum ab ea lecturos abducit, tantundem a scopo suo aberrat, vel certe a suis finibus quodammodo evagatur. Itaque cupiebamus ex eorum numero, quibus in hoc laboris genere theologiam iuvare hodie propositum est, unum aliquem exstare qui et facilitati studeret, et simul daret operam ne prolixis commentariis studiosos ultra modum detineret. Quanquam autem scio sententiam hanc non apud omnes receptam esse, et eos qui non recipiunt nonnullis quoque argumentis adduci ut ita iudicent, ego tamen dimoveri non possum ab amore compendii.

I remember that three years ago we had a friendly discussion concerning the best method of interpreting Scripture. The method which you favored most of all I myself preferred to all others. Both of us felt that the chief virtue of any interpreter lies in clear brevity. And indeed, since it is his only task to unfold the mind of the writer whom he has undertaken to expound, the more he leads the reader away from the meaning of the author, the more he deviates from his own purpose, and is sure to wander from his goal. It was our wish that, out of the number of those who have at the present day proposed to advance the cause of theology in this endeavor, someone might be found who would not only strive for facility, but at the same time try not to exhaust his readers with long and wordy commentaries. At the same time, however, I know that not everyone agrees with us, and those who do not have good reasons of their own. I, however, cannot be budged from my love of brevity.

We begin here to discover Calvin's methodological orientation as he, in 1540, introduced his first biblical commentary. Calvin had discussed with his friend the best method of interpreting Scripture. Both Calvin and his scholarly friend Grynaeus had come to the firm conclusion, first of all, that of all the possible goals an author might have, the only object that a commentator must hold clearly in view is the unfolding of the mind of the biblical author. The importance of this seemingly obvious statement lies not so much in what it includes as in what it rejects. No material that might in any way distract the reader from entering into the mind and intent of the biblical author will be admitted into the body of the commentary. The inclusion of such material will only defeat the primary reason for writing a biblical commentary, and cause the reader to wander from an understanding and appreciation of the biblical text. Two requirements are therefore of utmost importance: *brevitas* and *facilitas*. By the principle of *brevitas*, Calvin wishes to avoid *prolixis commentariis*, which only exhaust the reader. By the principle of *facilitas*, Calvin wishes to avoid discussions of other commentators, and come as quickly as possible to the primary meaning of the text. *Facilitas* here does not mean either a shortcut or superficiality. It means the absence of polemic, the exclusion of protracted excursuses, the purposive omission of detailed examinations from other sources. *Brevitas* and *facilitas* combine to exclude and reject discussions that may very naturally arise from the text, but which do not belong in the body of the commentary. Calvin is fully aware of the dangers inherent in his methodology. Not everyone will agree with his format. Those who do not agree, have good reasons. But, in Calvin's own words, "as for me, I cannot be budged from my love of brevity."

Calvin wrote the dedicatory preface to the Romans commentary in 1539, having formulated his basic methodological principles, if we may trust *ante triennium* as accurate, three years earlier, in 1536. Twenty-one years later, in 1557, he still holds firmly to his basic principles, for in his preface to the commentary on the Psalms, written in the last mentioned year, he affirms:[2]

Itaque non modo simplex docendi ratio ubique a me servata est, sed quo longius abesset omnis ostentatio, a refutationibus ut plurimum abstinui, ubi liberior patebat plausibilis iactiantiae campus. Neque unquam contrarias sententias attigi, nisi ubi periculum erat ne tacendo dubios ac perplexos relinquerem lectores.	I have maintained throughout not only a simple style of teaching, but, in order to be removed as far as possible from all ostentation, I have abstained for the most part from the refutation of others, although this would have presented much opportunity for plausible display. Neither have I mentioned opinions opposed to mine, unless there was danger that my silence would leave my readers in doubt or perplexed.

2. *Commentarii in Librum Psalmorum*, CO 31:33–34.

Nec me latet quanto suaviores multissint illecebrae, ex multiplici congerie suggerere materiam ambitiosi splendoris: sed nihil pluris fuit, quam ecclesiae aedificationi consulere. Faxit Deus, qui mihi hunc animum dedit, ut successus etiam respondeat.

I am aware, of course, that many would have been more delighted and allured had I heaped together a mass of glittering material in a great show. But I hold nothing to be of more importance than the edification of the Church. Nay God, who gave me strength, grant its success.

Here we not only see that Calvin has rigidly maintained his earlier established methodology, but also discover confirmation for our understanding of what Calvin meant by *brevitas* and *facilitas*. If Calvin will mention, in the body of his commentaries, the opinion of other authors, contemporary or ancient, it will never be for the purpose of examining in detail or painting a full and complete picture of their interpretations. Calvin's method will not allow him first to exhaust the interpretations offered by near or distant authorities. Even though Calvin is thoroughly familiar with historic and contemporary debates regarding the possible interpretations of any given text, he will not allow himself the pleasure of demonstrating his erudition by including such voluminous material in his commentaries. He will come straight to his own studied and considered opinion. To be sure, ancient and modern authorities will be mentioned, but only in the briefest possible manner, only to crystallize an opinion with which Calvin may agree. If an opinion of an author with whom Calvin disagrees is at all included, the author and his opinion will be given fleeting reference and summarily dismissed, not for fear of challenge, not on the grounds of inadequate documentation, but for the sake of the reader who should not be drawn into polemical examination but kept as near as possible to the mind and thought of the biblical author.

Calvin did not arrive at his method in a vacuum. He studied the commentaries of others, and, typically, attempts to steer a *via media* between two extremes. In order to demonstrate this, we must return to the Romans dedicatory. There, offering his own justification for attempting a commentary on Romans, Calvin enlarges upon the fact that many scholars of preeminent learning have devoted their abilities to an explanation and interpretation of Paul's epistle. Among his contemporaries, Calvin singles out two who, in his opinion, have produced significant work. He praises the writing of Philipp Melanchthon, but then adds the following interesting objection:[3]

Sed quia illi propositum modo fuisse apparet, quae inprimis essent animadversione digna excutere, in iis dum immoratur multa consulto praeterit, quae vulgare ingenium fatigare nonnihil possint.	But he [Melanchthon] evidently set himself to examine closely only those matters that were worthy of his own attention. He stopped with these, and deliberately passed by a great deal that could somewhat trouble the ordinary mind.

Calvin faults Melanchthon, not on the grounds of writing *prolixi commentarii*, but on the opposite extreme, a bias for certain portions of Scripture rather than producing a continuous commentary. Melanchthon expounds on only those portions of Scripture that he considers relevant *loci*, and in so doing omits many portions of Scripture important for the presentation of a balanced commentary. Melanchthon's method is open to the accusation of arbitrary selection.

Following a passing "tip of the hat" to Bullinger, Calvin remarks on the work of Bucer. There is no contemporary biblical commentator who receives more adulation than Bucer:[4]

Tandem Bucerus lucubrationibus suis emissis veluti colophonem imposuit. Siquidem vir ille, ut nosti, praeter reconditam eruditionem copiosamque multarum rerum scientiam, praeter ingenii perspicaciam, multam lectionem aliasque multas ac varies virtutes, quibus a nemine fere hodie vincitur, cum paucis est conferendus, plurimos antecellit, hanc sibi propriam laudem habet quod nullus hac memoria exactiore diligentia in scripturae interpretatione versatus est.	Finally there is Bucer, who said just about the last word on the subject with the publication of his writings. He is a man of profound learning, abundant knowledge, keenness of intellect, wide reading, and many other varied excellences in which he is surpassed by hardly anyone at the present day, equaled by few, and superior to very many. I can think of no one who has turned to the exposition of Scripture with equal diligence and precision.

3. *Calvinus Grynaeo*, Ep. 191, CO 10:404.

4. Ibid., CO 10:404.

Although Calvin has nothing but praise for his mentor in Strassburg, he nevertheless finds fault with Bucer's methodology as a biblical commentator:[5]

Bucerus et prolixior est quam ut ab hominibus aliis occupationibus districtis raptim legi, et sublimior quam [ut] ab humilibus et non valde attentis intelligi facile queat. Nam ad cuiuscunque argumenti tractationem se contulit, tam multa illi ad manum suggeruntur ab incredibili qua pollet ingenii foecunditate, ut manum de tabula tollere nesciat.	Bucer is too verbose to be read quickly by those who have other matters to deal with, and too profound to be easily understood by less intelligent and attentive readers. Whatever the subject with which he is dealing, so many subjects are suggested to him by his unbelievably forceful and fecund mind, that he does not know how to take his hands off the paper.

Although there is no author who can surpass Bucer as far as *content* is concerned, it is with Bucer's *method* that Calvin takes serious objection. Bucer's "forceful and fecund mind" suggests so many subjects that, regardless of the issue to which he addresses himself, "he cannot take his hands off the paper."

Hence Calvin arrives at his *via media*. Melanchthon's method is not satisfactory for he has selected only those texts for his commentary that, to him, seemed to be of worth. Melanchthon has failed to expound the entire text. Bucer's method is not satisfactory because he has done just the opposite, writing too much, exhausting the reader. Calvin, therefore, will write a continuous commentary at the expense of repetition, and be guided by the principles of *brevitas* and *facilitas*, at the expense of full treatment of other authors. Calvin tells us that he has considered including larger references to the interpretations of former and contemporary authors, but for the sake of readers who are easily distracted, hesitant to form an opinion, and do not have a solid basis for establishing sound judgment, he will proceed directly to what he considers to be the best interpretation:[6]

---

5. Ibid. For the insight into Calvin's division of labor between *loci communes* and the continual interpretation of Scripture in the commentaries, I am indebted to T. H. L. Parker, who raises the issue in *Calvin's New Testament Commentaries*, 49–50.

6. *Calvinus Grynaeo*, Ep. 191, CO 10:404–5.

verum quia illi non raro inter se variant, atque ea res multam praebet difficultatem lectoribus parum acutis, dum haesitant cuius sententiae potius debeant assentiri: putavi hunc quoque laborem non poenitendum fore, si optimam interpretationem indicando sublevarem eos a iudicandi molestia, quibus non stasis firmum est a se ipsis iudicium.	These writers, however, frequently vary from one another and this fact creates much difficulty for simpleminded readers, who are hesitant as to which opinion they ought to accept. I thought, therefore, that I should not regret having undertaken this task, if, by pointing to the best interpretation, I relieved them of the trouble of forming a judgment, especially those whose judgment does not stand on firm ground.

Our observations thus far are important for a proper understanding of Calvin as a biblical commentator, with particular regard for Calvin's use of Chrysostom, and others, as exegetical and interpretative sources. We would like to contend, furthermore, that these observations are crucial for an adequate appreciation of Calvin's entire theological enterprise, at least insofar as Calvin's methodological intent is concerned. Calvin's program, the format in which he intends to offer a theology based on Scripture, is most clearly seen in his *Epistola ad Lectorem*, which first appeared in the 1539 edition of the *Institutes*, just one year prior to the publication of his first biblical commentary. In this celebrated *Epistle* to the reader of the *Institutes*, Calvin begins by relating the *Institutes* to Scripture. Calvin has so arranged "the sum of religion" in the *Institutes* in such a manner that those interested in the pursuit of theology will have no difficulty with the complexities of Scripture:[7]

---

7. *Epistola ad Lectorem*, OS 3:6.

Porro hoc mihi in isto labore propositum fuit, sacrae Theologiae candidatos ad divini verbi lectionem ita praeparare et instruere, ut et facilem ad eam aditum habere, et inoffenso in ea gradu pergere queant; siquidem religionis summam omnibus partibus sic mihi complexus esse videor, et eo quoque ordine digessisse, ut siquis eam recte tenuerit, ei non sit difficile statuere et quid potissimum quaerere in Scriptura, et quem in scopum quicquid in ea continetur referre debeat.

Moreover, it has been my purpose in this labor to prepare and instruct candidates in sacred theology for the reading of the divine Word, in order that they may be able both to have easy access to it, and to advance in it without stumbling. For I believe I have so embraced the sum of religion in all its parts, and have arranged it in such an order, that if anyone rightly grasps it, it will not be difficult for him to determine what he ought especially to seek in Scripture, and to what end he ought to relate its contents.

Now, however, as Calvin continues, his mind shifts from the relationship between the *Institutes* and Scripture to the relationship between the *Institutes* and his commentaries:[8]

Itaque, hac veluti strata via, siquas posthac Scripturae enarrationes edidero, quia non necesse habebo de dogmatibus longas disputationes instituere, et in locos communes evagari: eas compendio semper astringam. Ea ratione, magna molestia et fastidio pius lector sublevabitur: modo praesentis operis cognitione, quasi necessario instrumento, praemunitus accedat. Sed quia huius instituti specimen praebebunt commentarii in Epistolam ad Romanos, re ipsa malo declarare quale sit, quam verbis praedicare.

If, after this road has, as it were been paved, I shall publish any interpretations of Scripture, I shall always condense them, because I shall have no need to undertake long doctrinal discussions, and to digress into *loci communes*. By this method, the godly reader will be spared great annoyance and boredom, provided he approaches [the commentaries] armed with a knowledge of the present work, as a necessary tool. But because the commentary on the Epistle to the Romans will furnish an example of this intention, I prefer to let this book speak for itself rather than forecast it by words.

8. *Epistola ad Lectorem*, CO 1:255–56.

This latter portion of the *Epistola* not only confirms what Calvin has elsewhere said regarding the use of his sources in the commentaries; but, in an incredible economy of words, also clarifies his intention with respect to his total theological program. As of the 1539 writing of this *Epistola*, Calvin has not produced, or at least not published, any biblical commentaries. Granted time, his commentaries that he shall produce will always be condensed and kept as brief as possible (*eas compendio semper astringam*); for in the commentaries there will be no need to digress into *loci communes*. That important function—the necessity of argumentation with the opinions of others, the refutation of errant interpretations of Scripture, and the polemic against deviant practices that have evolved from such errors—will be met in the *Institutes*. What Calvin intends, and indeed accomplished, is the separation into two works of that which made Bucer's commentaries prolix. Thus, the *Institutes* and the commentaries are two inseparable halves of the whole. This is a conscious and critical methodological step, but is taken for one important expedient (*ea ratione*): by this method the godly reader of the commentaries will be spared *molestia* and *fastidio*, annoyance and boredom. Calvin's reluctance to talk about method is seen as he concludes his letter. An example of his method will be seen fully when the commentary on Romans is published, and rather than elaborate on his method further, he will allow the forthcoming commentary to speak for itself.

Calvin well appreciated the necessity for doctrinal elaboration; he saw the necessity of Bucerian excursuses, refutation, and polemic. Standing apart from Bucer, however, and quite possibly as justification for producing his own commentaries, he will adopt another method, separating lengthy digressions from the Scriptural commentaries so that the reader of the latter might not be unduly taxed and burdened.

As far as the commentaries themselves are concerned, Calvin adopts a methodological *via media* between Melanchthon and Bucer. The commentaries will be continuous, but no digressions into *loci communes* will be allowed. Their guiding principles will be *brevitas* and *facilitas*. Is it not exactly here that we gain insight into Calvin's appreciation of John Chrysostom? It is an appreciation not only of content but in particular of method. Chrysostom, in Calvin's own words, "never veered to the right or to the left of the clear and straightforward meaning of Scripture." Of all the Fathers, Chrysostom is singular in his avoidance of doctrinal digressions and long excursuses that detract the reader from the clear meaning of Scripture. To be sure, Chrysostom is, according to Calvin, deficient in doctrine, as we have pointed out in chapter 3. He preached free-will to excess. Election is confused with the person's own efforts. To works he assigns a disproportionate emphasis. He cannot be compared to Augustine as a teacher of doctrine. But Augustine cannot be compared with Chrysostom as a biblical expositor. Methodologically, Augustine fell into the same trap as did Bucer. Both Augustine and Bucer did not restrict themselves in their biblical commentaries to the simple clarification of Scripture. Of Augustine, again and again Calvin will say: "What Augustine says is true, but it is not relevant to this passage."[9] "This is a godly observation, but it has nothing to do with Paul's meaning."[10] Augustine is *ultra modum argutus*.[11] But as a biblical interpreter, "the outstanding merit of our author Chrysostom is:[12]

quod ubique illi summo studio fuit a germana scripturae sinceritate ne minimum quidem deflectere, ac nullam sibi licentiam sumere in simplici verborum sensu contorquendo.	that it was his supreme concern always not to turn aside even to the slightest degree from the genuine, simple sense of Scripture, and to allow himself no liberties by twisting the plain meaning of the words.

Is this not an expression of methodological appreciation? Calvin will not always agree with Chrysostom's meaning of biblical words. He will not always adopt Chrysostom's final interpretation of a passage. Certainly he will not always agree with the doctrinal implication of Chrysostom's rendering of the text. But methodologically, there is none better. As an example of the way in which biblical interpretations should be offered to the common people, Chrysostom reigns supreme. Chrysostom has avoided the "picking and choosing" method of Melanchthon by rendering a continuous commentary on Scripture. He has avoided the *prolixi commentarii* of Bucer. Chrysostom represents, for Calvin, the best of one

---

9. *Comm. ad Cor. 1*, CO 49:159.

10. Ibid., CO 49:92.

11. *Praef. in Chry. Hom.*, CO 9:835; trans.: "over subtle" or "too verbose in his method."

12. Ibid.

side of the *via media* that Calvin embarked upon in his total theological enterprise. Thus Calvin can write:[13]

Certe haec mihi plus satis ius- ta excusatio est, quod causam habeo cum Chrysostomo coniunctam, quia nihil aliud quam cum plebe communico quae ille plebi nominatim inscripsit.	At least I myself am more than sufficiently justified in that I have common cause with Chrysostom, because I am doing nothing else than communicate to the people the things that he addressed specifically to the people.

We must examine one further document that will throw additional light on Calvin's methodological approach to the task of writing biblical commentaries. In October of 1554, Franciscus Burghardus, Chancellor to the Dukes of Saxony and one-time professor of Greek at the University of Wittenberg, wrote Calvin a letter complaining, among other matters:[14]

Qui aiunt te tuam opinionem diversam a sententia eccle- siarum nostrarum de coena Domini alicubi adspersisse, et summi viri Lutheri, piae memoriae, versionem et inter- pretationem in eosdem Mosis libros editam variis in locis odiose perstringere et insectari.	There are those who say that you have spread a different opinion from the judgment of our churches on the subject of the Lord's Supper, and that you have, in various places, angrily reproached and reviled the translation and interpretation of the books of Moses by that greatest of men, Luther, of pious memory.

Calvin had dedicated his second *Treatise on the Sacraments* to the church-es of Saxony and Germany, a dedication not received with overwhelming gratitude on the grounds that Calvin differed with Luther, not only on the Lord's Supper itself, but also on matters of interpretation regarding the books of Moses. In Calvin's response dated March 3, 1555, he dealt rather quickly with Burghardus's charge that an opinion on the Lord's Supper had been given that was at variance with the judgment of the churches of Saxony:[15]

13. Ibid., CO 9:833.

14. *Burghardus Calvino*, Ep. 2025, CO 15:260.

15. *Calvinus Burkardo*, Ep. 2123, CO 15:454.

Si quod dogma impium repre-
hendissent, nollem aequitatis
praetextu mihi parci. Sed ne
ipsi quidem id mihi obiicere
audebunt. In sacramentis non
consentimus, nempe quia ego
crassis loquendi formulis,
quas pertinacia magis quam
ratione urgent, ad verbum non
succino. Neque enim conce-
dam quemquam ipsorum esse
qui vim et usum finemque
sacramentorum splendidius
commendet, qui eorum dig-
nitatem ornet locupletius, qui
denique maiorem illis rever-
entiam conciliet. Verum quia
brevis huius causae explicatio,
quam tibi offeret nuncius,
omnem dubitationem eximet,
supervacuo sermone hom-
inem summo iudicio praeditum non morabor.

If they discovered in my doctrine on
the Lord's Supper any impious dogma, I would not wish to be spared
under the pretext of acquiescence.
Not even they themselves will dare to
reproach me with that. But we do not
agree in our view of the sacraments,
because I do not chime in with them
to the letter in their coarse manner
of expressions, which they insist on,
more from obstinacy than reason.
For I will not grant that there is any
of them who commends in higher
terms, the efficacy, use, and intention
of the sacraments, or who sets forth
more copiously their dignity, or
who brings to them more reverence.
But because a short explanation of
my reasons, which the messenger
will offer you, will clear up all your
doubts, I will not take up the time of
a man endowed with the greatest of
judgment by superfluous discourse.

But Calvin reacted even more vigorously to the charge that he did not always subscribe to the interpretations of Luther. This was an attack, not on an interpretation of doctrine, which would be answered in the communication sent with the bearer of Calvin's reply, but on something even more crucial than doctrinal differences, namely, the freedom of an interpreter to render his opinion independently. Calvin meets this challenge head on, and in so doing, reiterates his method with regard to citations in the body of his commentaries:[16]

---

16. Ibid.

Restat iam alterum crimen, quod non ubique Lutheri interpretationibus subscribam. Verum si iam cuique interpreti non licebit de singulis scripturae locis quod sentit in medium proferre, quorsum servitutis recidimus? Imo, si mihi usquam a Lutheri sententia discedere non licuit, munus interpretandi suscipere absurdum fuit ac ridiculum. Hoc modo videndum erat, an cupide accersam diversos sensus, an proterve exagitem, an odiose perstringam, an contumeliose insecter. Tu vero, ornatissime vir, si tantum suppeteret otii, totum librum perlegendo nihil tale reperies, quin potius, ubi videris me parce et sobrie attingere quae alius quispiam ostentationi deditus clamose iactasset, si quid ab aliis erratum est, vel tacitis nominibus vel sine contumelia reprehendere, et quidem silentio errores sepelire nisi dum ita cogit necessitas, modestiam cum humanitate coniunctam laudabis. Hoc quidem testari licet, nihil mihi fuisse propositum nisi ut publicae lectorum utilitati consulerem, quibus saepe in hallucinationem proclivis est lapsus, nisi admoniti caveant.

There remains now another charge, that I do not always subscribe to the interpretations of Luther. But now, if each interpreter is not allowed, in individual passages of Scripture, to bring forward his opinion, into what sort of slavery shall we have returned? Indeed, if I am not free to dissent from Luther's opinions, it would be absurdity bordering on the ridiculous to undertake the task of interpretation. The crucial point to be examined here is whether I was avidly seeking different meanings, whether I had wantonly attacked or spitefully carped or insultingly reviled them with abuse. Surely, most honored sir, if you will only take the trouble to read the whole book, you will find no such thing, but rather you will discover that I mention sparingly and soberly things which anyone fond of ostentation would clamor about. If others have erred, I reprove them with due respect to great names and without invective. I even bury in silence many mistakes unless when compelled by necessity I must do otherwise. You have good reason to commend both my modesty and my gentleness. It must certainly be affirmed that I have rendered no interpretation that would not benefit my readers, who are all too susceptible to wanderings of the mind, unless they are warned to be on their guard.

"Sparingly and soberly" and without the ostentation some clamor about— such is Calvin's mind-set when the opinions of others are to be mentioned in the commentaries. Here again is confirmed Calvin's basic disposition.

As a methodological principle Calvin will strive to omit the opinions of those with whom he does not agree. Even the opinions of those with whom he does agree will receive the briefest treatment. When referring to or citing the interpretations of contemporary or earlier scholars, Calvin's entire disposition is not exhaustive treatment, but brevity; it is not complete documentation, but sparsity. Where other authors are cited by name, only a portion of the total picture they have painted is alluded to, so that the reader is not distracted. For the most part, their names are unrevealed or cloaked in anonymity by such words as *alii* or *quidam*. An interpretation of a biblical passage by Chrysostom, Augustine, or Jerome that in their original may cover a page, will, in Calvin's commentary, be distilled in a sentence or two. The danger inherent in crystallizing the interpretations of near or distant commentators is risked with full knowledge that an incomplete picture may well be offered, yet the principles of *brevitas* and *facilitas* will be strictly adhered to, so that the commentator does not wander from his primary goal of introducing the reader to the mind of the biblical author.

2. Examples of Calvin's Procedure as Applied to John Chrysostom

Having examined Calvin's methodological principles, we must finally ask whether the employment of such principles clarifies, if not answers, the serious questions raised in chapter 4 regarding Calvin's representation of Chrysostom's position. We have selected a few of the more difficult problems there raised, as the basis for our reexamination. One methodological step of our own should be observed at this point. In order to establish as clearly as possible Chrysostom's interpretation of a given text, we quoted Chrysostom in the Greek. Now that we have established Calvin's use of the 1530 Basel Latin translation, we shall employ that text when citing Calvin's use of the Chrysostom material.

Let us first turn to the problem raised in connection with 1 Corinthians 5:13. There Paul, dealing with an issue of fornication in the Corinthian church, admonishes the congregation to maintain its purity by excising corrupt members. Verse 13b summarizes Paul's attitude to the fornicator: *eiicite scelestum ex vobis ipsis.* When Calvin comments on the verse, he observes that Chrysostom "compares the strictness of the Law with the clemency of the Gospel, because:[17]

17. *Comm. ad Cor. 1*, CO 49:387.

Paulus excommunicatione contentus fuit in eo scelere, de quo lex capitis poenam exigeret, nulla est ratio. Neque enim iudices gladio armatos Paulus alloquitur, sed inermem turmam, cui tantum fraterna correctio permissa erat.

Paul was content that the crime be dealt with by excommunication, whereas the law demanded the death penalty for it. But there is no justification for that view. For here, Paul is not speaking to judges armed with the sword, but to an unarmed company, allowed to use only brotherly reproof.

Now, it is absolutely true that Chrysostom makes the distinction between the severity of the punishment under the Old Covenant and the less severe correction meted out in this instance from the New Covenant. He even asks the question, why the lines were drawn one way in the former instance, and another way in the latter? He answers:[18]

Propter duas has causas: primam quidem, quod ad maius certamem hi vocabantur, & amiore indigebant patientia; alteram aut probabiliorem, quod hi facilius ab impunitate ad poenitentiam dirigebant, illi ad malitiam graviorem festinabant.

For the following two reasons. One because these were led into a greater trial, and needed greater endurance. The other, and more probable reason, because these by their impunity were more easily corrected, while the former hastened toward grievous malice.

Calvin is correct in observing that Chrysostom compares the strictness of the Law with the clemency of the Gospel. What troubled us repeatedly in our review of Calvin's use of Chrysostom was the question of why Calvin only drew a partial picture of Chrysostom's thought, and here is, if you will, a *locus classicus* of the problem. Calvin does not find it necessary to represent in his brief allusion to Chrysostom the Antiochene's extremely balanced treatment of the relationship between the two covenants. Chrysostom has no sooner made the observation to which Calvin alludes than he takes considerable pains to demonstrate that the covenants are in every way akin to each other and are derived from one and the same source. Further, according to Chrysostom, one may find many examples

18. Chrysostom, *In Epistolam Pauli ad Corinthios Primam* (1530), Hom. 16, 227. Hereafter cited as *EPCP, 1530*.

of more severe punishment in the New Testament than one discovers in the Old Testament. Also, in *both* covenants, one may find punishments following immediately upon the transgressions, as well as following the transgressions after a long interval. In support of his position, Chrysostom cites David of the Old Testament and Ananias of the New Testament:[19]

Siquidem in veteri testamento, adulterio & caede commissa, David per poenitentia saluatus est: & in novo exiguum quiddam ex agri precio auserens Ananias cum uxore periit. Quod si in veteri plura sunt punitionis exempla, in novo aut misericordiae, personarum differentia huius dispensationis differentia facit.	Thus in the Old Testament, David, who had committed adultery and murder, was saved by means of repentance. In the New Testament, Ananias, who took but a small portion of the land, perished together with his wife. Now if these instances are more frequent in the Old Testament, and those of the contrary kind are more frequent in the New, the difference of the persons produces the difference in the treatment in the two dispensations.

In order to avoid the conclusion that the Old Covenant is indicative of severity and the New of leniency, Chrysostom cites David who, following both murder and adultery, was forgiven; and Ananias who, following theft, perished. For Chrysostom, it is the difference in the persons involved, and not the difference in the dispensations, that produces the difference in punishment. With clarity and by way of examples, Chrysostom paints a balanced picture of the relationship between the two covenants. In one sense, therefore, Calvin may be challenged when he flatly observes that Chrysostom "compares the strictness of the Law with the clemency of the Gospel." Such a statement manifestly does not represent Chrysostom's full position.

The reason why Calvin drew only a partial picture of Chrysostom's thought is clarified by our conclusions regarding Calvin's methodological principles. Calvin's intention here is not to investigate Chrysostom's opinion on the matter and incorporate his finding in the body of his commentary. Rather, and characteristically, Calvin raises an issue, based on partial documentation to an ancient source, against which he wishes to warn his reader. If Calvin were here dealing with a studied consideration of the

19. Ibid.

relationship between the Old and New Covenants, and cited Chrysostom as an example of one who understood the Old Covenant in terms of severity and the New Covenant in terms of gentleness, there would be little difficulty supporting the contention that Calvin is superficial in his documentation to the point of being in error. But Calvin's interest here is not a discussion of the relationship between the covenants, but only to warn the reader, with brevity, facility, and without reference to historic debates or personages, against the conclusion that the New Covenant is considerably more lenient than the Old Covenant. To that end, he makes use of a single sentence in the body of Chrysostom's commentary that might suggest such a conclusion, and then refutes that conclusion.

We may perhaps clearly state the matter using a device Calvin himself frequently employs. It is as if Calvin thought, "some of my readers may conclude, since Paul's words are based on an Old Testament law (Deut 17:7), that Paul's solution to the problem is considerably less severe than the sentence of death imposed under the Old Covenant. But Chrysostom has already raised that issue, and it does not apply here, because Paul is not speaking to judges armed with the sword, but to a congregation allowed to use only brotherly reproof." In such a manner, Calvin introduces Chrysostom, not by way of offering an analysis of Chrysostom's understanding or interpretation, but by way of raising an issue against which Calvin wishes to speak.

Our contention that Calvin makes use of Chrysostom in the commentaries in the manner thus far described is further substantiated when we examine Calvin's comments on the word ἀγγέλους in 1 Corinthians 6:3. Paul asks, "Do you not know that we shall judge angels, not to mention everyday affairs?" Calvin notes that this passage is understood in various ways, and adds the following:[20]

Chrysostom refert, a quibusdam de sacerdotibus intelligi, sed illud est nimis coactum.	Chrysostom reports that some understand it as referring to priests, but this is forced indeed.

We are not told whether Chrysostom adopts such an interpretation, or similarly finds the notion that *angelos*, as referring to priests, is forced.

20. *Comm. ad Cor. 1*, CO 49:389.

As we have already shown,[21] Chrysostom, having raised the idea, rejects it immediately:[22]

Nescitis quoniam angelos iudicabimus, quanto magis secularia. Quidam hoc in loco inquiunt, sacerdotes signifi-cari: sed absit. De daemonibus enim ei sermo est, de malis autem sacerdotibus tunc locutus est, cum inquit, Quoniam in vobis iudicatur mundus.	Do you not know that we shall judge angels? How much more, then, the things that pertain to this life? Some say that here the priests are hinted at, but away with this. His speech is about demons. For had he been speaking about corrupt priests, he would have meant them above when he said, "the world is judged by you."

And further on,[23]

sed de illis loquitur angelis, de quibus Christus inquit, Discedite in ignem praepara-tum diabolo & angelis eius.	but he speaks concerning those angels about whom Christ said, "Depart into the fire prepared for the devil and his angels."

Here again we note the peculiar use of Chrysostom as an ancient reference in Calvin's commentaries. That Chrysostom's name is introduced into the body of the commentary is, in no way, an indication that Calvin means here to examine Chrysostom's position in complete or full treatment. The Antiochene's name is introduced almost as an aside, by way of saying that the idea of interpreting *angelos* as priests has already been raised, and the idea is far-fetched. Calvin's notation is not so much a comment on Chrysostom, whose position he does not feel called upon even to mention, as on the notion that some interpreters have understood *angelos* as referring to "priests." In fact, after mentioning several possible means of interpreting the text, the final conclusion to which Calvin comes is exactly that of Chrysostom's; but even here Chrysostom's name is not mentioned. This does not mean that Calvin has borrowed an idea without giving credit where credit is due. The foundation upon which Calvin draws his conclusions is considerably more grammatical and philological than

21. Chap. 4, p. 77.
22. *EPCP, 1530*, Hom. 16, 228.
23. Ibid.

simply adopting the interpretation of even so well respected an authority as Chrysostom. After rejecting the notion that *angelos* refers to priests, Calvin raises another possibility, and here we may note that Calvin refers now to no source in particular, but simply the frequently found word *alii* is employed:[24]

Alii de angelis coelestibus exponunt, hoc sensu, quod verbi Dei iudicio angeli subiaceant, et a nobis, si opus sit, per hoc verbum iudicari possint.	Others explain it as the heavenly angels, in this sense, that angels are subject to judgment by the Word of God, and, if need be, they can be judged by us through that Word.

At first glance, Calvin observes, such an explanation does not appear to be *a contextu Pauli*. Yet Calvin's final decision on the meaning of the text rests on further considerations:[25]

sed quia Paulus hic in futuro tanquam de extremo die loquitur, et actuale (ut vulgo dicitur) iudicium verba sonant: mea quidem opinione, angelos apostatas intelligere satius est. Neque enim minus quadrabi targumentum, hoc modo: daemones, qui ex origine adeo nobili orti sunt, et nunc quoque postquam exciderunt suo principatu creaturae sunt immortales et corruptibili mundo superiores, iudicabimus.	But as Paul uses the future tense here, referring to the last day, and as the words carry the sound of an actual judgment, as one commonly says, it would certainly seem better to me to understand what he says as referring to the apostate angels. For the argument will be no less conclusive in this way: Devils, who sprang from so illustrious an origin, and even now, when they have fallen from their high estate, are immortal creatures, and superior to this corruptible world, shall be judged by us.

Calvin grounds his interpretation of *angelos* as *angelos apostatos* on grammatical principles and the context; Paul uses the future tense, and the words carry the suggestion of an actual judgment, all of which is not *a contextu Pauli*. Calvin agrees with and even adopts the interpretation offered by Chrysostom, yet the final decision is derived not from any ill-

24. *Comm. ad Cor. 1*, CO 49:389.
25. Ibid.

documented borrowings, but from a studied consideration of the text as Calvin strives to enter into the mind of Paul.

When we move to an examination of the commentaries by both Calvin and Chrysostom on the Lord's Supper as given in 1 Corinthians 11:20–21, we are surprised to find that even though Calvin cites Chrysostom, there is little use of the Chrysostomic material and insights. To be sure, Calvin consults Chrysostom for an explanation of the abuse of the Lord's Supper by which the sacred meal became profaned. Calvin understands Chrysostom to be of the opinion that the abuse originated in the love feasts, and that[26]

quum divites soliti essent domo afferre unde promiscue cum pauperibus et in commune epularentur: postea exclusis pauperibus soli de suis lautitiis ingurgitare coeperunt.	While the rich had been accustomed to bring with them from their houses the means of feasting with the poor indiscriminately and in common, they afterwards began to exclude the poor, and to guzzle over their delicacies by themselves.

Yet there is little penetration into Chrysostom's thought or reflections on this verse. As we have shown in chapter 4.[27] Calvin understands the problem to which Paul is speaking as the preservation of a pure and spiritual feast from the corrupting influences of common and profane meals. More than that, they should be excluded from the Sacrament who are not properly prepared.

Chrysostom, on the other hand, understands Paul to be admonishing the Corinthians to be more inclusive. When Paul says, "it is not the Supper of the Lord that you eat," he means that the Corinthians were separating themselves off, making a supper which ought to be common into an affair that was private in character. The 1530 Basel text of Chrysostom is quite clear on this interpretation:[28]

26. *Comm. ad Cor. 1*, CO 49:482.
27. Pages 86–91.
28. *EPCP, 1530*, Hom. 27, 288–89.

Deinde interpretatur, quomodo non est dominicam coenam
manducare. Unusquisque
enim suam coenam praesumit
ad manducandum, & alius
guide esurit, alius est ebbrius.)
Vides quomodo eos se amiori
ignominia afficere ostendit.
Quod enim dominicum est,
privatum faciunt. Itaque ipsi
primi sunt ignominia affecti,
qui a mesa sua maxima abstu-
lerunt dignitatem. Quo nam
pacto. Quoniam dominica
coena, hoc est, domini, debet
esse communis. Quae enim
domini sunt, non huius sunt
servi, non alterius, sed omnibus communia. Quod enim
dominicum est, idem & commune. Nam si domini tui est,
quemadmodum est, non debes
tanquam propria titi a umere,
sed tanquam res domini com-
muniter omnibus proponere.
Siquidem hoc est dominicum,
nunc autem non sinis esse
commune, sed tibi comedis.

Next he explains how "it is not possible to eat the Lord's Supper." "For
when you come to the supper, each
one takes his own supper before
the other, and one is hungry, and
another is drunk.") Do you see how
he intimates that they were disgrac-
ing themselves? For that which is the
Lord's, they make a private matter, so
that they themselves are the first to
suffer indignity, depriving their own
table of its greatest dignity. How and
in what manner? Because the Lord's
Supper, that is, the Master's, ought to
be common. For the property of the
master belongs not to this servant
without belonging to that servant, but
must be in common to all. Thus, by
"the Lord's Supper," he expresses this,
the community of the feast. If it is the
Master's, as assuredly it is, you ought
not to withdraw it as private, but since
it belongs to your Lord and Master,
you ought to set it in common before
all. For this is the meaning of "the
Lord's." But now you do not allow it
to be the Lord's, not allowing it to be
common, but feasting all by yourself.

In accordance with our observations on Calvin's methodological principles, we have here a clear example of the way in which Calvin does *not*
use Chrysostom. There is much material in Chrysostom's commentary on
this single verse against which Calvin would take considerable exception.
Calvin would not allow the inclusiveness of the Lord's Supper, as expli-
cated by Chrysostom. Calvin understands Paul to be speaking about the
necessity of purity with respect to the sacraments, and not about conduct
at a love feast. But all such matters are buried in silence in the commentaries. For Calvin, the place for such debate is the *Institutes*, although on this
particular subject of the "commonality" of the Lord's Supper, Calvin does

not debate with Chrysostom. For that very reason, one would expect to find a rebuttal of Chrysostom's position in the commentaries, the lack of which even further suggests Calvin's restraint. Since Calvin explicitly mentions Chrysostom's name as a source for understanding one of the problems connected with the Supper, it is fair to assume Calvin has consulted Chrysostom on the interpretation of the verse. Yet there is not a hint of debate with Chrysostom in the body of Calvin's discussion on Paul's meaning. In chapter 4, we raised the question, since Calvin quotes or cites Chrysostom constantly throughout the 1 Corinthians commentary, takes pains to point out those places where he is in disagreement with Chrysostom over fine points of grammar, and has apparently read Chrysostom's interpretation of these words of Paul, why does Calvin not offer a rebuttal? The reason is now clear. As a methodological principle, Calvin will not allow himself the pleasure of protracted debate in the commentary.[29] Where Calvin is in disagreement with the Antiochene, for his purposes in the commentaries, Calvin will not include polemical material. If anything distracts the reader from the primary objective, namely, entering into the mind of Paul as Calvin understood it, it will be omitted.

The distinctive use of sources with whom Calvin disagreed and the unflinching practice in the commentaries of not becoming entangled in disputes also provide an answer to the problem raised in connection with the word *pistis*. We noted[30] that, for Chrysostom, Paul employs the word *pistis* as meaning the ability to perform miracles, and that *pistis* does not mean doctrinal faith. Moreover, that Paul is not here referring to doctrinal faith means that he is referring to a faith superior to doctrinal faith. For Chrysostom, *pistis* is the "faith that can move mountains"; it is the faith the apostles prayed for when they said, "increase our faith."

29. The reason Calvin adopts the interpretation that Paul has in mind the reproving of an abuse that had crept in among the Corinthians, namely, the confusion of ordinary banquets with sacred feasts, which should be kept holy and spiritual, would be interesting to pursue. Such a question would need to be answered in connection with Calvin's manifest Augustinian position on the Supper, in the light of Bucer's influence on Calvin, and in connection with Calvin's growing concern with church discipline. The question of whether the Lord's Supper should be maintained in its purity, from which the undeserving should be excluded, or whether the greatest dignity of the Supper lies in its inclusiveness is of course an unsettled issue. For our purposes here, we have confined ourselves to an examination of the methodological principles employed by Calvin as he sets himself the task of writing biblical commentaries.

30. Ibid.

For Chrysostom, the fact that *pistis* here does not embrace doctrinal faith means that Paul has in mind the highest faith possible.

Calvin also qualifies the word *pistis*, and, as with Chrysostom, Calvin understands Paul to be speaking of faith that does not encompass doctrinal faith. Unlike Chrysostom, however, the qualification that Calvin places on the word means that Paul is talking, not about the highest reach of faith, but an incomplete faith that does not comprehend the "whole Christ." *Pistis* for Calvin means "faith that does not lay hold of Christ in His wholeness for redemption, justification, sanctification, but only insofar as miracles are performed in His name."[31] Hence there is radical disagreement between Chrysostom and Calvin here. While both place qualifications on the word *pistis*, and both are in agreement that *pistis* as employed by Paul in this context means the "faith of miracles" rather than doctrinal faith, for Chrysostom Paul has in mind the most superior and highest reaches of faith; while for Calvin *pistis* here is inadequate for it is incomplete in its comprehension of the totality of Christ's work. Now this radical distinction in the commentary Calvin alludes to in exactly two words: *paulo aliter:*[32]

Chrysostomus paulo aliter distinguit, fidem appellans signorum, non dogmatum: quod tamen a priore sensu non admodum discrepat.	Chrysostom asks a slightly different distinction, calling it the faith of miracles, and not dogmatic faith. But there is not much divergence between that and the interpretation that I have given.

A basic qualitative difference in the meaning of the word *pistis* is buried in the two words *paulo aliter*. Calvin acknowledges that Chrysostom understands the word *pistis* "somewhat differently," and Calvin therewith drops the entire matter.

Here again is an example of Calvin's strict adherence to the basic principles of method that we delineated earlier in this chapter. Calvin will not be budged from his love of brevity. He will not distract his reader by long excursuses that have no place in the commentary. Opinions of others, if they find any place in the commentary, will be kept as brief as possible, even to two words! The inclusion of a source will rarely, if ever, mean that a full and complete picture of the source will be presented.

31. Ibid.
32. *Comm. ad Cor. 1*, CO 49:500.

We wish to contend, therefore, that an understanding of Calvin's methodological principles and appreciation of Calvin's intended limited goals in the writing of the commentaries answer the question, not of the correctness or aptness of Calvin's interpretation on any given text, but the central question repeatedly raised in chapter 4, why Calvin's representation of his sources' position is often incomplete. Calvin's entire frame of reference to the use of his sources as he writes his commentaries is precisely the absence of exhaustive treatment, the avoidance of extensive documentation, and a rigorous application of the principles of *brevitas* and *facilitas*. As a matter of methodological procedure Calvin deliberately omits all opinions that would distract his reader from that which Calvin considered to be the central thrust of Paul's meaning. What appeared to be a sin of omission has turned out to be disciplined restraint. What appeared to be conclusions over-hastily reached have turned out to be studied caution for the sake of brevity. What appeared to be less than adequate documentation has, at the expense of protracted debate and the delight of readers who relish disputation, turned out to be an accommodation to readers who wish the Word of God interpreted with brevity and facility.

The conclusions to which we have come, however, should not be construed to be an uncritical evaluation of Calvin's commentaries from the standpoint of our investigation of Calvin's major source, Chrysostom. There are occasions when Calvin is simply in error, whether one wants to subsume such errors under the category of "quoting faultily from memory," writing under personal physical duress, or the heat of external attack. For example, on the subject of "baptism for the dead," Calvin rather off-handedly numbers Chrysostom with "the Fathers and Ambrose" as those who were of the opinion that Paul brought forward the issue of baptism for the dead in order to argue for the validity of the resurrection. We have seen that Chrysostom does not allow for this argument.[33] Calvin may well have had Tertullian's position in mind. Tertullian most notably of the Fathers contends that Paul refers to the abnormal practice of baptism for the dead, which would be meaningless without belief in the resurrection.[34] While writing his commentary, Calvin may well have recalled

---

33. Chap. 4, pp. 108–15.

34. In two places, *De resurrectio carnis*, chapter 48, and *Adversus Marcionem* 5.10, Tertullian speaks of the reference in 1 Corinthians 15:29 to a baptism for the dead.
In *De resurrectio carnis* (PL 2:864–65), he uses it as an argument for the resurrection of the flesh: Si autem et baptizantur quidam pro mortuis, videbimus an ratione; certe

Chrysostom's name in this context, for Chrysostom writes graphically about the distortion, but nowhere allows that Paul was content with the practice of baptism for the dead as a means for validating belief in the resurrection.

Other minor errors are of course observable, as one might naturally expect from the pen of a person whose literary output was prodigious. For example, in verse two of the very first chapter of Corinthians, Paul is writing *ecclesiae Dei quae est Corinthi, sanctificatis in Christo Iesu, vacatis sanctis, una cum omnibus qui invocant nomen Domini nostri Iesu Christi in quovis loco, tam sui quam nostri.* Calvin is aware that the words *sui* and *nostri* may refer either to *Iesu Christi* or to *in quovis loco,* and, adopting the former, indicates that he follows Chrysostom:[35]

---

illa praesumptione hoc eos instituisse contendit, qua alii etiam carni, ut vicarium bap-
tisma profuturum existimarent ad spem resurrectionis; quae nisi corporalis, non alias
hic baptismate corporali obligaretur. "But since some are baptized for the dead, we will
see whether there is good reason. Now it is certain that they adopted this practice with
such presumption that it made them suppose vicarious baptism would be beneficial to
the flesh of another in hope of the resurrection. For unless it were a bodily resurrection,
there would be no pledge derived from corporeal baptism."

In *Adversus Marcionem* (PL 2:494) Tertullian has the following: Revertamur nunc
ad resurrectionem, cui et alias quidem proprio volumine satisfecimus omnibus haer-
eticis resistentes; sed nec hic desumus propter eos qui illud opusculum ignorant. Quid,
ait, facient qui pro mortuis baptizantur, si mortui non resurgunt? Viderit institutio ista.
Kalendae si forte Februariae respondebunt illi, pro mortuis petere. Noli ergo Apostolum
novum statim auctorem aut confirmatorem eius denotare, ut tanto magis sisteret carnis
resurrectionem, quanto illi qui vane pro mortuis baptizarentur, fide resurrectionis hoc
facerent. "Let us now return to the resurrection, to the defense of which, against all sorts
of heretics, we have given sufficient attention. But we will not neglect those who are
unaware of that little work. 'What,' he asks, 'shall they do who are baptized for the dead,
if the dead do not rise?' Now, never mind that practice itself. The 'Februarian lustrations'
will certainly answer him, in those prayers for the dead. Do not suppose that the apostle
here indicates some new author as advocate for this practice. His only intention in alluding to baptism for the dead is that he might all the more firmly insist upon the resurrection of the body, to the degree that those who vainly baptized for the dead resorted to
such a practice on the basis of belief in such a resurrection."

Thus, according to Tertullian's interpretation of this text, Paul was using an argument
from the Roman custom of special sacrifices for the departed.

35. *Comm. ad Cor. 1,* CO 49:309.

Iam vero quod istas particulas nostri et sui in genitivo posui, ut ad Christum referantur, quas alii ad locum referentes, per ablativum reddunt: in eo Chrysostomum sum sequutus.	I have placed the little words *nostri* and *sui* (ours and theirs) in the genitive, understanding them as referring to Christ. Others, understanding them as referring to place, render them in the ablative. In doing so, I have followed Chrysostom.

When we examine the 1530 Basel Latin translation of Chrysostom, however, it is clear that Chrysostom does not understand the two words in question as referring to "Christ," but to "place":[36]

In omni loco ipsorum & nostro. Licet enim ad Corinthios haec scribatur epistola: non tamen eorum duntaxat, sed omnium qui in orbe sunt fidelium meminit. Ostendit enim in universo orbe unam oportere esse ecclesiam, quanquam locis divisam pluribus, & longe magis quae est Corinthi. Quae & si locis separatur, deus tamen eam coniungit, cum omnibus sit communis. Quamobrem cum in unum ipsam contrahat, has addidit particulas ipsorum & nostro.	"In every place, both theirs and ours." For while the letter is written to the Corinthians only, yet he makes mention of all the believers that are in the entire earth; showing that the Church throughout the world must be one, however separate in diverse places; and much more, than in Corinth. And though the place be separate, the Lord binds them together, being common to all. Therefore uniting them, he adds, "both theirs and ours."

Calvin recalls correctly that he follows Chrysostom by placing the two words *sui* and *nostri* in the genitive, but he is in error when he suggests that he follows Chrysostom referring them to *Iesu Christi*, as Chrysostom adopts *in quovis loco* as the referent of *sui* and *nostri*.

Faults such as these may be both expected and overlooked, given the immensity of Calvin's total contribution. The problems raised elsewhere, however, which we have now reviewed, would constitute serious charges against Calvin were it not for our understanding of Calvin's method and intention, were it not for our appreciation of the limits Calvin imposed upon himself as he sought to bring the mind of biblical authors to the

36. *EPCP,* 1530, Hom. 1, 1.

hearts of his readers. Let us take one more example from our findings in chapter 4 in order to demonstrate how an understanding of Calvin's method and intention explains Calvin's highly condensed employment of Chrysostomic remarks. When we examined the respective commentaries on 1 Corinthians 14:2, we were perplexed to read Calvin's remark on the meaning of "speaking mysteries in the spirit." On this matter, Calvin writes:[37]

Loquitur spiritu: hoc est, dono spirituali (sic enim cum Chrysostomo interpretor) mysteria et res occultas, ideoque nullius utilitatis.	He speaks in the spirit: that is, by a spiritual gift (for that is the way I interpret it, along with Chrysostom) mysteries and hidden things, therefore that are of no profit.

We are informed here that speaking in the spirit is a spiritual gift, for that is how Calvin along with Chrysostom explains *loquitur spiritu*. Following the parenthetical reference to Chrysostom, Calvin continues the sentence observing that the one who speaks in the spirit speaks "mysteries" and "things which remain secret," and therefore are of no utility or bring no benefit. We were perplexed because, when we examined Chrysostom's interpretation of this text, we discovered that while Chrysostom does understand *loquitur spiritu* as a *dono spirituali*, Chrysostom in no way understands *mysteria et res occultas* to be of *nullius utilitatis*. For Chrysostom, to speak mysteries in the spirit is a great gift and not something that is of no value or use. The gift is not, according to Chrysostom, given as a "useless or superfluous gift, nor is it given in vain." One would think that within the confines of a single sentence, Calvin would not quote a source, yet come to a contrary conclusion with the same source. The reader of Calvin's commentary would undoubtedly understand Chrysostom to be in full support of Calvin's contention that speaking mysteries in the spirit is of little value, whereas in fact Chrysostom placed a high value on speaking in the spirit.

Now, it should be observed first of all that Calvin does not misrepresent Chrysostom. Calvin writes that he interprets *loquitur spiritu* as a spiritual gift, and in so doing he follows Chrysostom, which is exactly correct. However, Calvin does not agree with Chrysostom that there is value in speaking mysteries or things that remain in secret. Without even

37. *Comm. ad Cor. 1*, CO 49:517.

so much as raising the issue that there are contrary opinions, Calvin proceeds directly to his conclusion that speaking in the spirit is of no value. To be sure, Calvin in the next sentence informs us that Chrysostom understands "mysteries" in a good sense, as extraordinary revelations from God. But the point is that we here have an excellent example of the way Calvin will employ an interpretation of Chrysostom, bringing forth an insight based on but a segment of Chrysostom's total picture, and either accept or reject the insight raised. Furthermore, when Calvin does mention the opinion of Chrysostom, he does not offer anything resembling a refutation of that opinion. We simply have, "Chrysostom says thus and so, but I say the following," and that ends the matter. Even in one sentence Calvin will quote a source to show that he agrees with that source on one particular matter, but then go directly back to his own opinion, which may well differ from the source. Such limitations Calvin imposed upon himself for the sake of brevity and the ease of reading.

We have examined Calvin as a biblical exegete, with particular reference to the manner in which he employs his source material. Virtually at every point, Calvin employs Chrysostomic material in the body of his commentary with acute brevity. The nature of highly compressed references to his sources opens Calvin to the charge of inadequate documentation and incomplete representation. We have found that the words "Chrysostom says" rarely will be followed by a full explanation of Chrysostom's position. The nature of Calvin's use of sources raises many doubts concerning the accuracy of Calvin's references. That Calvin's representation of Chrysostom crystallizes the latter's thought, we cannot be at all sure, when we are informed that Chrysostom says thus and so. We may suspect that the full import of the Antiochene's position is not to be found in Calvin. When Calvin gives reference to Chrysostom, we may understand that Calvin is giving acknowledgment to the fact that an issue has been raised by Chrysostom, but that the reference or quotation does not include a balanced treatment of Chrysostom's position. For Calvin the reference often means, "I ran across the idea in Chrysostom," but not, "here is the conclusion to which Chrysostom has come."

We do wish to contend that Calvin's methodology was not arbitrary, but the result of a studied consideration on the nature of biblical commentaries. For Calvin, the commentaries were purposely to be devoid of the opinions of contemporary or ancient scholars. Calvin is consciously reacting to the inclusion of excursuses in the commentaries that distract the reader from the thought of the biblical author. There is a deliberate absence of references to the opinions of other commentators. Calvin reduces such opinions as he does include, to an absolute minimum, in order that no extended refutations will be necessary. His mindset is the absence of showmanship, which might delight the learned but deflect the common reader. If Calvin's biblical commentaries are to be evaluated from the standpoint of his highly abbreviated source documentation, they must also be judged from the standpoint of their methodological foundations. Such foundations were crucial for determining not only what was to be included in the commentaries but, equally important, what was to be excluded.

Conclusions

WE HAVE BY NO means answered all the problems raised in chapter 4. Our intention is not to explain why Chrysostom adopts one interpretation of a given text and Calvin another. Our goal has been to propose a plausible explanation to the major question of why Calvin so inadequately represented the full import of Chrysostom's thought on so many occasions. The findings of chapter 4 raise further questions that merit investigation. Of interest would be the extent to which Calvin's rigorous devotion to church discipline imposed a particular interpretation on Paul's letter to the Corinthians. An investigation into Calvin's concept of *ignavia* might well prove fruitful as a means of understanding why, when Chrysostom understands Paul to be speaking to a definite problem of, for example, fornication, Calvin develops from such passages a full-blown system of church government, organization, authority, power of the keys, and the right of excommunication. Of interest would be the extent to which Calvin's perception of the historical situation in Geneva colored his interpretation of a given text. A study along these lines might be especially helpful as a means of understanding both Calvin's and Chrysostom's commentaries on the Lord's Supper. For example, Chrysostom's Homilies on 1 Corinthians, while the date is not exactly known, were most probably delivered at Antioch. According to Homily 66 on St. Matthew, the church of Antioch was flourishing, "maintaining 3000 widows, virgins, maimed persons, prisoners, and ministers at the altar."[1] The church was also in a state of division, on account of the disputed succession in the episcopate between the followers of Paulinus and Meletius. Does Chrysostom emphasize the importance of "the commonality of the Lord's Supper" with an eye to this schism? On

---

1. PG 58; quoted in NPNF 12:iv.

the other hand, Calvin, according to his preface to the commentary on the Psalms, perceived his mission as bringing order out of civil chaos.[2] "Those unfit for the Lord's Supper eat Christ's sacred bread." Does Calvin emphasize the importance of maintaining the purity of the Supper with an eye to establishing order and discipline? Research along such lines undoubtedly would enhance our understanding of the positions taken by Calvin in the commentaries, and in turn provide additional answers for questions and problems raised in our investigation of Calvin's use of Chrysostom.

Our investigation entailed a critical examination of all the explicit and implicit references Calvin made to Chrysostom, combined with an examination of Chrysostom's treatment of the issue to which Calvin alluded or explicitly referred. The basis for our selection of Chrysostom is presented in part 1, combined with the fact that of all the sources mentioned by Calvin in the commentaries Chrysostom is by far the author most cited. Given the fact that Chrysostom was an Eastern Father representing a tradition quite at variance with the Reformed Church of sixteenth-century Geneva, we asked the question, why would Calvin not only quote Chrysostom so frequently, but embark on the publication of these ancient homilies? As a means toward understanding Calvin as a biblical commentator, we were looking for dependence on critical issues, for exegetical similarities, and for theological similarities. It was to our surprise that Calvin, while he would consult Chrysostom frequently as a historical authority, rarely entered into the theological and especially ethical implications of Chrysostom's thought. Ethical implications were avoided because Chrysostom founded his patterns of behavior on principles too closely allied with the doctrine of works-righteousness. Calvin would often adopt the final interpretation offered by Chrysostom, but Calvin showed here no easy dependence. Always Calvin founded his interpretation on historical, grammatical, philological, or contextual grounds. In the course of the comparative reading, however, a new and unforeseen problem soon became evident. When Calvin quoted Chrysostom, the quotations, while for the most part accurate, were always incomplete, distilling into a sentence or two a fraction of Chrysostom's total position or interpretation of any given text. These findings in turn raised other questions. Did Calvin misread Chrysostom? Did he have only fragments of Chrysostom's text? Did he understand Chrysostom through an intermediary source? Such questions sent us to a detailed investigation

2. *Commentarii in Librum Psalmorum*, CO 31:23.

of what texts Calvin might have had at his disposal. The results of that investigation convinced us that Calvin made use of the Erasmus work on the Chrysostom *Opera*, published by Frober. A word-for-word comparison of Calvin's citations of Chrysostom and the 1530 Basel text substantiated that Calvin had access to a reputable text.

Such findings still left open the question initially raised: why Calvin kept his references to Chrysostom incredibly brief. It was at this point that we had to step back from the texts themselves and inquire into Calvin's own understanding of what a commentary is, what it should do. At this point we came to an understanding of the principles upon which Calvin determined to write his commentaries. An explanation of the problem raised in our detailed examination of Calvin's commentary began to emerge. Calvin, during discussions with his friend Grynaeus, probably in 1533, had come to the conclusion that the twofold principle of *brevitas* and *facilitas* is to be rigorously applied to the writing of biblical commentaries. The only goal and purpose for writing biblical commentaries is to lay open the mind of the biblical writer whom the commentator endeavors to explain. This seemingly obvious methodological step turns out to be an important statement by virtue of what the statement excludes. It means that all attempts at ostentation and showmanship by which the opinions of others might be challenged and refuted will not be admitted into the body of the commentary. Calvin adopts his method, partly on the grounds of his acquaintance with other biblical commentators, partly on the grounds of justification for his own attempts at commentating on Scriptures when so many other erudite scholars have already produced their own commentaries.

With respect to the commentaries of contemporary authors, he finds the writing of Melanchthon inadequate, for he offers comments only on those portions of Scripture that were considered to be relevant *loci*. Opposed to this method of arbitrary selection, Calvin will write a continuous commentary at the risk of repetition. Calvin praises his mentor's work in Strassburg, but finds Bucer's long and involved excursuses tedious for the untutored reader; Bucer is too prolix. Therefore Calvin arrives at his own *via media*, and in so doing justifies the production of yet another set of commentaries on Scripture. The commentaries will seek only to draw out the mind of the biblical author, and will be devoid, unless necessary warnings must be sounded for the sake of the reader, of polemical, argumentative issues. What Calvin methodologically accomplishes is the division of Bucer's work into two parts. The commentaries of Scripture will be continuously readable for the common man, containing no digressions. The opinions of others will be treated with the greatest brevity. It is in the *Institutes* that the sum of religion will be so ordered that anyone familiar with the content of this work may find what is necessary for a more adequate and complete appreciation of Scripture. It is in the *Institutes* that refutation of ancient and modern errors will be dealt with. But for Calvin, the *Institutes* and the *Commentaries* are two parts of a whole, though separated for the ease and convenience of the reader.

Calvin's intentions, methodological principles, and structural arrangements all focus on one object, the reader. As one reviews the several references we have brought together concerning Calvin's method as it pertains to the writing of commentaries, one is struck by the number of times the reader is mentioned. Moreover, Calvin seems to have in mind a particular kind of reader. In the *Praefatio in Chrysostomi Homilias*, Calvin responds to a possible objection that his proposed publication of Chrysostom's homilies should not be ventured on the grounds that Chrysostom wrote only for the learned and scholarly reader:[3]

Equidem non me fugit quid hic obiectari mihi queat: Chrysostomum, quem vulgo hominum publicare instituo, doctus tantum et literarum peritis lucubrationes suas destinasse. At vero, nisi et titulus et orationis compositio mentitur, quos ad universum populum sermones habuit hic complexus est. Ita certe et rerum tractationem et dictionem attemperat, quasi hominum multitudinem instituere velit. Proinde frustra quis contendat, eum inter doctos reconditum esse oportere, quum data opera studuerit esse popularis.	Now I am not unaware of an objection that can be raised against me at this point: that Chrysostom, whom I am on the point of making available to the common people, intended his studies only for the learned and the educated. But, on the contrary, unless both the title and style of his oratory are lying, this man composed sermons which he delivered to the people at large. Thus, without doubt, he modifies both his method of treatment and his language as though wishing to instruct the general run of men. Accordingly, anyone who maintains that he ought to be hidden away among the learned is quite wrong, seeing that he has taken pains specifically to be popular.

3. *Praef. in Chry. Hom.*, CO 9:333.

Certe haec mihi plus satis iusta excusatio est, quod causam habeo cum Chrysostomo coniunctam, quia nihil aliud quam cum plebe communico quae ille plebi nominatim inscripsit.

At least I myself am more than sufficiently justified in that I have common cause with Chrysostom, because I am doing nothing else than communicate to the people the things which he addressed specifically to the people.

Calvin here identifies himself as at one with the Antiochene as far as the object of the commentaries are concerned. Calvin intends his writings, as did Chrysostom, not for the learned and highly trained, but for the *universum populum*; the method of writing the commentaries, the treatment of language must all be geared so that the commentaries may be readily understood by *quasi hominum multitudinem*. Calvin understands himself to be doing nothing else (and here the *nihil aliud* is important for what it rejects) than communicate to the common people (*cum plebe communico*) the same straightforward sense of Scripture. Calvin, like Chrysostom, wishes above all else to strive for facility in his commentaries, which might best be rendered "readability." In order to maintain the simplest style of teaching, he will abstain from refutation and all pretension. Calvin directs his commentaries not to readers who would welcome derogation of Papists or Anabaptists, but to the *universum populum*; the commentaries are offered not for "a splendid show" but for the edification of the church. The reader must not be faced with a wide variety of interpretations for such excursuses only create difficulty for *lectoribus parum acutis*, especially those who easily vacillate from one opinion to another. The reader must be spared *molestia et fastidio*.

But this method, these principles, do not imply a speaking down to the reader, or accommodation to the point of superficiality. The key word for an understanding of Calvin's commentaries, by which he understood that he was making an advancement over the commentaries of the highly praised Bucer, is separation, the division of that which must be kept brief and simple from that which of necessity would involve length and complexity. The reader of the commentaries will be spared annoyance and boredom provided he approaches the commentaries armed with a knowledge of the *Institutes*, which serves as a *necessario instrumento* for a full and complete appreciation of Scripture. The reader of the commentaries who happens upon *loci* that need further elaboration, debate, or refutation of errant opinions is directed by Calvin to the other half of his theological enterprise, the *Institutes*. Does this not explain why so many readers of the *Institutes* alone come away with impressions of Calvin as an argumentative, polemical, and vituperative author? The reader of the commentaries receives no such dominant impression. In the commentaries Calvin demonstrates, for the large part, a warm pastoral concern that is markedly restrained, devoid of invective. Is this not why Calvin reacted so strongly to Burghardus in the 1555 response to that *ornatissime vir*? The Lutherans charged Calvin with a differing opinion on the subject of the Lord's Supper. That charge could be met. The Lutherans charged Calvin with possessing different opinions on "the books of Moses," again a charge that could easily be met. But, according to Calvin in the same letter, the crucial issue to be examined should have been whether he "avidly sought different meanings, had wantonly attacked, spitefully carped at, or insultingly reviled" the Lutheran interpretations. Against that possibility Calvin reacts with heated anger, for his whole program in the commentaries on Scripture was the very avoidance of such a disposition. Against such a possibility, Calvin responds with the flat statement, "you have good reason to commend both my modesty and my gentleness."

Issues that anyone fond of ostentation would love to clamor about Calvin mentions with sobriety and reticence. If, in the commentaries, errors must be pointed out, they are done so with utmost respect, and most errors are simply buried in silence. This is the Calvin of the commentaries. If the author of the *Institutes* began that work by writing a politico-theological tract to the reigning Catholic King of France in defense of the new religion, the author of the commentaries began writing with nonpolemical methodological principles solidly in mind. The only duty of the commentator is *patefacere mentem scriptoris, quem explicandum sumpsit*, to lay open the mind of the writer whom he has undertaken to explain. He misses his mark, or at least strays outside his limits, by the extent to which he leads his readers away from the meaning of his author.

The man whom Calvin found to be most in line with his own goal and intentions as a biblical commentator, the author who stayed closest to the text, the church father who most closely represented the pastoral attitude with which Calvin wrote for the *universum populum*, was John Chrysostom. Calvin calls upon Chrysostom as a respected "great name"; he refers to Chrysostom when the latter's remarks are striking; he consults Chrysostom for principles of grammar, for clarification of historical settings by virtue of the proximity of Chrysostom to the age of the apostles; he frequently adopts the interpretation rendered by Chrysostom, but of all the reasons Calvin frequently cites Chrysostom, the essential basis for Calvin's great appreciation of the Antiochene commentator is methodological affinity. Chrysostom accomplished two primary objectives to which Calvin dedicated himself; he never strayed from a clear elaboration and explanation of the biblical text, and he spoke with the common people in mind. Given that fact, however, it must be observed that Calvin employs Chrysostom as a source for the commentaries in a characteristic manner. The citation of Chrysostom's name in the body of the commentaries more often than not means that Calvin uses his ancient source in a "punctiliar" fashion, to bring forth a single issue raised by Chrysostom, but which in no way reflects Chrysostom's complete or studied interpretation.

In the context of Chrysostom's discussion on the relationship between the two covenants, Calvin will only mention the fact that Chrysostom compares the strictness of the Law with the clemency of the Gospel. The point is raised, not to send the reader to Chrysostom, nor to offer documentation to Chrysostom's position. The point is raised only to warn the reader that such a comparison has, on other occasions, been raised, and that the position has no validity. On another issue, Calvin wishes to warn his readers that the word *angelos* has, in the past, been understood as referring to "priests." Calvin recalls that Chrysostom mentions such an interpretation, but the inclusion of Chrysostom's name is secondary to the issue. There is no attempt to elaborate on the final position to which Chrysostom came. The accurate conjunction of names with ideas simply does not represent Calvin's mind-set, his disposition, in the commentaries. To the contrary, the dominant impulse away from anything that might appear to be ostentation, or the raising of opinions from other sources, or the inclusion of concepts that might deflect the reader from the text itself, or the inclusion of an interpretation that would necessitate refutation, all combine to the predisposition of Calvin's mind away from meticulous documentation. A reference to Chrysostom means "Chrysostom mentions," and not always "Chrysostom's interpretation is."

As an outstanding example of one who wrote commentaries according to the goals and upon the principles that Calvin established for his own work, the Reformer identified himself with the patriarch. As the

"Golden Mouth" spoke to and wrote for the people, Calvin composed his commentaries only for the edification of the church. As Chrysostom made it his supreme concern never to turn aside even to the slightest degree from the simple sense of Scripture, Calvin wrote his commentaries according to principles that would contribute to but one goal, the unfolding of the mind of biblical authors to *universum populum*.

Appendix A

Proposed Dating of Calvin's
Praefatio in Chrysostomi Homilias

O UR TASK HERE IS to assign a plausible date for Calvin's Latin *Preface* to the intended French translation of Chrysostom's homilies. Before turning to the document itself, we may first establish a *terminus a quo*. Taking the successive editions of the *Institutes* as our guide, we find that with the 1536 edition there appears only one reference to Chrysostom. With the publication of the 1539 edition, twenty-six references appear, ten additional in the 1543 edition, and only one more in the 1559 edition. As reflected in the *Institutes*, we may assume that Calvin's effective work on Chrysostom roughly coincided with his sojourn in Strassburg, establishing a minimum date 1538.

Let us turn now to evidence within the document itself:[1]

Atqui memoria tenet, qui statum orbis per aetatem ante annos viginti videre potuerunt, in maiori hominum multitudine nihil fere reliquum fuisse Christi praeter nomen; memoriam virtutis eius et raram et exiguam exstitisse.	Now those who are able to see the condition of the world twenty years ago recall clearly that among the majority of men almost no knowledge of Christ remained except the name; such memory of His power as prevailed was faint and feeble.

To what might Calvin refer by *ante annos viginti*? Undoubtedly "twenty" is a round number, but he must have in mind a time prior to that in which

1. *Praef. in Chry. Hom.*, CO 9:832.

Scriptures became generally available to the public. One possibility therefore would be Luther's translation of the New Testament into German.
While he was sequestered in Wartburg, from December 1521 until early
spring of 1522, Luther, encouraged by his friend Melanchthon, translated
the New Testament into German. In May of 1522 the printing had begun
and was completed shortly before September 21, 1522. This first edition
appeared under the title *Das Neue Testament Deutzsch* in an edition of
3000 copies. Calvin may therefore have in mind the round figure of 1520
in his *ante annos viginti* reference, which would place the writing of the
Preface approximately in the year 1540.

Let us propose another hypothesis closer to Calvin's own experience.
The years 1533 and 1534 were decisive for Calvin. On November 1, 1533,
Nicholas Cop delivered his rectorial address at the University of Paris.
Whether or not, as Beza suggests, Calvin was Cop's ghostwriter, a strong
probability lingers that Calvin was associated with the biblical, evangelical,
and anti-Sorbonnist address. Calvin was charged with "familiarity with
the rector" and forced to flee from Paris to his native Noyon, where his
books and papers were seized. In the following year, Calvin met Jacques
Lefèvre, whose biblical translations and commentaries both shocked the
Sorbonne and greatly stimulated Luther. Already having worked on the
Psalms (1509), a Latin translation of Paul's epistles with commentary
(1512), and a translation of the four Gospels into French (1523), Lefèvre
welcomed from the press the final edition of his French Bible on April 6,
1534. It was this year, 1534, that Lefèvre received the twenty-five year old
Calvin for an interview. Given Calvin's later biblical work, the interview
must have been formative, if not decisive.

That Calvin was soon to become personally involved in the publication of Scriptures for the common people may be seen in the two prefaces
to his cousin Olivétan's translation of the New Testament, published in
1534. The first preface, addressed to "Emperors, Kings, Princes, and to
All Nations Subject to Christ's Rule," consists of a passionate plea for
the Bible in the vernacular.[2] The second preface stands before the New
Testament and begins with the greeting, "To all those who love Christ and
His Gospel."[3] There follows a defense of the Reformed faith and an appeal
to kings and magistrates, bishops and pastors that they maintain the right
preaching of the Gospel and the health of the church.

2. *Praefationes Bibliis Gallicis Petri Roberti Olivetani*, CO 9:787–90.
3. Ibid., CO 9:791–822.

If Calvin is recalling events that were crucial for his own life as they related to his work of biblical exposition, the words *ante annos viginti* may well refer to the early 1530s, which would place the writing of the *Preface* in the 1550s.

Let us examine further evidence from the *Preface*. From several sections of the document, we may infer that Calvin is well into the process of writing and publishing commentaries on Scripture. Introducing the reasons he intends to publish the Chrysostom homilies, Calvin says:[4]

Certe haec mihi plus satis iusta excusatio est, quod causam habeo cum Chrysostomo coniunctam, quia nihil aliud quam cum plebe communico quae ille plebi nominatim inscripsit.	At least I myself am more than sufficiently justified in that I have a common cause with Chrysostom, because I am doing nothing else than communicate to the people the things which he addressed specifically to the people.

Calvin is beyond the initial stages of intending to produce commentaries. Further, there are several indications that he has advanced to the stage where he is at work on the Old Testament commentaries. Calvin is of the opinion that while Chrysostom excels as an interpreter of the New Testament, he did not demonstrate much skill with the language of the Old Testament:[5]

Sunt autem homiliae, quae quum variis partibus constent, primum tamen in illis locum tenet scripturae interpretatio, in qua Chrysostomum nostrum vetustos omnes scriptores qui hodie exstant antecedere nemo sani iudicii negaverit. Praesertim ubi novum testamentum tractat. Nam quominus in veteri tantum praestaret, obstabat hebraicae linguae imperitia.	Homilies are such that although they consist of a variety of elements, they are primarily concerned with the interpretation of Scripture, and that is a function in which all men of sound judgment agree that our writer Chrysostom excels all the ancient writers presently extant. Especially this is true when he deals with the New Testament; for his unfamiliarity with the Hebrew language prevented him from showing such skill in the Old Testament.

4. *Praef. in Chry. Hom.*, CO 9:833.
5. Ibid., CO 9:834.

Calvin may well have already addressed himself to the commentary on the Psalms, or that commentary may have been completed. He is familiar with Hilary's work on the Psalms, and found it of little use:[6]

Quantum ad Latinos attinet, Tertulliani, Cypriani labores istius generis exciderunt. Nec Hilarii multa habentur. Commentarii in Psalterium parum ad intelligendam prophetae mentem faciunt.	As far as the Latins are concerned, works of the kind we are considering are lost in the case of Tertullian and Cyprian, and not many of Hilary's survive. The latter's commentaries on the Psalter have little value for understanding the mind of the prophet.

He has not been able to derive a great deal from Jerome on the Old Testament:[7]

Quae in vetus testamentum scripsit Hieronymus merito exiguam laudem inter doctos habent. Est enim totus fere in allegoriis demersus, quibus nimium licentiose scripturam contorquet.	Jerome's writings on the Old Testament have deservedly little recognition among the yearned; for he is almost completely sunk in allegories in which he twists Scripture in far too free a manner.

Since Calvin's observations on the Old Testament works of Chrysostom, Hilary, and Jerome are not tenuous but decided in nature, it may be inferred that Calvin has completed his work on the Psalms. This would suggest the date of the Psalms commentary, published in 1555.

From 1557 until his death, Calvin worked through the remaining Old Testament books as time allowed him. A revised edition of Isaiah was published in 1559, along with all the Minor Prophets. The commentary on Daniel came in 1560; Jeremiah and Lamentations, in 1563; Genesis and the Harmony of the remainder of the Pentateuch, in 1563; and posthumously, Joshua, in 1564, and Ezekiel 1–20, in 1565.

Let us examine the year 1559. Calvin has produced a large number of biblical commentaries, but there remains a substantial portion of the Old Testament on which work must be completed. Haunted by the

6. Ibid.

7. Ibid.

insistent demands of a waiting public, Calvin's anxiety is compounded by a serious illness from which he never recovered. From 1558 onward Calvin suffered from the quartan fever, and his diseases multiplied. The year 1559 saw the culmination of many editions of the *Institutio*, which, together with the 1560 French translation, had now reached logical structure and orderly precision. Calvin's mind could not rest, however, for the commentaries were not completed.

We mentioned that in the year 1559, Calvin issued a revised edition of the commentary on Isaiah. Was it not in the first dedicatory preface to Edward VI that Calvin had so clearly insisted that Scripture must be given to the common people as well as kings? The themes that are sounded so strongly in the dedicatory preface to Edward VI are sounded again in the *Praefatio in Chrysostomi Homilias*: the manner in which the sacred Word was bound up in monasteries and interpreted by priests; the urgency that the truth of God be freely and boldly maintained; the personal references that Calvin made to himself and his vocation as an expositor of Scripture; the necessity to allow the pure and simple doctrine of Scripture to shine forth as it ought. The original preface to Edward VI was published in 1551, and were it not for the dominant impression that Calvin has completed or been industriously at work on the Psalms, one would be willing to assign 1551 as the date of the *Preface* to the Chrysostom Homilies. But now in 1559 Calvin publishes a revised edition of the earlier work on Isaiah that brings sharply to mind the earlier promises of commentaries on Scripture. But Calvin is now older, and also ill. There are others whom God has given as aids to the study of Scripture; we must make free use of what the Lord intended for our use. With such thoughts then, Calvin may well have composed a *Preface* to an intended French translation of the Homilies of John Chrysostom.

Based on the above evidence and confluence of events in Calvin's life, the year 1559 is proposed as the date for Calvin's *Praefatio in Chrysostomi Homilias*.

Appendix B

An Outline of John Calvin's *Preface* to
the Homilies of Chrysostom
CO 9:831–38

I. Brief explanation of the purpose and object in publishing the Homilies of John Chrysostom:
   A. At first, there were strong objections to reading the Gospel to the common people.
      1. Some thought it a dastardly crime for the mysteries of God to be made public for ordinary people to hear.
      2. But such complaining has changed into approval.
      3. Now that the Word of God has been restored to the universal Church, Christ, the Sun of Righteousness, has shined on his own.
   B. Twenty years ago, almost no knowledge of Christ remained except his name.
      1. Reason: the common people had consigned the reading of Scripture to priests and monks.
      2. We take pride that in our own age this treasury has been opened.
   C. But it is necessary to know what we ought to look for in Scripture, and what the goal is towards which we ought to direct ourselves in reading it.
      1. Otherwise, we will wander far afield without much fruit for our labor.

      2. While the Holy Spirit is of course our only teacher, the Lord has bestowed upon us aids that should assist us in the investigation of his truth.

  D. If it is right that the people have the Word of God, it is right that they should have instruments that will prove of use in the search for its true interpretation.

      1. Since most people are without training, they should be helped by the work of interpreters who have advanced in the knowledge of God.

      2. A great injustice would be done if men well-versed in Scripture did not help those who are simple and uneducated.

      3. Therefore, the sole object in the forthcoming publication is to lay down a pathway to the reading of sacred Scripture for the simple and uneducated.

II. Response to possible objection:

  A. Some say Chrysostom wrote only for the learned and educated.

      1. On the contrary, Chrysostom accommodated his language and method so as to reach the general run of men.

      2. Anyone who says he ought to be hidden away among the learned is quite wrong.

  B. The aim of the proposed work is the same as Chrysostom's own aim: communication to the people of that which belongs to them.

      1. All the capacities that God has conferred on his servants ought to be contributed towards the upbuilding of all.

      2. We would be hateful to God if we did not share with his people what is their own.

  C. Further, pastors are not always sufficiently skilled in Greek and Latin to hear the ancient writers in their own language.

      1. It is important for pastors to hold to the ancient form of the church and have at least some knowledge of antiquity.

2. The publication of the homilies is important because those who carry out the teaching office should be familiar with this kind of writing.

III. Why Chrysostom has been chosen as the most outstanding of all:
   A. In the homily as a literary form, Chrysostom excels all the Greeks.
      1. Origen obscures the straightforward sense of Scripture by endless allegories.
      2. Athanasius, Basil, and Gregory were more fitted for oratory than written systematic teaching.
      3. Cyril can be rated second to Chrysostom, but cannot rival him.
      4. Whatever in Theophylact is praiseworthy, he got from Chrysostom.
   B. Chrysostom also excels the Latins.
      1. Any homilies of Tertullian and Cyprian are not extant.
      2. Clarity is lacking in the case of Hilary.
      3. Jerome's writings smack of one who is not sufficiently experienced in the church.
      4. Ambrose is by far the closest to Chrysostom in excellence.
      5. Augustine, while the greatest of all in dogma, is over-subtle as an interpreter of Scripture.
   C. The outstanding merit of Chrysostom:
      1. He did not turn aside even to the slightest degree from the genuine simple sense of Scripture.
      2. He never twists the plain meaning of words.

IV. Areas in which Chrysostom is inferior to other writers:
   A. The doctrine of election:
      1. He strives to work into the idea of election some reference to our own efforts.
      2. But Scripture everywhere proclaims that the only ground of our election is our utter wretchedness, and the only source of our help is God's own goodness.
   B. The doctrine of free-will:
      1. He speaks of free-will as if it had great importance for the pursuit of virtue and the observance of the divine law.

    2.   But Scripture denies to us all capacity to do good and leaves to us no virtue except what he supplies by his Spirit.

  C. The doctrine of works:

    1.   He makes our righteousness before God depend, to some extent, on works.

    2.   But Scripture urgently insists that God alone is just, and he justifies his servants not for merit but on the ground of faith in Jesus Christ.

V. Reasons that drove Chrysostom to his position.

  A. Debate with the philosophers of his time:

    1.   There is little agreement between the pronouncements of the philosophers and the doctrine handed down in the Scriptures concerning the corruption of our total nature.

    2.   In meeting the philosophers' quibbles, he modified his standpoint to avoid revolting too strongly from the common opinion of men.

    3.   This, however, was no adequate reason to turn from the plain sense of Scripture.

    4.   But since his object was to deliver himself from the enemies of the cross of Christ, his motive deserves some excuse.

  B. Men within the church living impure and licentious lives:

    1.   These men claimed no fault could be laid to their charge for their actions, since they were being driven to sin by the corruptness of their nature.

    2.   These men in an impious and unworthy way transferred the blame for their sins to God himself.

    3.   Since the method of direct attack did not suit the saintly Chrysostom, he denied that a man was prepared for the good life by the grace of God in such a way that he himself could contribute nothing at all.

    4.   While this method is little in harmony with Scripture, Chrysostom in no sense turned the faithful servant of Christ from the way, since he always kept the highest end in view.

VI. Finally, beyond straightforward interpretation of Scripture, the reader of the homilies will find reminders of the old way of things.

    A. The type of function and authority bishops had:

        1. The kind of discipline that prevailed in the priestly order

        2. The restraints practiced among bishops themselves to prevent them from misusing their power

        3. The character of the sacred communities

        4. The nature of their ties and the purpose for which they were instituted

    B. The nature of the laws by which the people were kept within the bounds of duty:

        1. The kind of discipline that prevailed among the people

        2. The degree of sobriety among the people that prevented them from scorning the responsibility entrusted to the bishops

Appendix C

Table of Chrysostom References in Calvin's Works Arranged in Order of Migne's *Patrologia Graeca*

Chrysostom	PG	Calvin	CO or Inst.
Adv. opp. vit. mon.			
2.2	47.399f.	*Inst.*	4.13.8n12
3.4	47.355f.		2.5.2n4
3.14	47.372ff.		2.8.57n64
3.14	47.372		4.13.12n19
De compunc. cordis			
1.4	47.399f.	*Inst.*	2.8.57n64
1.4	47.399f.		4.13.12n19
		Comm. Harm. Ev.	
1.4	47.399f.	Matt 5:44	
		Luke 6:28	
1.9	47.408	*Inst.*	3.22.8
De prov. ad Stag.			
3.14	47.493f.	*Inst.*	3.4.35n72
De sacerdotio			
3.4	48.642	*Inst.*	4.18.11n19
3.4		*Interim*	7.581
De incomp. Dei Natura			
(Contra Anomeonos)			
1.5	48.706	*Comm. Is.* 53:8	37.261
1.5	48.706	*Comm. Acts* 8:33	48.194
5.7	48.745ff.	*Inst.*	1.13.21n47
5.7	48.746		3.4.8n18
Adv. Jud.			
5.	48.891	*Inst.*	3.4.31n67
7.5	48.923	*Interim*	7.580
Hom. de non anath.			

Chrysostom	PG	Calvin	CO or Inst.
	48.943ff.	*Inst.*	4.12.8n19
De Lazaro Concio			
3.1 (Luke 16.25)	48.992	*Pref. Bibl.*	
4.4	48.	*Art. fac. Par.* 3, *Poen.*	7.11
De poenitentia			
7.1 (5.1?)	49.338	*Inst.*	3.4.1n2
6.3	49.317		3.5.9n21
De fer. repr.			
3.6	51.143	*Inst.*	2.3.10n25
3.6	51.143	*Adv. Pigh.*	6.395
3.6	51.143	*Inst.*	3.24.13n23
De profectu ev.			
2.	51.312	*Inst.*	2.2.11n49
12.	51.319		3.20.27
De Canaanita			
6.	52.453	*Inst.*	3.20.20
9.	52.456f.		3.4.4n10
		Art. fac. Par. 3	7.11
Ep. ad Innocentium			
	52.533	*Inst.* 1536	OS 5.415
In Gen.			
10.2	53.83ff.	*Inst.*	3.4.38n78
10.4	53.85	*Comm. Gen.* 1:26	23.26
10.4	53.85	*Psychopann.*	5.181
10.4	53.85	*Inst.*	1.15.4
18.7	53.158		2.2.4n15
19.1	53.158f.		2.2.4n15
22.1	53.187		2.5.2n4
23.5	53.204		2.5.3n8
26.5f.	53.235–39		3.16.3n5
25.7 ?	53.228		2.2.4
34.6	53.321		3.15.2n5
36.3	53.336f.	*Interim*	7.580
53.2	53.466	*Inst.*	2.2.4n15
Expos. in Ps.			
41 (.2) ?	55.157	*Ep. Lect.* 1545	6.171
109 (8)	55.276f.	*Interim*	7.580
Hom. in illud: Domine,			
non est in homine via eius			
5	56.160f.	*Inst.*	2.5.2n4
	56.153–62	*Adv. Pigh.*	6.336
In Matt. Hom.			
9.4	57.180	*Comm. Harm. Ev.* Mark 2:23	45.102
10.1	57.183–85	*Inst.*	4.15.7n11
19.2	57.275f.		3.20.29
19.6	57.282	*Comm. Harm. Ev.* Matt 6:13	45.202

Chrysostom	PG	Calvin	CO or Inst.
23 (24).1	57.307f.	*Comm. Harm. Ev.* Matt 7:1	45.214
24.3	57.324	*Inst.*	3.18.4
44 (45).1	57.464	*Comm. Harm. Ev.* Luke 8:19	45.350
57 (58).2 ?	57.561	*Comm. Harm. Ev.* Mark 9:17	45.493
82 (83).4	58.742	*Adv. Pigh.*	6.391
82 (83).4	58.743	*Inst.*	4.17.14
82 (83).4ff.	58.743ff.		4.17.43n40
82 (83).5	58.744 ?	*Ratisbonne*	5.552
82 (83).4ff.	58.743ff.	*Interim*	7.581
82 (83).6		*Ratisbonne*	5.635
82 (83).6	58.745f.	*Inst.*	4.12.5n9
83 (84).1	58.745f.		2.16.12
83 (84).4	58.752		4.17.45
85 (86).4	58.762f.		4.5.18
In Jo. Hom.			
10.1	59.73	*Inst.*	2.3.10n25
10.1	59.73	*Adv. Pigh.*	6.395
17 (16).1	59.108	*Comm.* John 1:29	47.26
21 (20).1	59.129	*Comm.* John 2:3	47.38
25 (24).2	59.151	*Comm.* John 3:5	47.55
26 (25).1	59.154	*Comm.* John 3:7	47.58
47 (46).2	59.265	*Comm.* John 6:63	47.159
53 (52).1	59.293	*Comm.* John 8:25	47.198
55 (54).2	59.304	*Comm.* John 8:58	47.216
68 (67).3	59.373	*Comm.* John 12:32	47.294
88.1	59.477f. ?	*Comm.* John 21:15	47.452
In Act. Ap. Hom.			
19.2	60.151	*Comm.* Acts 8:36	48.196
21.4	60.169	*Eccl. Ref. Rat.*	7.656
39.1 ?	60.275	*Comm.* Acts 18:3	48.425
In Rom. Hom.			
2.1 (Rom 1:8)	60.401–2	*Inst.*	4.8.9
8.8	60.465		4.18.11n19
11.1 (Rom 6:5)	60,483f. ?	*Comm. Rom.*	49.107
23.1 (Rom 13:1)	60.615	*Ratisbonne*	5.641
In 1 Cor. Hom.			
1.1 (1 Cor 1:2)	61.13	*Comm. 1 Cor.*	49.309
2.1 (1 Cor 1:2)	61.17f.		49.310
3.1 (1 Cor 1:2)	61.23		49.315
12.2 (1 Cor 1:2)	61.99		49.369
15.2 (1 Cor 5:5)	61.123	*Inst.*	4.12.5n11
15.2 (1 Cor 5:5)	61.123	*Comm. 1 Cor.*	49.380
16.1 (1 Cor 5:10)	61.129f.		49.384
16.2 (1 Cor 5:13)	61.131f.		49.387
16.3 (1 Cor 6:4)	61.133		49.389

Chrysostom	PG	Calvin	CO or Inst.
23.1 (1 Cor 9:24)	61.189		49.449
27.2 (1 Cor 11:19)	61.226f.		49.481
27.3 (1 Cor 11:21)	61.228		49.482
27.4 (1 Cor 11:21)	61.230	Vera Part.	9.501
28.1 (1 Cor 11:28)	61.231ff.	Inst.	4.17.40
29.3 (1 Cor 12:7)?	61.244	Comm. 1 Cor.	49.499
29.3 (1 Cor 12:8)	61.245		49.500
32.1 (1 Cor 12:27)	61.264		49.505
32.2 (1 Cor 12:28)	61.266		49.507
32.4 (1 Cor 13:2)	61.269		49.509
35.1 (1 Cor 14:2)	61.295f.		49.517
35.3 (1 Cor 14:14)	61.300		49.521
36.1 (1 Cor 14:24)	61.307f.		49.527
36.2 (1 Cor 14:23)	61.308		49.526
38.4 (1 Cor 15:5)	61.326		49.539
43.1 (1 Cor 16:2)	61.368		49.566
In 2 Cor. Hom.			
6.	61.438	Inst.	2.7.7
4.3 (2 Cor 2:5)	61.421	Comm. 2 Cor.	50.28
4.5 (2 Cor 2:11)	61.424		50.30
8.1 (2 Cor 4:2)	61.454		50.48
8.2 (2 Cor 4:4)	61.455		50.50
8.5 (2 Cor 4:6)	61.457		50.53
9.2 (2 Cor 4:16)	61.461		50.58
10.1 (2 Cor 5:3)	61.468		50.61
12.1 (2 Cor 6:1)	61.481		50.75
12.2 (2 Cor 6:5)	61.483		50.78
13.2 (2 Cor 6:13)	61.492		50.80
14.1 (2 Cor 7:4)	61.498		50.86
15.2 (2 Cor 7:12)	61.505		50.93
18.1 (2 Cor 8:18)	61.523		50.103
18.3 (2 Cor 8)	61.527	Inst.	4.17.48n54
18.3 (2 Cor 8)	61.527	Art. fac. Par. 7	7.18
18.9 (2 Cor 8)	61.527	Ratisbonne	5.636
21.2 (2 Cor 10:3)	61.543	Comm. 2 Cor.	50.113
24.2 (2 Cor 11:20)	61.566		50.131
26.2 (2 Cor 12:7)	61.578		50.139
27.2 (2 Cor 12:13)	61.585		50.144
29.2 (2 Cor 13:3)	61.587		50.149
In Gal.			
ch. 2, par. 2 (Gal 2:6)	61.637	Comm. Gal.	50.186
ch. 2, par. 4 (Gal 2:11)	61.640		50.191f.
ch. 2, par. 5 (Gal 2:14)	61.642		50.193
ch. 2, par. 6 (Gal 2:17)	61.646		50.197
ch. 2, par. 6 (Gal 2:17)	61.644	Inst.	2.7.7
ch. 4, par. 4 (Gal 4:25)	61.662	Comm. Gal.	50.239
ch. 5, par. 3 (Gal 5:12)	61.668		50.249

Chrysostom	PG	Calvin	CO or Inst.
In Eph. Hom.			
1.1 (Eph 1:3)	62.11	*Comm. Eph.*	51.146
3.4 (Eph 1)	62.28	*Inst.*	4.17.40 ?
3.4f.	62.28–30		PA4n25
3.5	62.29–30		4.17.45n44
3.4	62.29	*Ratisbonne*	5.635
3.4	62.29	*Act. Syn. Tr. 2s*	7.404
10.1 (Eph 4)	62.78	*Inst.*	4.2.6 (cf.)
11.2 (Eph 4:11)	62.82f.	*Comm. Eph.*	51.197
In Philip. Hom.			
1 & 2	62.181–98	*Inst.*	2.8.46 ?
2.1 (Phil 1:10) ?	62.191	*Comm. Phil.*	52.12
In Col. Hom.			
1.2f. (Col 1:8)	62.302f.	*Comm. Col.*	52.80
3.1 (Col 1:15)	62.317f.		52.84
7. (Col 2:16)	62.343		52.110
9.2 (Col 3)	62.362f.	*Ep. Lect.* 1545	6.171
In 1 Thess. Hom.			
1.2 (1 Thess 1:4)	62.395	*Comm. 1 Thess.*	52.141
5.2 (1 Thess 4:6)	62.424		52.161
10.2 (1 Thess 5:18)	62.457		52.175
11.2 (1 Thess 5:22)	62.463		52.177
2 Thess. Hom.			
4.1 (2 Thess 2:6)	62.485f.	*Comm. 2 Thess.*	52.200
4.3 (2 Thess 3:2)	62.489		52.209
5.1 (2 Thess 3:6)	62.493f.		52.212
5.2 (2 Thess 3:13)	62.495		52.215
In 1 Tim. Hom.			
7.2 (1 Tim 2:3)	62.536	Ep. 3345 (Feb. 1561) Leopolitanus to Calvin	18.371
8.1 (1 Tim 2:8)	62.540f.	*Comm. 1 Tim.*	52.274
10.1 (1 Tim 3:1)	62.547 ?		52.279
10.1 (1 Tim 3:2)	62.547ff. ?		52.281
10.1 (1 Tim 3:1)	62.548	*Inst.*	4.4.2 ?
10.1 (1 Tim 3:3)	62.548	*Comm. 1 Tim.*	52.283
10.2 (1 Tim 3:6)	62.550		
15.2 (1 Tim 5:17)	62.581		52.315
In 2 Tim. Hom.			
1.1 (2 Tim 1:3)	62.602 ?	*Comm. 2 Tim.*	52.347
3.1 (2 Tim 1:13)	62.613 ?		52.356
8.2 (2 Tim 3:6)	62.644		52.377
8.2 (2 Tim 3:9)	62.644f.		52.378
In Philemon Hom.			
2.4	62.713f.	*Inst.*	3.14.15n23
In Heb. Hom.			
Pref. 1	63.11	*Comm. Heb. arg.*	55.5
4.2 (Heb 2:9)	63.39f.		55.26f.

Chrysostom	PG	Calvin	CO or Inst.
8.1 (Heb 5:7)	63.69		55.62
8.1f. (Heb 5:6)	63.69	*Interim*	7.580
8.1 (Heb 5)	63.69	Ep. 3345 (Feb.1561) Leopolitanus to Calvin	18.375
9.1 (Heb 6.2)	66.77 ?	*Comm. Heb.*	55.69
9.4 (Heb 6)	63.81	*Inst.*	3.4.1n2
12.3 (Heb)	63.99		2.2.27n85
13.1 (Heb 7.11)	63.101f.	*Interim*	7.580
16.2 (Heb 9.22)	63.124	*Comm. Heb.*	55.116
17.3 (Heb)	63.131f.	*Inst.*	4.18.10n18
17.3	63.131		4.18.11n19
27.2 (Heb 11.34)	63.187	*Comm. Heb.*	55.167
28.1 (Heb 11.37f.)	63.192	*Psychopann.*	5.215

Table of Pseudo-Chrysostom References Printed in Migne, PG

Work	PG	Calvin	CO or Inst.
Contra Jud., Gent. & haer.			
	48.1078	*Inst.*	3.4.31n67
De fide et lege naturae			
3.	48.1085	*Inst.*	3.4.31n67
De Spiritu Sancto			
8. ff.	52.822ff.	*Sadolet*	5.393
10.	52.824	*Inst.*	4.8.13n16
10.	52.824	*Art. fac. Par.*	7.33
In Ps. 50 Hom.			
2.5	55.580ff.	*Inst.*	3.4.8n18
2.5	55.580ff.	*Art. fac. Par.*	7.11
Opus imperf. in Matt. Hom.			
11.	56.691	*Inst.* 1536	OS 1.151
14.	56.715	*Inst.*	3.20.35n71
49.	56.910	*Inst.*	2.8.12n20

Table of Pseudo-Chrysostom References Not Printed in Migne, PG

Work	Ed. 1530 (unless otherwise specified)	Calvin	CO or Inst.
Hom. ad Naeophitos	2.82 (leDuc. 2.52f)	*Inst.*	4.14.19n43
Dom. I Adv. Dom. Hom. 35	2.124	*Inst.*	2.2.9n47
De inventione crucis	2.130	*Inst.*	4.12.28n52
Hom. "Provida Mente"	2.347A	*Inst.*	3.4.1n3
Hom. 60 ad populum	4.581	*Inst.*	4.14.3n4
	4.581	*Inst.*	4.17.6n19
	4.581	*Art. fac. Par.*	7.17
Hom. 61 ad populum		*Inst.*	4.17.40
Hom. 80 ad populum		*Inst.*	3.3.8
Hom. Spir. Sanct.	5.379	*Inst.*	4.17.12n35
Serm. de poen. & conf.	5.512		
	5.574D (ed. 1539)	*Inst.*	3.4.8n18
	5.512	*Art. fac. Par.*	7.11
	5.514	*Inst.*	3.4.31n69
Hom. in illud Simile est regn. coel. patrif. &c.	6.544ff. (leDuc.)	*Contre Anab.*	7.126

References As Yet Unlocated

Topic	Calvin	CO
	Adv. Pigh.	6.287
		6.396
Supererogatory works	*Interim*	7.559
Daily offering of the Mass	*Interim*	7.579
Lord's Supper to infants & children	*Eccl. Ref. Rat.*	7.657
Fathers called "Sophists"	*Ref. Err. Serv.*	8.574
Christ's table	*Ult. Adm. Westph.*	9.157
Sursum Corda	*Ult. Adm. Westph.*	9.214

Topic	Calvin	CO
The Mediator Divine/Human	*Resp. Min. Eccl. Gen.*	9.357
(*Hom. de Ascensione*)		9.358
Schism from the Church	*Grat. ad Praec. Lugd.*	9.435
Hoc est corpus		9.439
		9.443
Heshusius on L/S	*Vera Partic.*	9.483
Lay possession of Scriptures	*Pref. Bibl.*	9.788f
(*Hom. Gen.* 17)	*Cons. ad Disc.*	
	Eccl. de Luxu	10.203 ?
Usury	*Quaest. Jurid.*	10.247
(*De Sacerd.*)	Ep. 25	10.b.47f
	Ep. 26	
	Ep. 187	10.b.383
(Rom ch. 13)	Ep. 3515	18.701
(Chrys. Prol. Matt.)	Ep. 3541	18.766
Trinity	Ep. 4125	20.343
	Comm. Is. 5.8	36.108
		45.293 ?
(Luke 7.35/17.25)		45.308
(Mark 13.57)		45.426
		47.98
		49.139
(Rom 16:16) or (Cor 13:12)		49.287
(2 Cor 1:9)		50.14
		50.236
(Phil 3:7)		52.48
(Col 3:16)		52.125

Bibliography

Latin and Greek Primary Sources

Calvin

Ioannis Calvini Opera quae supersunt omnia (CO). Edited by Guilielmus Baum, Eduardus Cunitz, and Eduardus Reuss. 59 vols. Corpus Reformatorum. Vols. 29–87. Brunswick: C. A. Schwetschke et filium, 1863–1900.

Ioannis Calvini Opera Selecta (OS). Edited by Petrus Barth et Guilielmus Niesel. Vols. 1–4. Munich: Kaiser, 1926–1936.

INSTITUTIO

Institutio Religionis Christianae. 1536, 1539–1554, 1559. CO 1–2.
Institutio Christianae Religionis. 1559. OS 3–5.
Institution de la Religion Chretienne. 1560. CO 3–4.

COMMENTARII ET PRAELECTIONES

Commentarius in Genesin. 1554. CO 23.
Commentarius in Mosis reliquos quatuor libros. 1563. CO 24–25.
Commentarius in Librum Iosue. 1564. CO 25.
Commentarius in Librum Psalmorum. 1557. CO 31–32.
Commentarius in Librum Isaiae. 1550. CO 36–37.
Praelectiones in Librum Ieremiae. 1563. CO 37–39.
Praelectiones in Lamentationes Ieremiae. 1563. CO 39.
Praelectiones in Ezechielis viginti capita priora. 1565. CO 40.
Praelectiones in Danielem. 1561. CO 40–41.
Praelectiones in XII Prophetas Minores. Hosea, Ioel. 1559. CO 42. Amos, Obadias, Ionas, Michaeas, Nahum, Habacuc. 1559. CO 43. Sophonias, Haggaeus, Zacharias, Malachias. 1559. CO 44.
Commentarius in Harmoniam Evangelicam. 1555. CO 45.
Commentarius in Evangelium Ioannis. 1552. CO 47.

189

Commentarius in Acta Apostolorum. 1552–1554. CO 48.

Commentarius in Epistolam Pauli ad Romanos. 1540. CO 49.

Commentarius in Epistolam Pauli ad Corinthios I. 1546. CO 49.

Commentarius in Epistolam Pauli ad Corinthios II. 1548. CO 50.

Commentarius in Epistolam Pauli ad Galatas. 1548. CO 50.

Commentarius in Epistolam ad Ephesios. 1548. CO 51.

Commentarius in Epistolam Pauli ad Philippenses. 1548. CO 52.

Commentarius in Epistolam Pauli ad Colossenses. 1548. CO 52.

Commentarius in Epistolam Pauli ad Thessalonicenses I. 1550. CO 52.

Commentarius in Epistolam Pauli ad Thessalonicenses II. 1550. CO 52.

Commentarius in Epistolam Pauli ad Timotheum I. 1548. CO 52.

Commentarius in Epistolam Pauli ad Timatheum II. 1548. CO 52.

Commentarius in Epistolam Pauli ad Titum. 1549. CO 52.

Commentarius in Epistolam ad Philemonem. 1549. CO 52.

Commentarius in Epistolam ad Hebraeos. 1549. CO 55.

Commentarius in Epistolas Catholicas. 1551. CO 55.

L. Annaei Senecae libri de clementia cum Io. Calvini commentario. 1532. CO 5.

Praefationes

Praefatio in Chrysostomi Homilias. n.d. CO 9.

Praefationes Bibliis Gallicis Petri Roberti Olivetani. 1535. CO 9.

Epistolae

Calvinus Grynaeo. Epistula 191. November 15, 1539. CO 10.

Farellus Calvino. Epistula 825. September 3, 1546. CO 12.

Calvinus Farello. Epistula 832. October 6, 1546. CO 12.

Balduinus Calvino. Epistula 4144. n.d. CO 20.

Pollanus Calvino. Epistula 729. December 16, 1545. CO 12.

Calvinus Fallestio. Epistula 753. February 9, 1546. CO 12.

Moibanus Calvino. Epistula 1615. March 24, 1552. CO 14.

Calvinus Regi Eduardo. Epistula 1443. February 9, 1551. CO 14.

Burghardus Calvino. Epistula 2025. October 7, 1554. CO 15.

Calvinus Burkardo. Epistula 2123. March 3, 1555. CO 15.

Miscellanea

Psychopannychia. 1542. CO 5.

Chrysostom

Joannis Chrysostomi Opera Omnia Quae Exstant. Edited by J. P. Migne. Patrologiae Cursus Completus, Series Graeca (PG). Vols. 47–64. Paris: J. P. Migne, 1863.

Homiliae, Expositio, Interpretatio, Commentarius, Enarratio

Homiliae in Genesin. 386–88. PG 53–54.

Expositio in Psalmum. n.d. PG 55.

Interpretatio in Isaiam Prophetam. 390. PG 56.
Homiliae in Matthaeum. 390. PG 57.
Commentarius in Sanctum Joannem Apostolum et Evangelistam. 391. PG 59.
Commentarius in Acta Apostolorum. 400. PG 60.
Commentarius in Epistolam ad Romanos. n.d. PG 61.
In Epistolam Pauli ad Corinthios Primam. Edited by Desiderius Erasmi. Translated by Francisco Aretino. Basil: Froben, 1530.
Commentarius in Epistolam ad Corinthios I. n.d. PG 61.
Commentarius in Epistolam ad Corinthios II. n.d. PG 61.
In Epistolam ad Galatas, Interpretatio. n.d. PG 61.
In Epistolam ad Ephesios Commentarius. n.d. PG 62.
In Epistolam ad Philippenses Commentarius. n.d. PG 62.
In Epistolam ad Colossenses Commentarius. 399. PG 62.
In Epistolam Primam ad Thessalonicenses Commentarius. n.d. PG 62.
In Epistolam Secundam ad Thessalonicenses Commentarius. n.d. PG 62.
In Epistolam Primam ad Timotheum Commentarius. n.d. PG 62.
In Epistolam Secundam ad Timotheum Commentarius. n.d. PG 63.
In Epistolam ad Titum Commentarius. n.d. PG 62.
In Epistolam ad Philemonem Commentarius. n.d. PG 62.
Enarratio in Epistolam ad Hebraeos, ex notis post eius obitum Constantino presbytero Antiocheno edita. 403–404. PG 63.

HOMILIA SELECTA

De Incomprehensibili Dei Natura. 386–387, 397. PG 48.
Homilia adversus eos qui ecclesia relicta ad circenses ludos et ad theatra transfugerunt. July 3, 399. PG 56.
Homiliae XXI De Statuis ad Populum Antiochenum Habitae. 387. PG 49.
Salutate Priscillam et Aquilam. n.d. PG 51.
Vidi Dominum. n.d. PG 56.

MISCELLANEA

De Sacerdotio. n.d. PG 48.
De Compunctione, ad Demetrium. n.d. PG 47.
Adversus qui ad Monasticam Vitam Inducunt. n.d. PG 47.

Erasmus

Opus Epistolarum Des. Erasmi Roterodami. Edited by P. S. Allen and H. M. Allen. 12 vols. Oxford: In Typographeo Clarendoniano, 1906.

Translations of Calvin's Works

Institutes

Institutes of the Christian Religion. Edited by John T. McNeill. Translated and indexed by Ford Lewis Battles. 2 vols. The Library of Christian Classics 20–21. Philadelphia: Westminster Press, 1960–1961.

Institution of the Christian Religion; embracing almost the whole sum of piety, & whatever is necessary to know the doctrine of salvation: a work most worthy to be read by all persons zealous for piety, and recently published. *Christianae religionis institutio*, Basil, 1536. Now Englished completely for the first time by Ford Lewis Battles. Pittsburgh: Pittsburgh Theological Seminary, 1972.

Commentaries

Commentaries on the First Book of Moses Called Genesis. Translated by John King. 2 vols. Grand Rapids: Eerdmans, 1948.

Commentaries on the Four Last Books of Moses Arranged in the Form of a Harmony. Translated by Charles William Bingham. 4 vols. Grand Rapids: Eerdmans, 1950.

Commentaries on the Book of Joshua. Translated by Henry Beveridge. Grand Rapids: Eerdmans, 1949.

Commentary on the Book of Psalms. Translated by James Anderson. 5 vols. Grand Rapids: Eerdmans, 1949.

Commentary on the Book of the Prophet Isaiah. Translated by William Pringle. 4 vols. Grand Rapids: Eerdmans, 1948.

Commentaries on the Book of the Prophet Jeremiah and the Lamentations. Translated by John Owen. 5 vols. Grand Rapids: Eerdmans, 1950.

Commentaries on the Book of the Prophet Ezekiel. Translated by Thomas Myers. 2 vols. Grand Rapids: Eerdmans, 1948.

Commentaries on the Book of the Prophet Daniel. Translated by Thomas Myers. 2 vols. Grand Rapids: Eerdmans, 1948.

Commentaries on the Twelve Minor Prophets. Translated by John Owen. 5 vols. Grand Rapids: Eerdmans, 1950.

Commentary on a Harmony of the Evangelists, Matthew, Mark, and Luke. Translated by William Pringle. 3 vols. Grand Rapids: Eerdmans, 1956.

The Gospel according to St. John, 1–10. Translated by T. H. L. Parker. Edited by David W. and Thomas F. Torrance. Calvin's Commentaries 4. Grand Rapids: Eerdmans, 1961.

The Gospel according to St. John, 11–21 and the First Epistle of John. Translated by T. H. L. Parker. Edited by David W. and Thomas F. Torrance. Calvin's Commentaries 5. Grand Rapids: Eerdmans, 1961.

The Acts of the Apostles, 1–13. Translated by John W. Fraser and W. J. G. McDonald. Edited by David W. and Thomas F. Torrance. Calvin's Commentaries 6. Grand Rapids: Eerdmans, 1965.

The Acts of the Apostles, 14–28. Translated by John W. Fraser. Edited by David W. and Thomas F. Torrance. Calvin's Commentaries 7. Grand Rapids: Eerdmans, 1966.

The Epistles of Paul the Apostle to the Romans and to the Thessalonians. Translated by Ross Mackenzie. Edited by David W. and Thomas F. Torrance. Calvin's Commentaries 8. Grand Rapids: Eerdmans, 1961.

The First Epistle of Paul to the Corinthians. Translated by John W. Fraser. Edited by David W. and Thomas F. Torrance. Calvin's Commentaries 9. Grand Rapids: Eerdmans, 1960.

The Second Epistle of Paul the Apostle to the Corinthians and the Epistle to Timothy, Titus, and Philemon. Translated by T. A. Small. Edited by David W. and Thomas F. Torrance. Calvin's Commentaries 10. Grand Rapids: Eerdmans, 1964.

The Epistles of Paul the Apostle to the Galatians, Ephesians, Philippians, and Colossians. Translated by T. H. L. Parker. Edited by David W. and Thomas F. Torrance. Calvin's Commentaries 11. Grand Rapids: Eerdmans, 1965.

The Epistle of Paul the Apostle to the Hebrews, and the First and Second Epistles of St. Peter. Translated by William B. Johnston. Edited by David W. and Thomas F. Torrance. Calvin's Commentaries 12. Grand Rapids: Eerdmans, 1963.

Calvin's Commentary on Seneca's 'De Clementia.' With introduction, translation, and notes by Ford Lewis Battles and André Malan Hugo. Renaissance Text Series 3. Leiden: Brill, 1969.

Calvin: Commentaries. Edited and translated by Joseph Haroutunian and Louise Pettibone Smith. The Library of Christian Classics 23. Philadelphia: Westminster Press, 1958.

Other Works

"Preface to Olivétan's New Testament." In *Calvin: Commentaries.* Edited and translated by Joseph Haroutunian and Louise Pettibone Smith. The Library of Christian Classics 23. Philadelphia: Westminster Press, 1958.

"Preface to the Homilies of Chrysostom." Translated by J. H. McIndoe. *Hartford Quarterly* 5 (Winter 1965): 19–26.

Calvin's Tracts and Treatises. Edited by Thomas F. Torrance. Translated by Henry Beveridge. 3 vols. Grand Rapids: Eerdmans, 1958.

Letters of John Calvin. Edited by Jules Bonnet. Translated by Marcus Robert Gilchrist. 4 vols. Philadelphia: Presbyterian Board of Publication, 1858.

Translations of Chrysostom's Works

Homilies on the Gospel of St. Matthew. Edited by Philip Schaff. Translated by Sir George Prevost. Revised with notes by M. B. Riddle. A Select Library of the Nicene and Post Nicene Fathers 10. Grand Rapids: Eerdmans, 1969.

Homilies on the Acts of the Apostles. Edited by Philip Schaff. Translated by J. Welder, J. Sheppard, and H. Browne. Revised with notes by George B. Stevens. A Select Library of the Nicene and Post Nicene Fathers 11. Grand Rapids: Eerdmans, 1969.

Homilies on the Epistle of St. Paul and Apostle to the Romans. Edited by Philip Schaff. Translated by J. B. Morris and W. H. Simcox. Revised, with notes by George B. Stevens. A Select Library of the Nicene and Post Nicene Fathers 11. Grand Rapids: Eerdmans, 1969.

Homilies on the Epistles of Paul to the Corinthians. Edited by Philip Schaff. Translated by Talbot W. Chambers. A Select Library of the Nicene and Post Nicene Fathers 12. Grand Rapids: Eerdmans, 1969.

Homilies on the Epistles of St. Paul the Apostle to the Galatians, Ephesians, Philippians, Colossians, Thessalonians; to Timothy, Titus, and Philemon. Edited by John A. Broadus. Translated by Gross Alexander and John A. Broadus. A Select Library of the Nicene and Post Nicene Fathers 13. Grand Rapids: Eerdmans, 1969.

Homilies on the Gospel of St. John and the Epistle to the Hebrews. Edited by Frederic Gardiner and Charles Marriott based on the Oxford "Library of the Fathers" edition. A Select Library of the Nicene and Post Nicene Fathers 14. Grand Rapids: Eerdmans, 1969.

On the Priesthood; Ascetic Treatises; Select Homilies and Letters; Homilies on the Statues. Edited by Philip Schaff. Translated by W. R. W. Stephens, T. P. Brandbram, and R. Blackburn. A Select Library of the Nicene and Post Nicene Fathers 9. Grand Rapids: Eerdmans, 1968.

Translation of Erasmus

The Epistles of Erasmus. Edited and translated by Francis Morgan Nichols. 3 vols. London: Longmans, 1918.

Books and Articles

Allen, P. S. *The Age of Erasmus.* New York: Russell & Russell, 1963.

Battles, Ford Lewis. *An Analysis of the Institutes of the Christian Religion of John Calvin.* By Ford Lewis Battles assisted by John Walchenbach. 2d rev. ed. Pittsburgh: Pittsburgh Theological Seminary, 1970.

———. *A Computerized Concordance to Institutio Christianae Religionis 1559 of Ioannes Calvinus.* Pittsburgh: Pittsburgh Theological Seminary, 1972.

———. *The Piety of John Calvin: An Anthology Illustrative of the Spirituality of the Reformer of Geneva.* Pittsburgh: Pittsburgh Theological Seminary, 1969.

Baur, Chrysostomus. *John Chrysostom and His Time.* Translated by M. Gonzaga. 2 vols. Westminster, MD: The Newman Press, 1958.

Bury, J. B. *History of the Later Roman Empire.* Vol. 1. London: Macmillan, 1923.

Dorey, T. A. *Erasmus.* Studies in Latin Literature. London: Routledge Kegan Paul, 1970.

Doumergue, Emile. *Jean Calvin, les hommes et les choses de son temps.* 7 vols. Genève: Slatkine, 1969. Reprint of 1899–1927 Lausanne edition.

Imbart de La Tour, Pierre. *Les Origines de la Réforme.* Vol. 4: *Calvin et l'Institution chrétienne.* Paris: Librairie D'Argences, 1948.

Long, J. H. "Calvin as an Interpreter of the Bible." *Reformed Church Review* 13 (1909): 165–82.

McIndoe, John H. "Chrysostom on St. Matthew: A Study in Antiochene Exegesis." STM thesis. Hartford Seminary Foundation, 1960.

Parker, Thomas H. L. "Calvin the Biblical Expositor." *The Churchman* 78 (1964): 23–21. Reprinted in John Calvin. Edited by G. E. Duffield. Grand Rapids: Eerdmans, 1966.

————. *Calvin's New Testament Commentaries*. Grand Rapids: Eerdmans, 1971.

Peters, Robert, ed. *Desiderius Erasmus: Preface to the Fathers [and] The New Testament [and] On Study*. Menston: Scolar Press, 1970.

Schaff, Philip. "Calvin as a Commentator." *Presbyterian and Reformed Review* 3 (1892): 462–69.

————. "The Canons and Decrees of the Council of Trent." In *The Creeds of Christendom*. Vol. 2. New York: Harper & Brothers, 1877.

Smits, Luchesius. *Saint Augustin dans L'Oeuvre de Jean Calvin*. 2 vols. Assen: Van Gorcum, 1957.

Socrates. *The Ecclesiastical History*. Translated in *A Select Library of the Nicene and Post Nicene Fathers*. Edited by P. Schaff. 2d series. Vol. 2. New York: The Christian Literature Company, 1890.

Sozomen. *The Ecclesiastical History*. Translated in *A Select Library of the Nicene and Post Nicene Fathers*. Edited by P. Schaff. 2d series. Vol. 2. New York: The Christian Literature Company, 1890.

Spitz, Lewis W. *The Religious Renaissance of the German Humanists*. Cambridge: Harvard University Press, 1963.

Stauffer, Richard. *The Humanness of John Calvin*. Translated by George H. H. Shriver. Nashville: Abingdon, 1971. Original title: *L'humanité de Calvin*. Neuchâtel: Éditions Delachaux et Niestlé, 1964.

Stephens, W. R. W. *Saint John Chrysostom*. London: John Murray, 1883.

Theodoret. *The Ecclesiastical History*. Translated in *A Select Library of the Nicene and Post Nicene Fathers*. Edited by P. Schaff. 2d series. Vol. 3. New York: The Christian Literature Company, 1892.

Woollcambe, K. J. "The Biblical Origins and Patristic Development of Typology." In *Essays on Typology*, ed. G. W. H. Lampe and K. J. Woollcambe, 39–75. Naperville, IL: Alec R. Allenson, 1957.